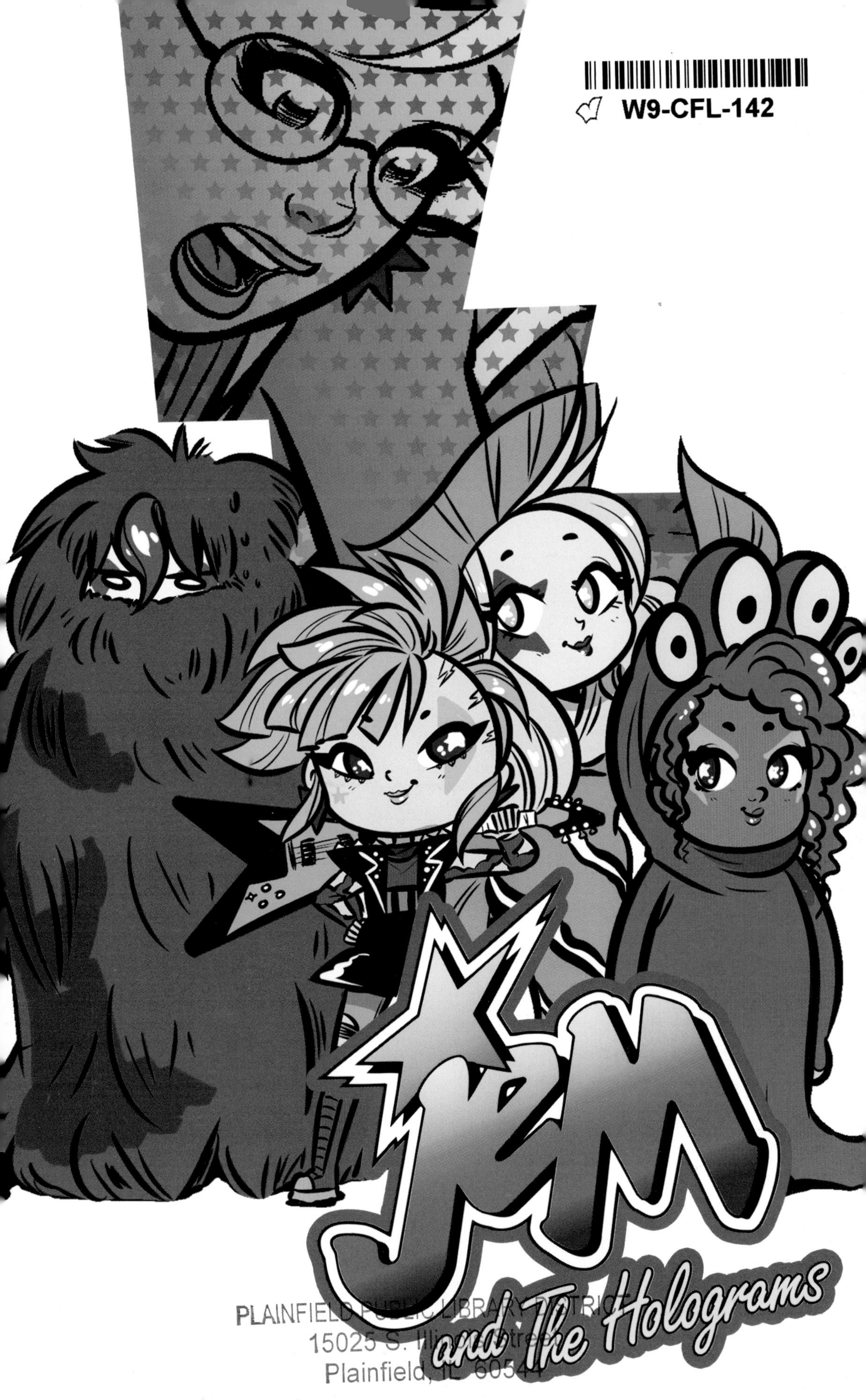
Jem
and The Holograms

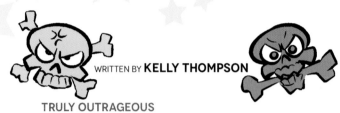

WRITTEN BY **KELLY THOMPSON**

TRULY OUTRAGEOUS

ART BY **GISELE LAGACE** • COLORS BY **M. VICTORIA ROBADO**

ANNUAL 2017

AN EXQUISITE CORPSE

ART BY **GISELE LAGACE** • COLORS BY **JASON MILLET**

KIMBER

ART AND COLORS BY **M.J. BARROS**

AJA

ART AND COLORS BY **M. VICTORIA ROBADO**

SHANA

ART AND COLORS BY **KATARZYNA WITERSCHEIM**

JEM

ART AND COLORS BY **SAVANNA GANUCHEAU**

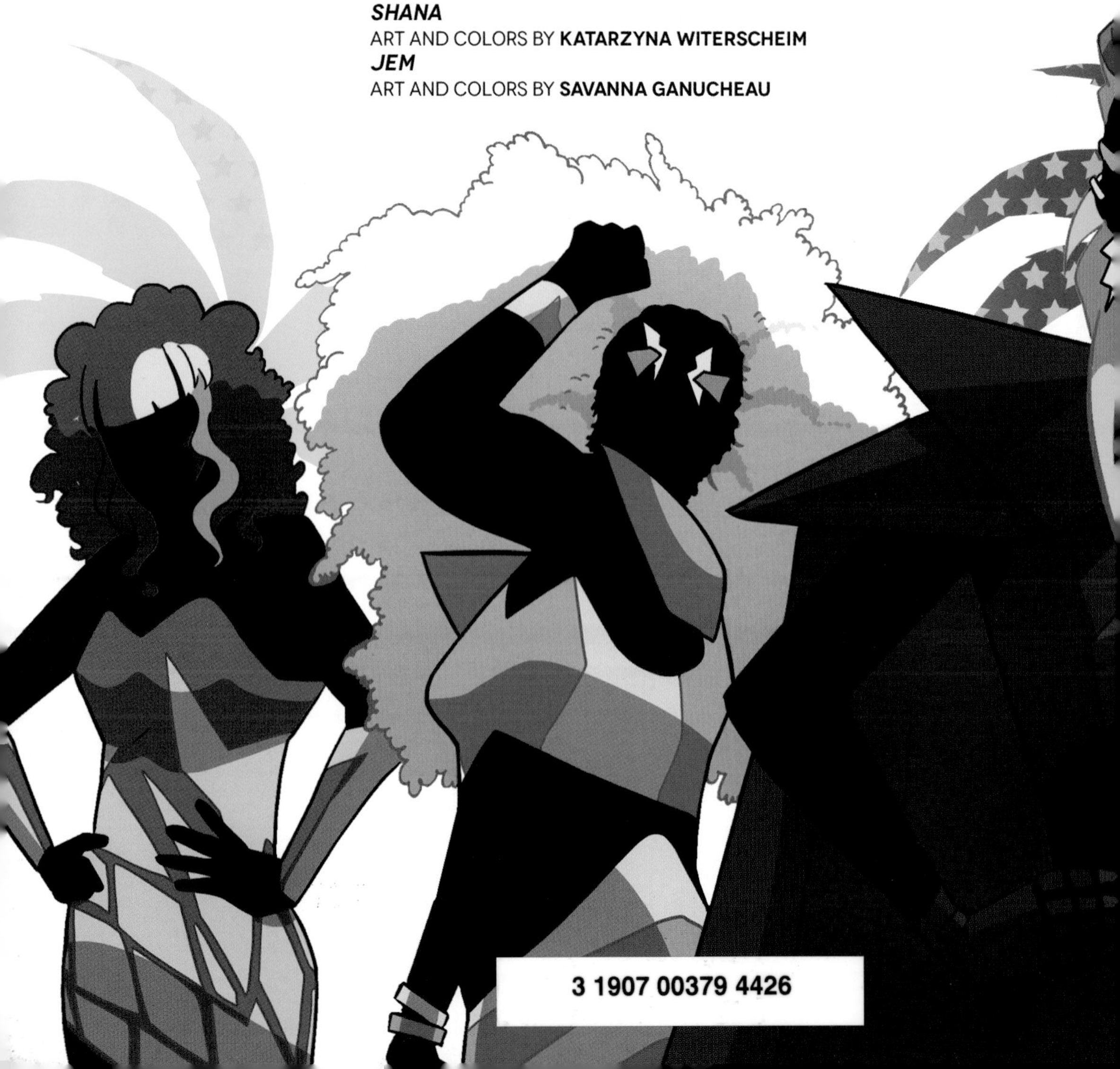

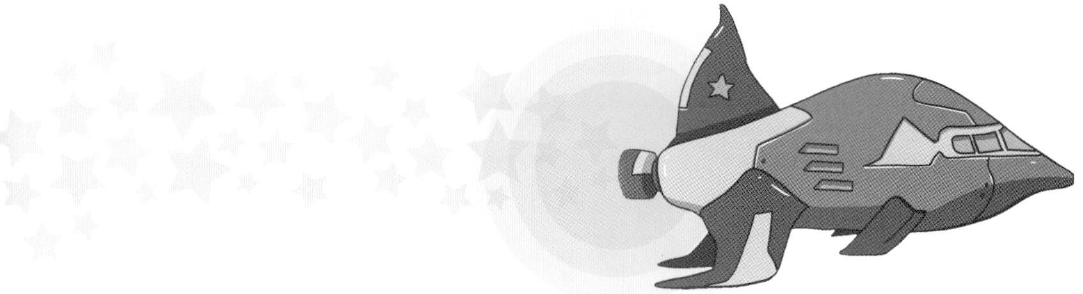

LYRICAL LETTERING BY **M. VICTORIA ROBADO**
LETTERS AND COLLECTION DESIGN BY **SHAWN LEE**
SERIES EDITS BY **SARAH GAYDOS**

COVER BY **JEN BARTEL**
COLLECTION EDITS BY **JUSTIN EISINGER** AND **ALONZO SIMON**
PUBLISHED BY **TED ADAMS**

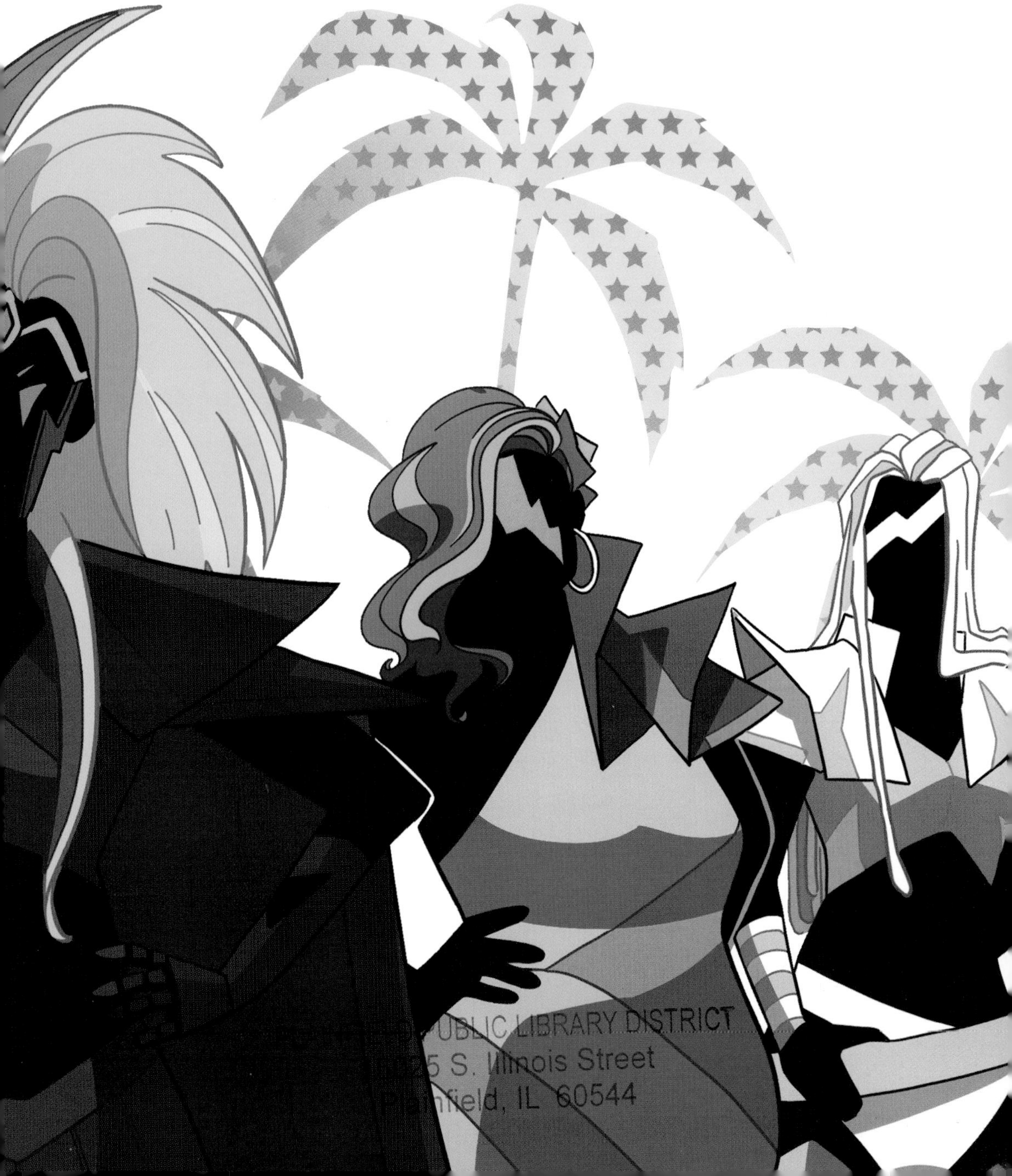

JEM • KIMBER • SHANA • AJA

RAYA • RIO • SYNERGY • PIZZAZZ

JETTA • STORMER • ROXY • RIOT

MINX • RAPTURE

SMILE FOR THE GUESTLIST!

Special thanks to John Barber; Hasbro's Andrea Hopelain, Elizabeth Malkin, Ed Lane, Beth Artale, and Michael Kelly for their invaluable assistance.

For international rights, contact licensing@idwpublishing.com

ISBN: 978-1-63140-914-1 | 20 19 18 17 1 2 3 4

Licensed By: Hasbro

  You Tube ⓘ

Facebook: facebook.com/idwpublishing
Twitter: @idwpublishing • YouTube: youtube.com/idwpublishing
Tumblr: tumblr.idwpublishing.com
Instagram: instagram.com/idwpublishing

www.IDWPUBLISHING.com

Ted Adams, CEO & Publisher • Greg Goldstein, President & COO • Robbie Robbins, EVP/Sr. Graphic Artist
Chris Ryall, Chief Creative Officer • David Hedgecock, Editor-in-Chief Laurie Windrow, Senior Vice President of
Sales & Marketing • Matthew Ruzicka, CPA, Chief Financial Officer • Lorelei Bunjes, VP of Digital Services
Jerry Bennington, VP of New Product Development

Originally published as JEM AND THE HOLOGRAMS issues #24–26 and JEM AND THE HOLOGRAMS ANNUAL 2017.

PREVIOUSLY

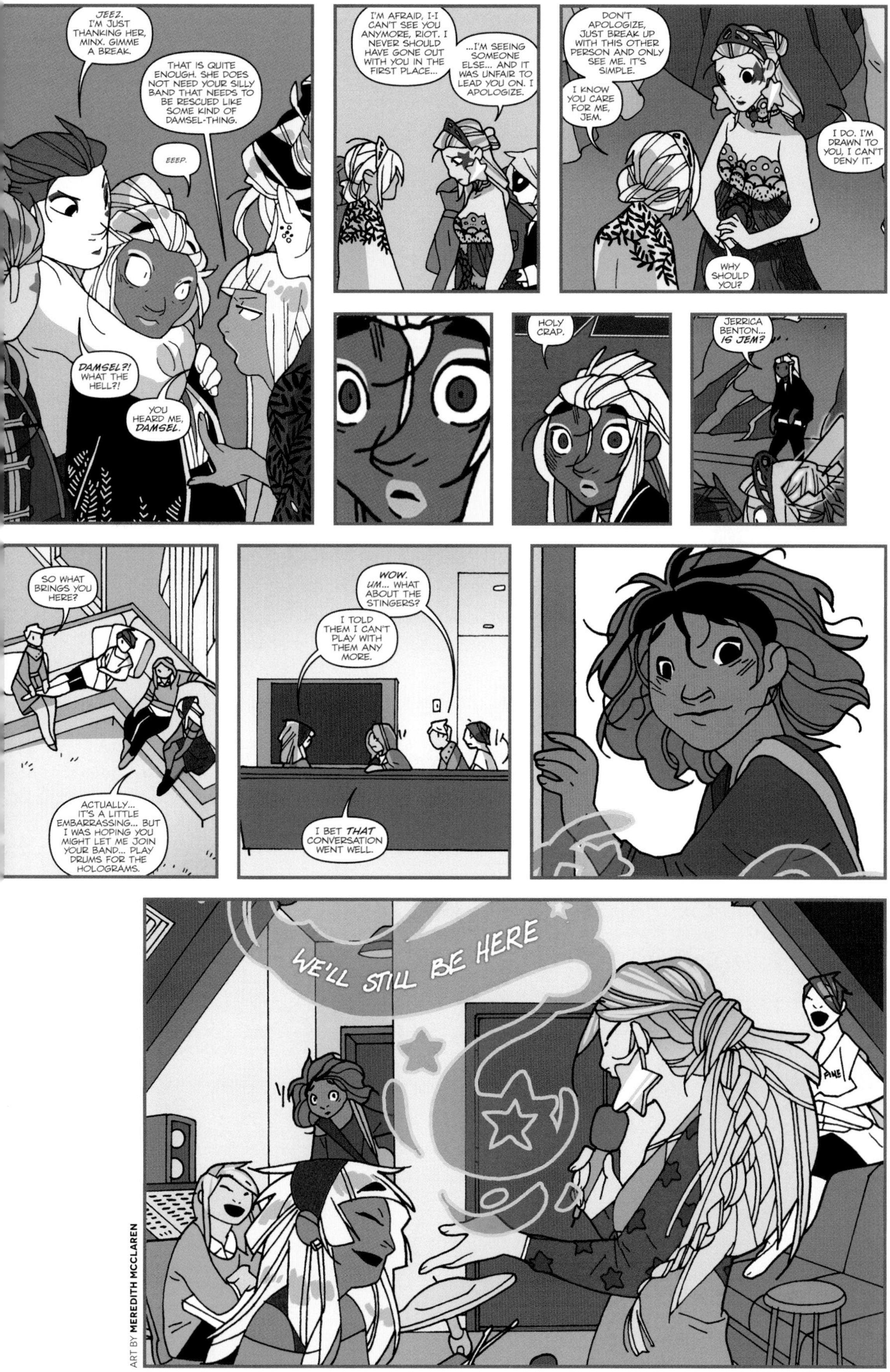
JEEZ. I'M JUST THANKING HER, MINX. GIMME A BREAK.
THAT IS QUITE ENOUGH. SHE DOES NOT NEED YOUR SILLY BAND THAT NEEDS TO BE RESCUED LIKE SOME KIND OF DAMSEL-THING.
EEEP.
DAMSEL?! WHAT THE HELL?!
YOU HEARD ME, DAMSEL.
I'M AFRAID, I-I CAN'T SEE YOU ANYMORE, RIOT. I NEVER SHOULD HAVE GONE OUT WITH YOU IN THE FIRST PLACE...
...I'M SEEING SOMEONE ELSE... AND IT WAS UNFAIR TO LEAD YOU ON. I APOLOGIZE.
DON'T APOLOGIZE, JUST BREAK UP WITH THIS OTHER PERSON AND ONLY SEE ME. IT'S SIMPLE.
I KNOW YOU CARE FOR ME, JEM.
I DO. I'M DRAWN TO YOU, I CAN'T DENY IT.
WHY SHOULD YOU?
HOLY CRAP.
JERRICA BENTON... IS JEM?
SO WHAT BRINGS YOU HERE?
ACTUALLY... IT'S A LITTLE EMBARRASSING... BUT I WAS HOPING YOU MIGHT LET ME JOIN YOUR BAND... PLAY DRUMS FOR THE HOLOGRAMS.
WOW. UM... WHAT ABOUT THE STINGERS?
I TOLD THEM I CAN'T PLAY WITH THEM ANY MORE.
I BET THAT CONVERSATION WENT WELL.
WE'LL STILL BE HERE

ART BY MEREDITH MCCLAREN

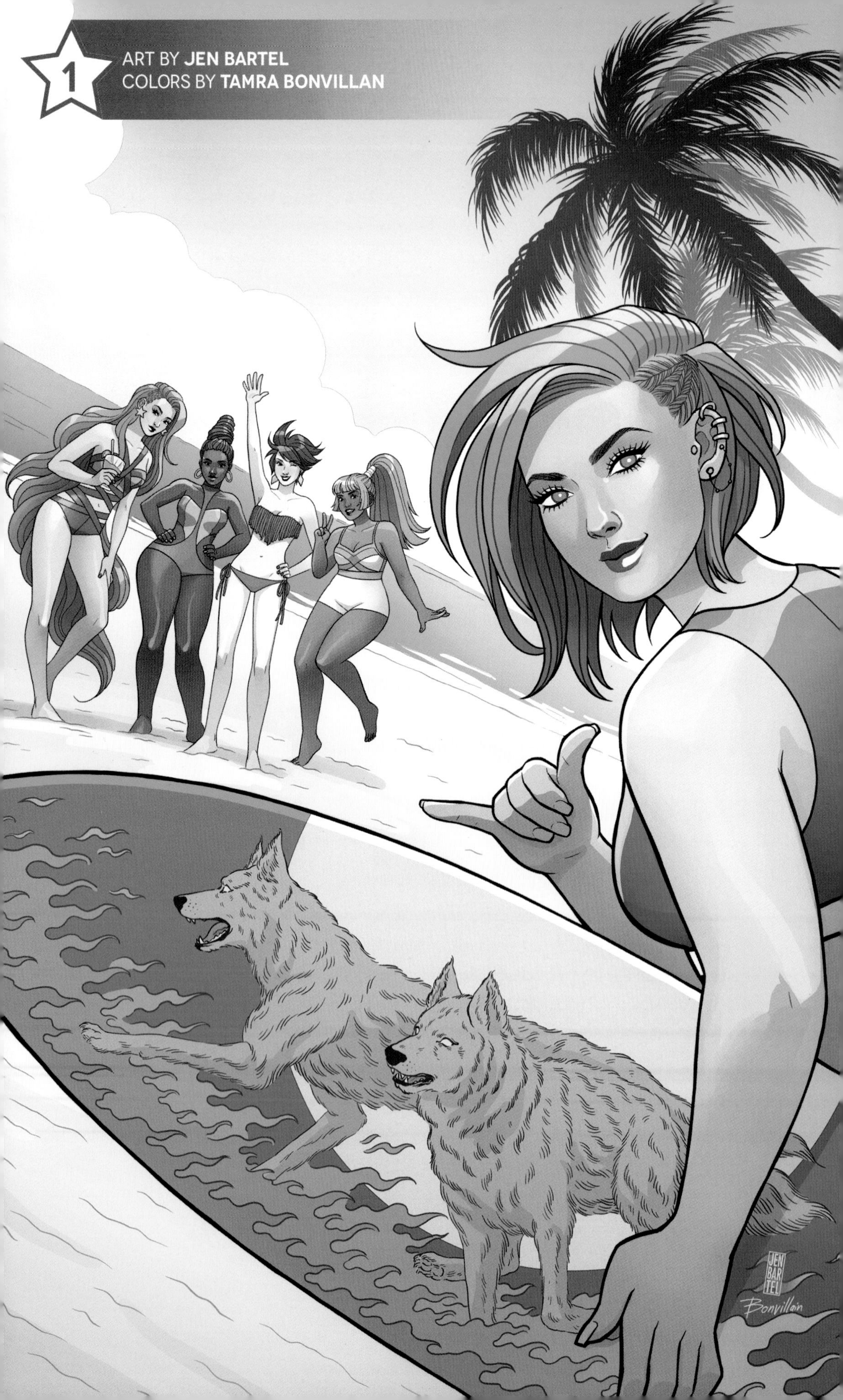
1
ART BY JEN BARTEL
COLORS BY TAMRA BONVILLAN
JEN BARTEL
Bonvillain

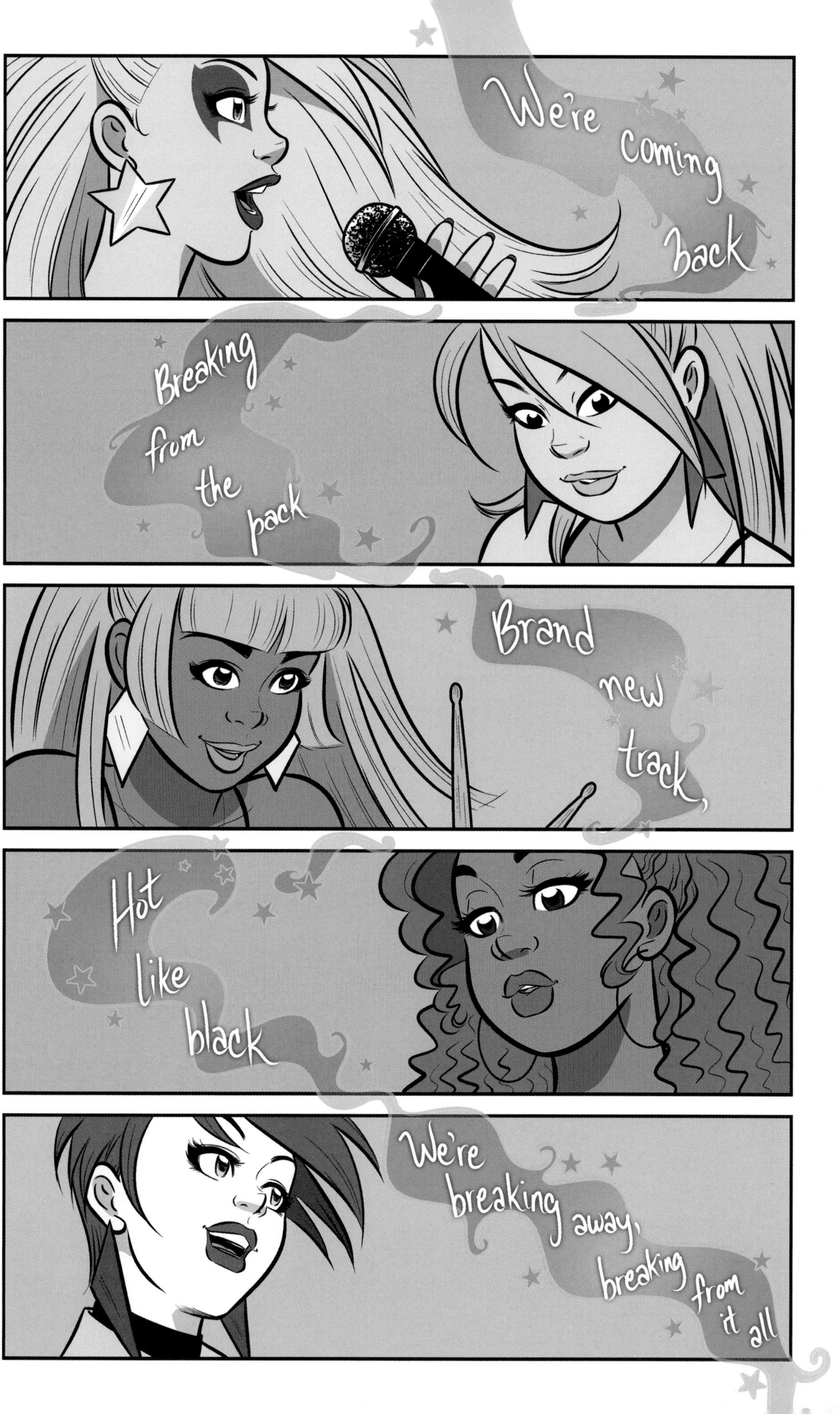

We're coming back
Breaking from the pack
Brand new track,
Hot like black
We're breaking away, breaking from it all

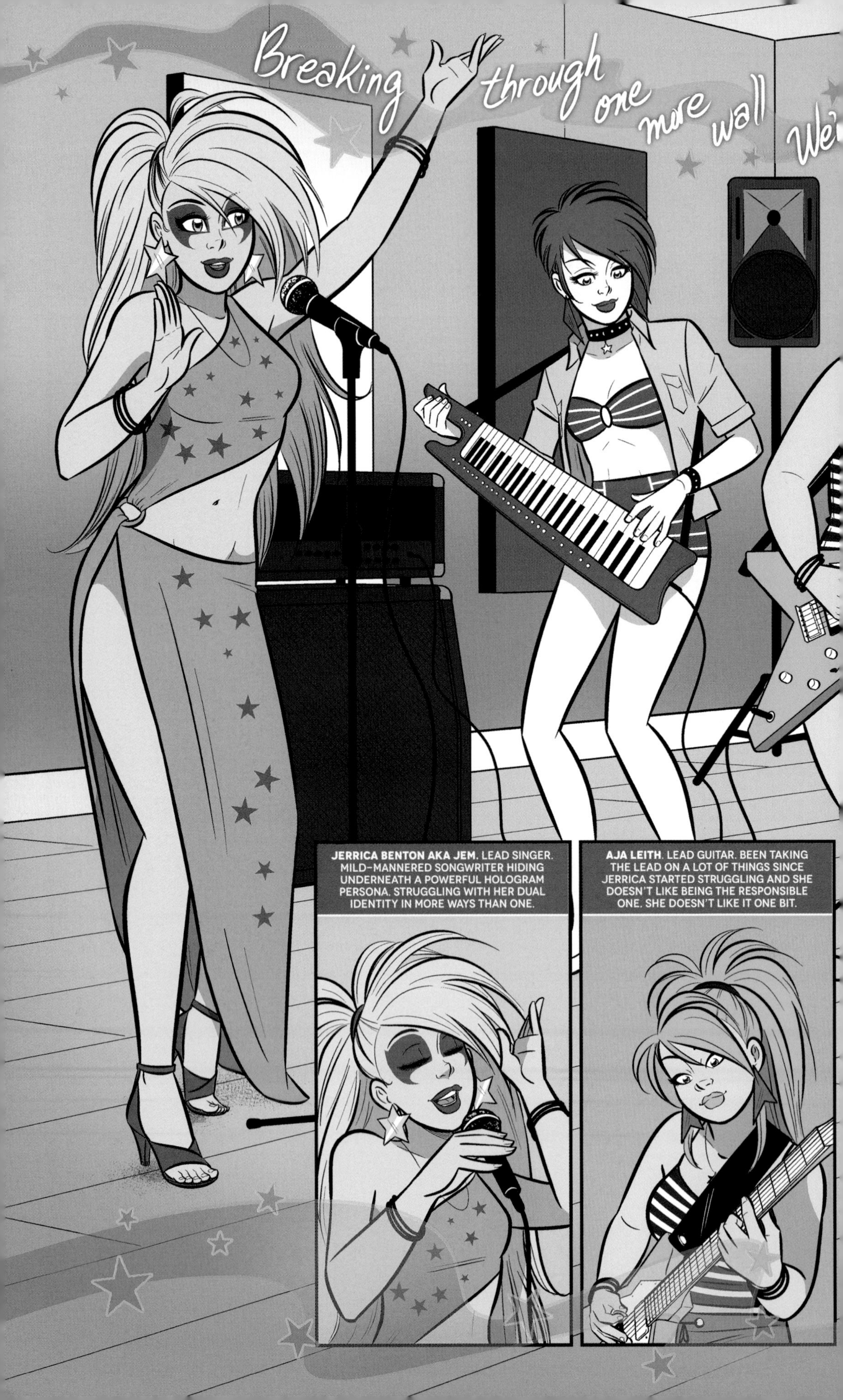
Breaking through one more wall
We'
JERRICA BENTON AKA JEM. LEAD SINGER. MILD-MANNERED SONGWRITER HIDING UNDERNEATH A POWERFUL HOLOGRAM PERSONA. STRUGGLING WITH HER DUAL IDENTITY IN MORE WAYS THAN ONE.
AJA LEITH. LEAD GUITAR. BEEN TAKING THE LEAD ON A LOT OF THINGS SINCE JERRICA STARTED STRUGGLING AND SHE DOESN'T LIKE BEING THE RESPONSIBLE ONE. SHE DOESN'T LIKE IT ONE BIT.

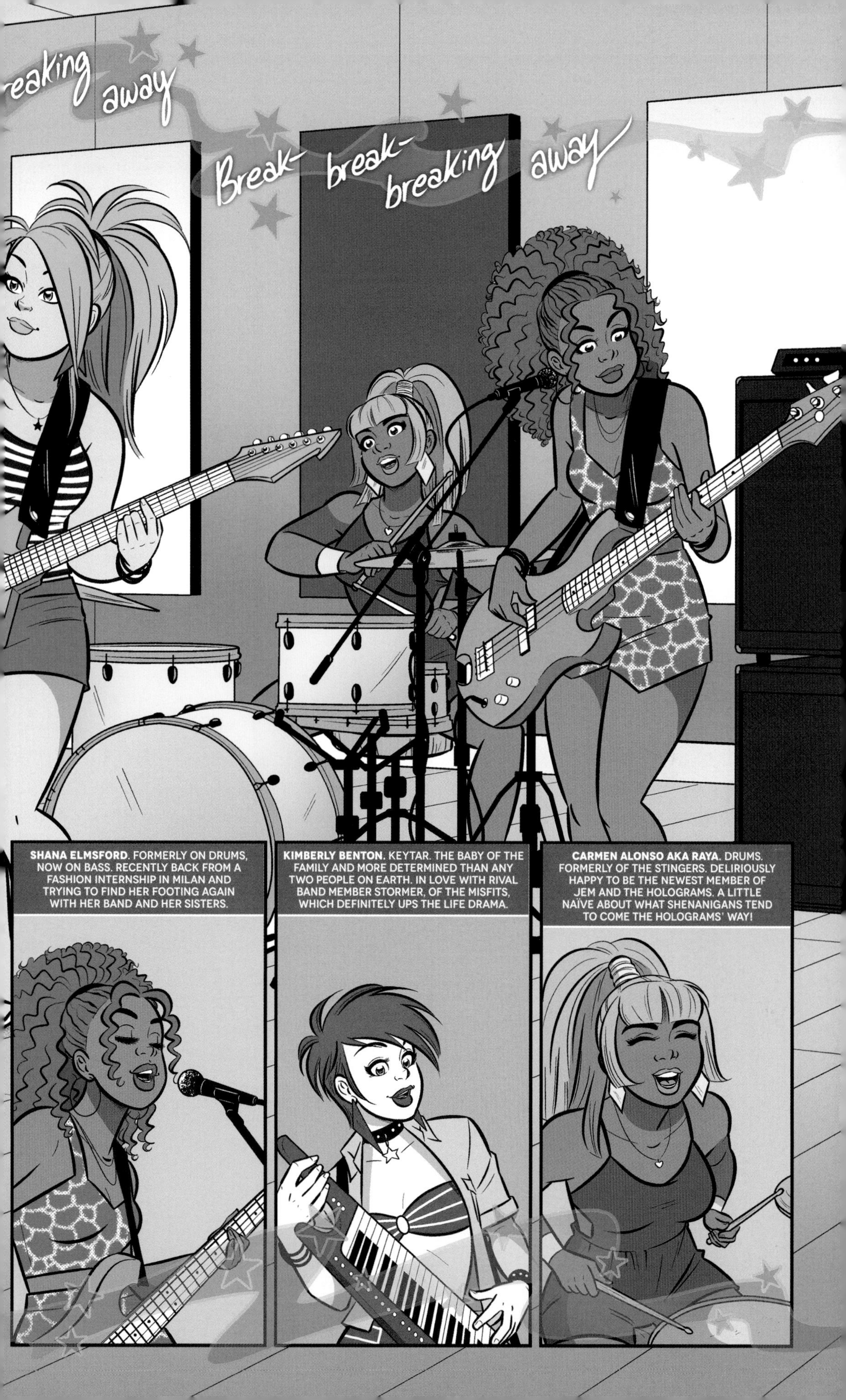

eaking away
Break- break- breaking away
SHANA ELMSFORD. FORMERLY ON DRUMS, NOW ON BASS. RECENTLY BACK FROM A FASHION INTERNSHIP IN MILAN AND TRYING TO FIND HER FOOTING AGAIN WITH HER BAND AND HER SISTERS.
KIMBERLY BENTON. KEYTAR. THE BABY OF THE FAMILY AND MORE DETERMINED THAN ANY TWO PEOPLE ON EARTH. IN LOVE WITH RIVAL BAND MEMBER STORMER, OF THE MISFITS, WHICH DEFINITELY UPS THE LIFE DRAMA.
CARMEN ALONSO AKA RAYA. DRUMS. FORMERLY OF THE STINGERS. DELIRIOUSLY HAPPY TO BE THE NEWEST MEMBER OF JEM AND THE HOLOGRAMS. A LITTLE NAÏVE ABOUT WHAT SHENANIGANS TEND TO COME THE HOLOGRAMS' WAY!

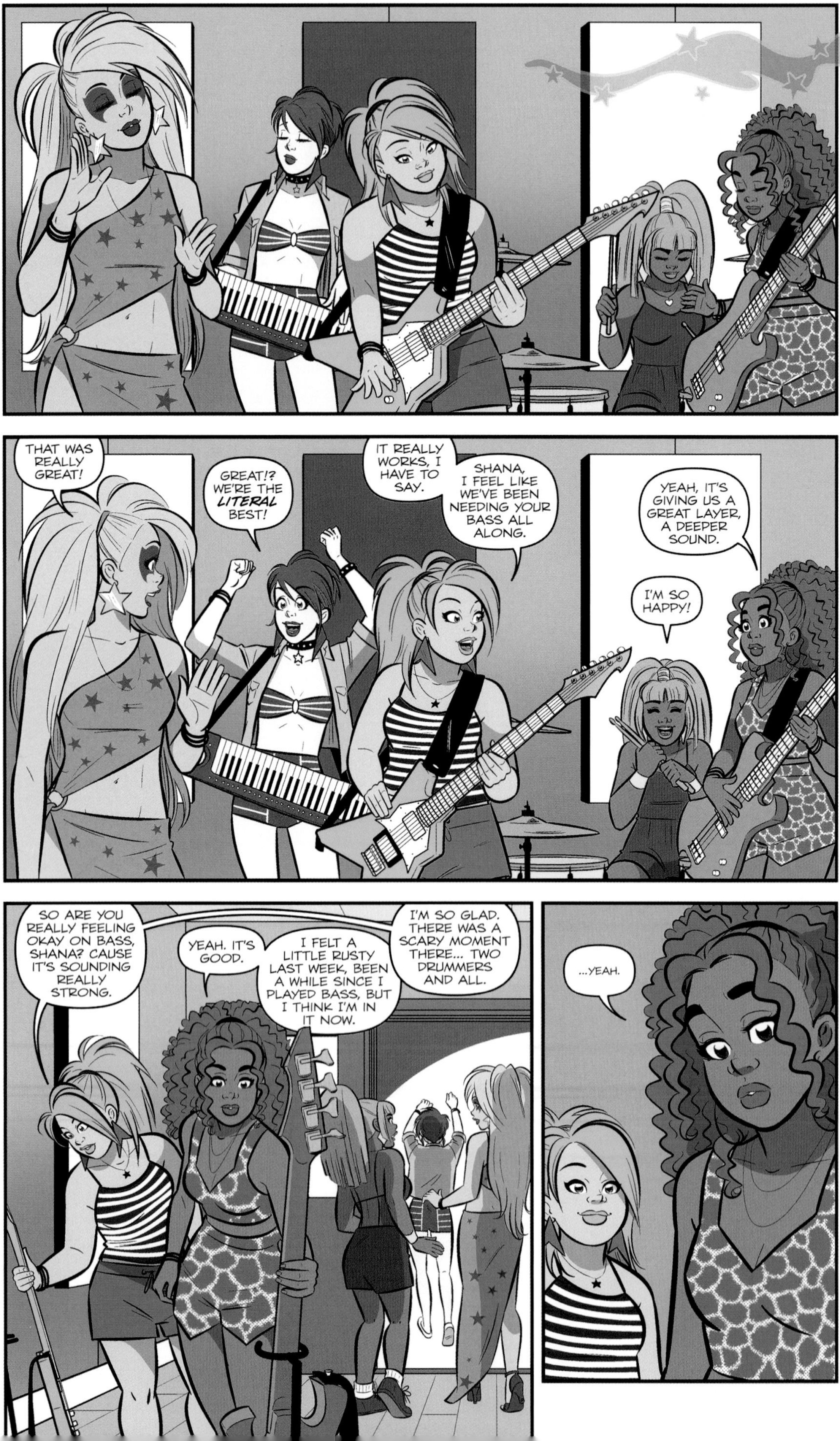
THAT WAS REALLY GREAT!
GREAT!? WE'RE THE *LITERAL* BEST!
IT REALLY WORKS, I HAVE TO SAY.
SHANA, I FEEL LIKE WE'VE BEEN NEEDING YOUR BASS ALL ALONG.
YEAH, IT'S GIVING US A GREAT LAYER, A DEEPER SOUND.
I'M SO HAPPY!
SO ARE YOU REALLY FEELING OKAY ON BASS, SHANA? CAUSE IT'S SOUNDING REALLY STRONG.
YEAH. IT'S GOOD.
I FELT A LITTLE RUSTY LAST WEEK, BEEN A WHILE SINCE I PLAYED BASS, BUT I THINK I'M IN IT NOW.
I'M SO GLAD. THERE WAS A SCARY MOMENT THERE... TWO DRUMMERS AND ALL.
...YEAH.

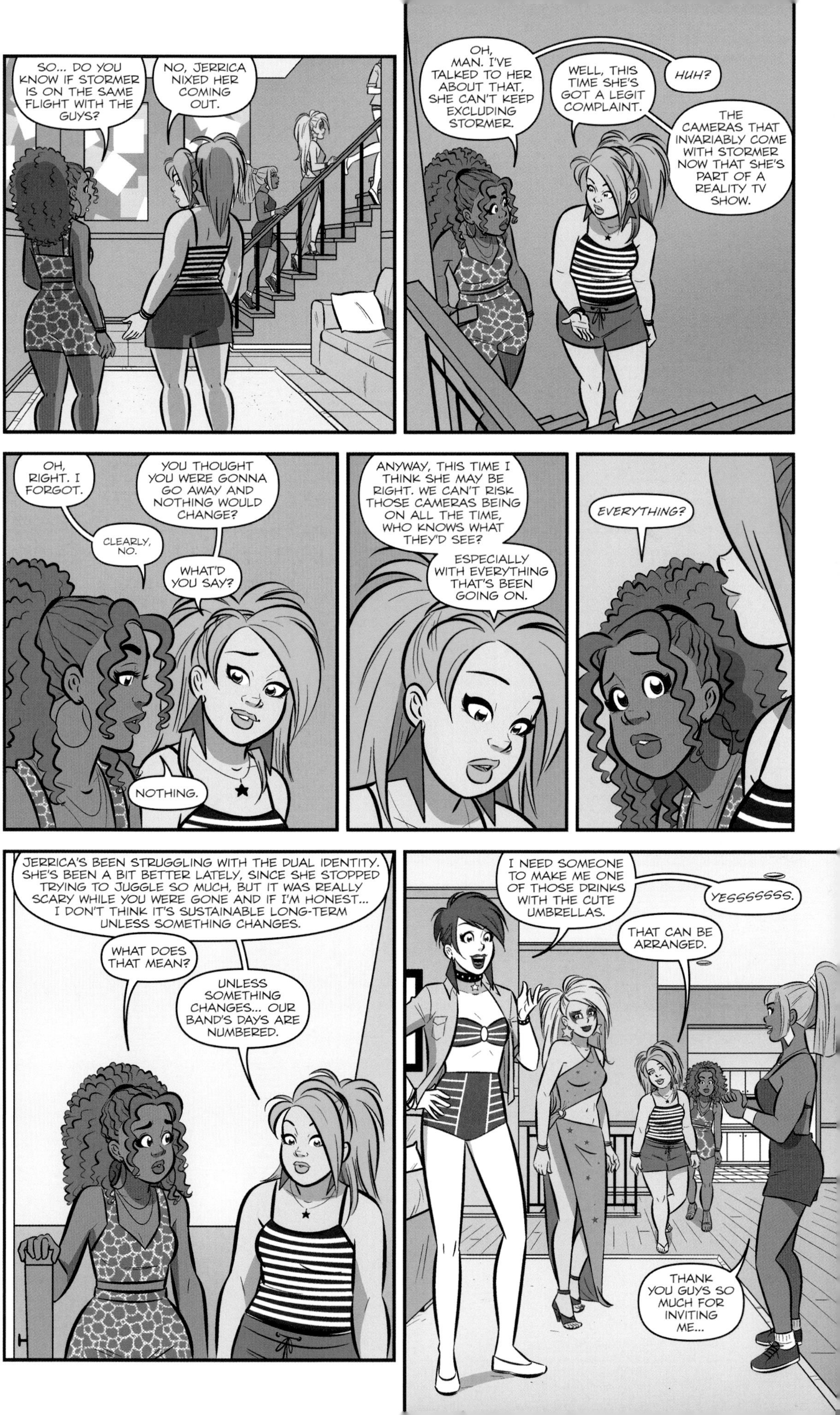

SO... DO YOU KNOW IF STORMER IS ON THE SAME FLIGHT WITH THE GUYS?
NO, JERRICA NIXED HER COMING OUT.
OH, MAN. I'VE TALKED TO HER ABOUT THAT, SHE CAN'T KEEP EXCLUDING STORMER.
WELL, THIS TIME SHE'S GOT A LEGIT COMPLAINT.
HUH?
THE CAMERAS THAT INVARIABLY COME WITH STORMER NOW THAT SHE'S PART OF A REALITY TV SHOW.
OH, RIGHT. I FORGOT.
YOU THOUGHT YOU WERE GONNA GO AWAY AND NOTHING WOULD CHANGE?
CLEARLY, NO.
WHAT'D YOU SAY?
NOTHING.
ANYWAY, THIS TIME I THINK SHE MAY BE RIGHT. WE CAN'T RISK THOSE CAMERAS BEING ON ALL THE TIME, WHO KNOWS WHAT THEY'D SEE?
ESPECIALLY WITH EVERYTHING THAT'S BEEN GOING ON.
EVERYTHING?
JERRICA'S BEEN STRUGGLING WITH THE DUAL IDENTITY. SHE'S BEEN A BIT BETTER LATELY, SINCE SHE STOPPED TRYING TO JUGGLE SO MUCH, BUT IT WAS REALLY SCARY WHILE YOU WERE GONE AND IF I'M HONEST... I DON'T THINK IT'S SUSTAINABLE LONG-TERM UNLESS SOMETHING CHANGES.
WHAT DOES THAT MEAN?
UNLESS SOMETHING CHANGES... OUR BAND'S DAYS ARE NUMBERED.
I NEED SOMEONE TO MAKE ME ONE OF THOSE DRINKS WITH THE CUTE UMBRELLAS.
YESSSSSSS.
THAT CAN BE ARRANGED.
THANK YOU GUYS SO MUCH FOR INVITING ME...

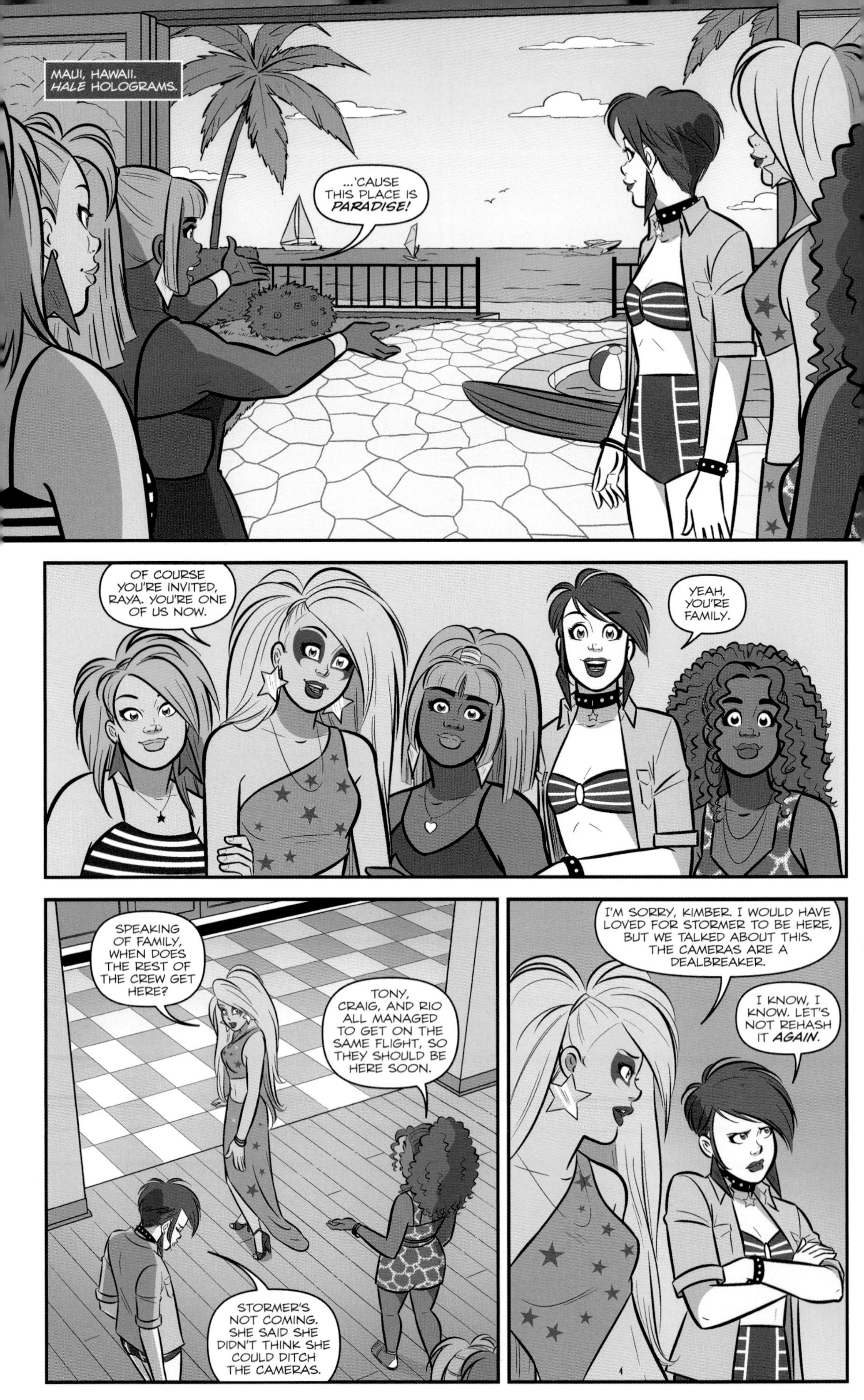

MAUI, HAWAII.
HALE HOLOGRAMS.
...'CAUSE THIS PLACE IS *PARADISE!*
OF COURSE YOU'RE INVITED, RAYA. YOU'RE ONE OF US NOW.
YEAH, YOU'RE FAMILY.
SPEAKING OF FAMILY, WHEN DOES THE REST OF THE CREW GET HERE?
TONY, CRAIG, AND RIO ALL MANAGED TO GET ON THE SAME FLIGHT, SO THEY SHOULD BE HERE SOON.
STORMER'S NOT COMING. SHE SAID SHE DIDN'T THINK SHE COULD DITCH THE CAMERAS.
I'M SORRY, KIMBER. I WOULD HAVE LOVED FOR STORMER TO BE HERE, BUT WE TALKED ABOUT THIS. THE CAMERAS ARE A DEALBREAKER.
I KNOW, I KNOW. LET'S NOT REHASH IT *AGAIN*.

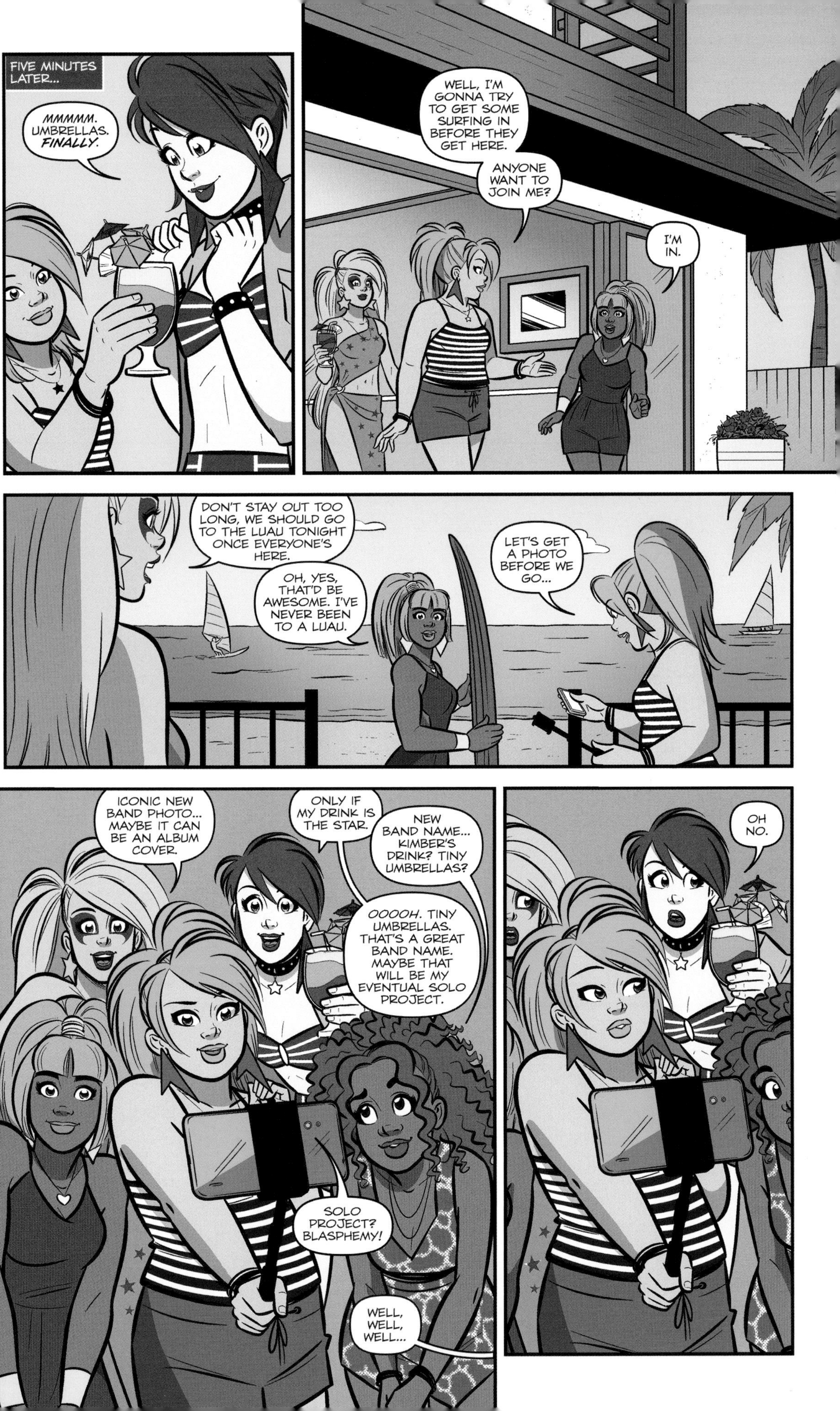
FIVE MINUTES LATER...
MMMMM. UMBRELLAS. FINALLY.
WELL, I'M GONNA TRY TO GET SOME SURFING IN BEFORE THEY GET HERE.
ANYONE WANT TO JOIN ME?
I'M IN.
DON'T STAY OUT TOO LONG, WE SHOULD GO TO THE LUAU TONIGHT ONCE EVERYONE'S HERE.
OH, YES, THAT'D BE AWESOME. I'VE NEVER BEEN TO A LUAU.
LET'S GET A PHOTO BEFORE WE GO...
ICONIC NEW BAND PHOTO... MAYBE IT CAN BE AN ALBUM COVER.
ONLY IF MY DRINK IS THE STAR.
NEW BAND NAME... KIMBER'S DRINK? TINY UMBRELLAS?
OOOOH. TINY UMBRELLAS. THAT'S A GREAT BAND NAME. MAYBE THAT WILL BE MY EVENTUAL SOLO PROJECT.
SOLO PROJECT? BLASPHEMY!
WELL, WELL, WELL...
OH NO.

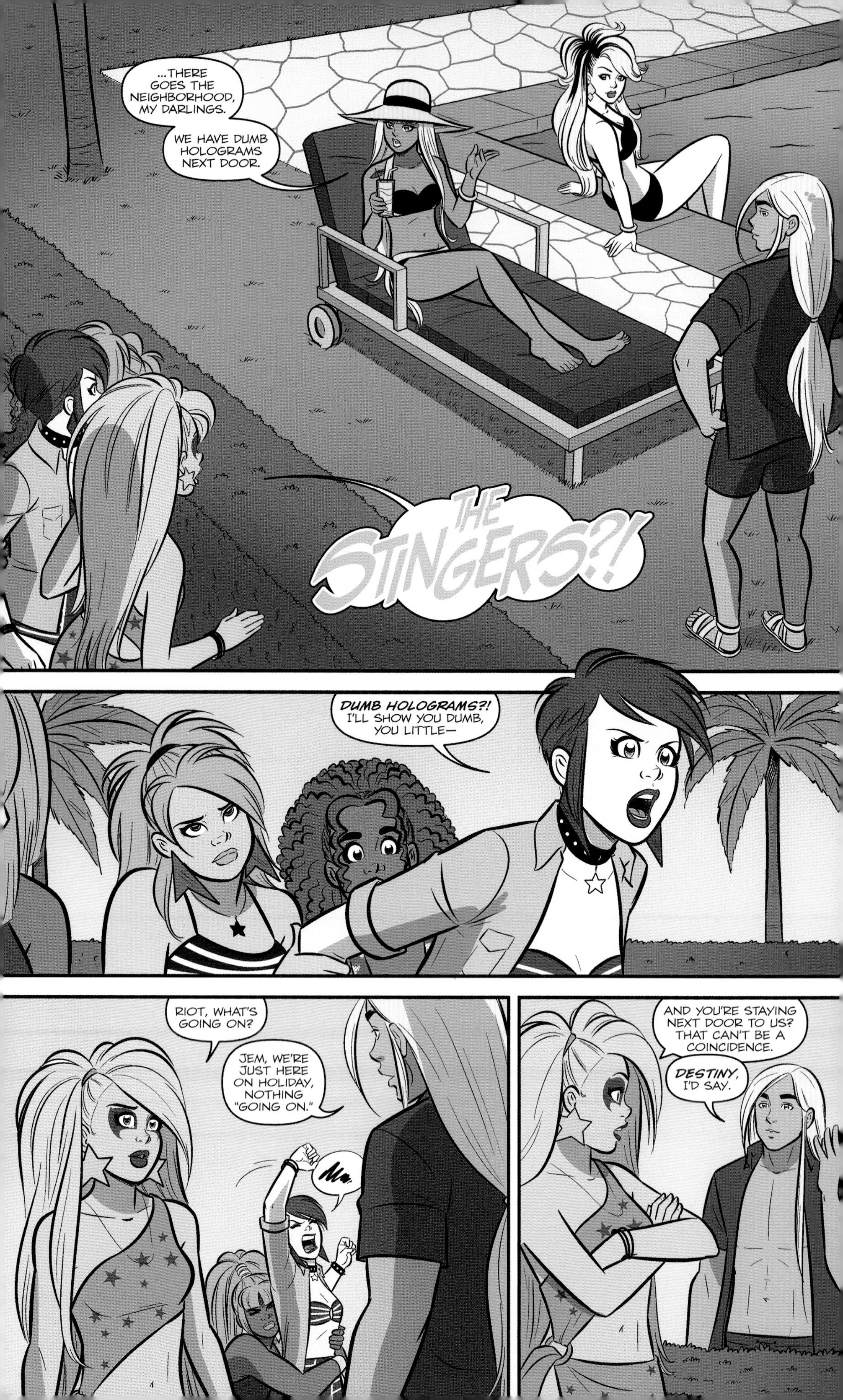

...THERE GOES THE NEIGHBORHOOD, MY DARLINGS.
WE HAVE DUMB HOLOGRAMS NEXT DOOR.
THE STINGERS?!
DUMB HOLOGRAMS?! I'LL SHOW YOU DUMB, YOU LITTLE—
RIOT, WHAT'S GOING ON?
JEM, WE'RE JUST HERE ON HOLIDAY, NOTHING "GOING ON."
AND YOU'RE STAYING NEXT DOOR TO US? THAT CAN'T BE A COINCIDENCE.
DESTINY, I'D SAY.

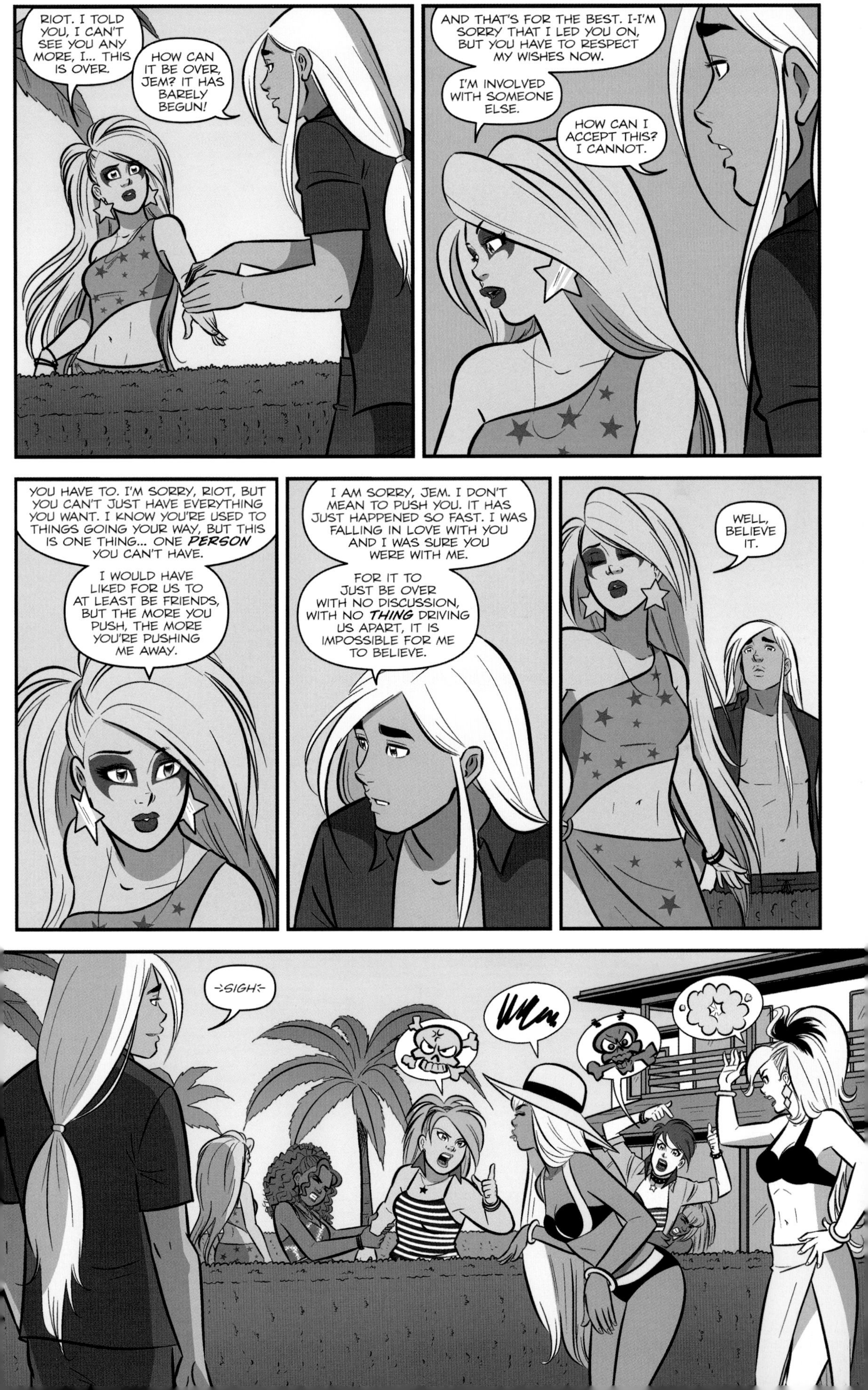

RIOT. I TOLD YOU, I CAN'T SEE YOU ANY MORE, I... THIS IS OVER.
HOW CAN IT BE OVER, JEM? IT HAS BARELY BEGUN!
AND THAT'S FOR THE BEST. I-I'M SORRY THAT I LED YOU ON, BUT YOU HAVE TO RESPECT MY WISHES NOW.
I'M INVOLVED WITH SOMEONE ELSE.
HOW CAN I ACCEPT THIS? I CANNOT.
YOU HAVE TO. I'M SORRY, RIOT, BUT YOU CAN'T JUST HAVE EVERYTHING YOU WANT. I KNOW YOU'RE USED TO THINGS GOING YOUR WAY, BUT THIS IS ONE THING... ONE PERSON YOU CAN'T HAVE.
I WOULD HAVE LIKED FOR US TO AT LEAST BE FRIENDS, BUT THE MORE YOU PUSH, THE MORE YOU'RE PUSHING ME AWAY.
I AM SORRY, JEM. I DON'T MEAN TO PUSH YOU. IT HAS JUST HAPPENED SO FAST. I WAS FALLING IN LOVE WITH YOU AND I WAS SURE YOU WERE WITH ME.
FOR IT TO JUST BE OVER WITH NO DISCUSSION, WITH NO THING DRIVING US APART, IT IS IMPOSSIBLE FOR ME TO BELIEVE.
WELL, BELIEVE IT.
-SIGH-

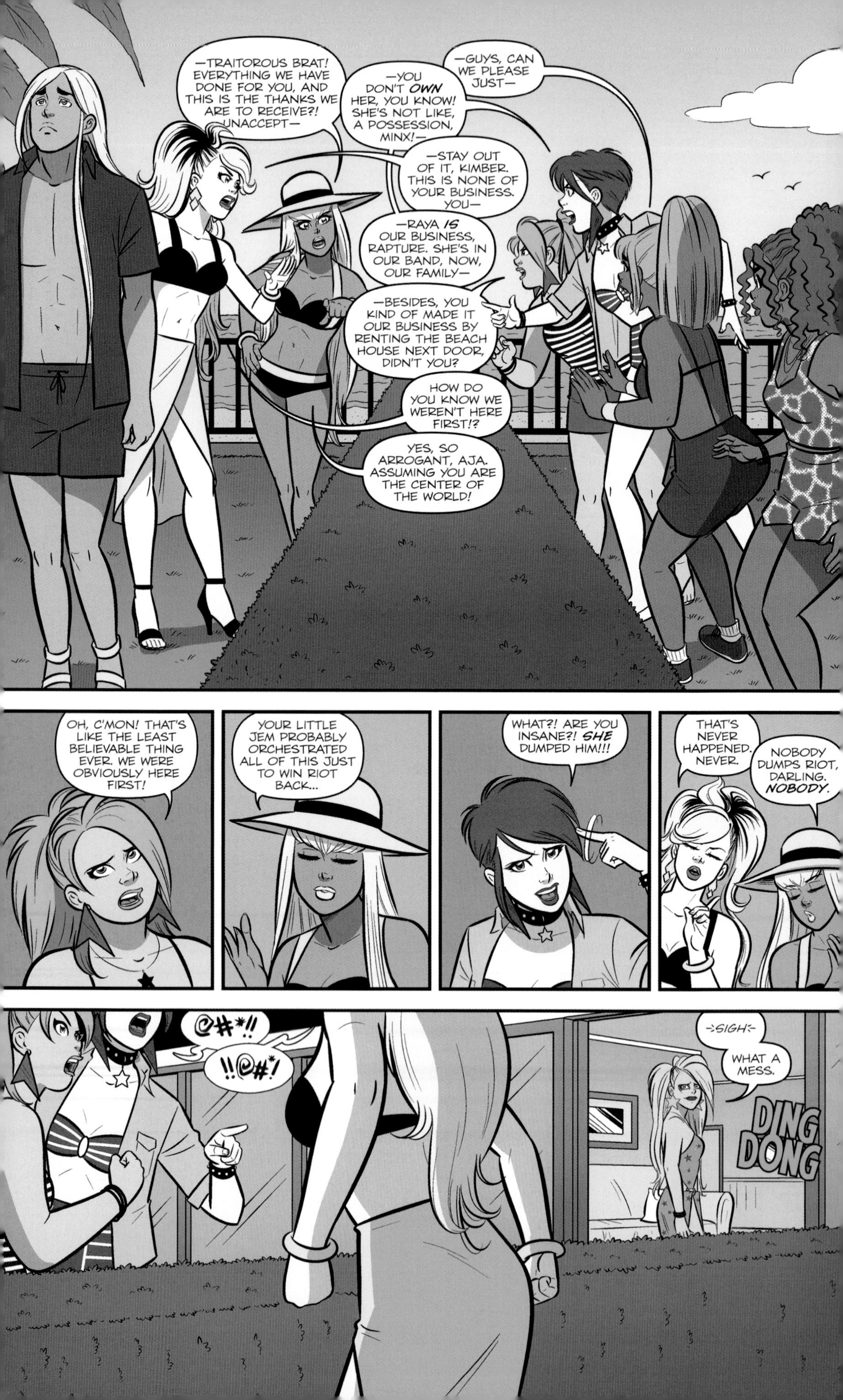

—TRAITOROUS BRAT! EVERYTHING WE HAVE DONE FOR YOU, AND THIS IS THE THANKS WE ARE TO RECEIVE?! UNACCEPT—
—YOU DON'T *OWN* HER, YOU KNOW! SHE'S NOT LIKE, A POSSESSION, MINX!—
—GUYS, CAN WE PLEASE JUST—
—STAY OUT OF IT, KIMBER. THIS IS NONE OF YOUR BUSINESS. YOU—
—RAYA *IS* OUR BUSINESS, RAPTURE. SHE'S IN OUR BAND, NOW, OUR FAMILY—
—BESIDES, YOU KIND OF MADE IT OUR BUSINESS BY RENTING THE BEACH HOUSE NEXT DOOR, DIDN'T YOU?
HOW DO YOU KNOW WE WEREN'T HERE FIRST!?
YES, SO ARROGANT, AJA. ASSUMING YOU ARE THE CENTER OF THE WORLD!
OH, C'MON! THAT'S LIKE THE LEAST BELIEVABLE THING EVER. WE WERE OBVIOUSLY HERE FIRST!
YOUR LITTLE JEM PROBABLY ORCHESTRATED ALL OF THIS JUST TO WIN RIOT BACK...
WHAT?! ARE YOU INSANE?! *SHE* DUMPED HIM!!!
THAT'S NEVER HAPPENED. NEVER.
NOBODY DUMPS RIOT, DARLING. *NOBODY*.
@#*!!
!!@#*!
-SIGH-
WHAT A MESS.
DING DONG

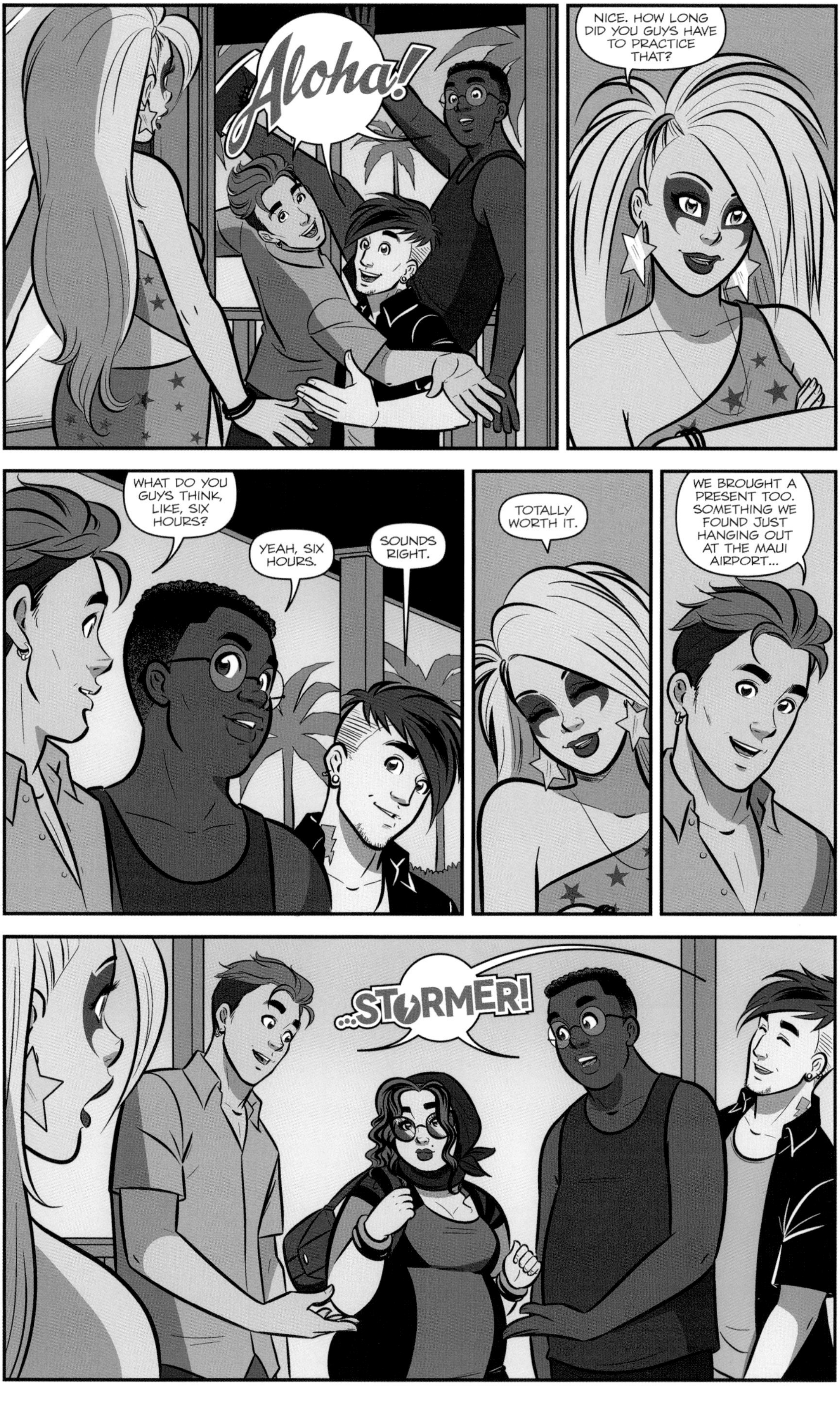
Aloha!
NICE. HOW LONG DID YOU GUYS HAVE TO PRACTICE THAT?
WHAT DO YOU GUYS THINK, LIKE, SIX HOURS?
YEAH, SIX HOURS.
SOUNDS RIGHT.
TOTALLY WORTH IT.
WE BROUGHT A PRESENT TOO. SOMETHING WE FOUND JUST HANGING OUT AT THE MAUI AIRPORT...
...STORMER!

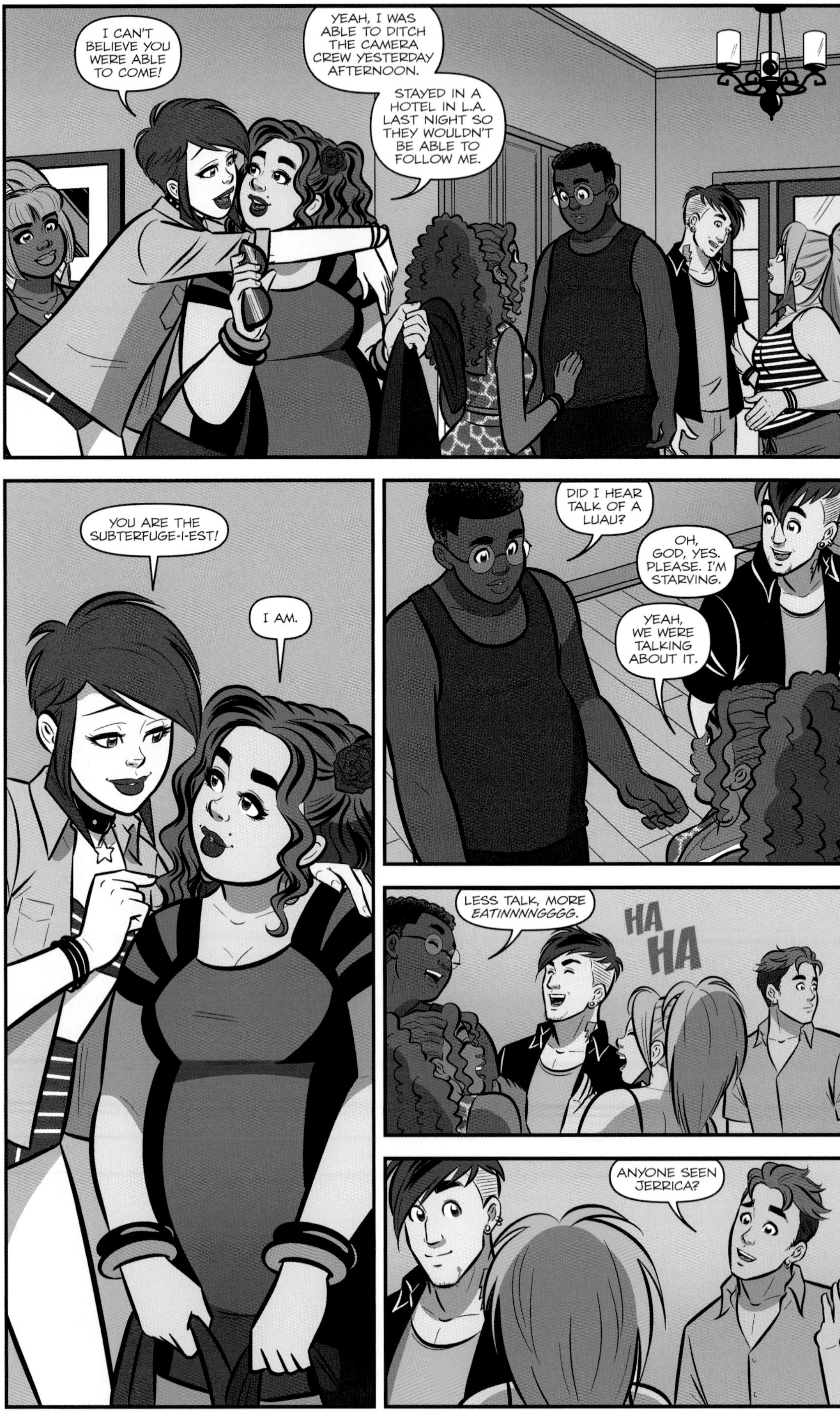

I CAN'T BELIEVE YOU WERE ABLE TO COME!
YEAH, I WAS ABLE TO DITCH THE CAMERA CREW YESTERDAY AFTERNOON.
STAYED IN A HOTEL IN L.A. LAST NIGHT SO THEY WOULDN'T BE ABLE TO FOLLOW ME.
YOU ARE THE SUBTERFUGE-I-EST!
I AM.
DID I HEAR TALK OF A LUAU?
OH, GOD, YES. PLEASE. I'M STARVING.
YEAH, WE WERE TALKING ABOUT IT.
LESS TALK, MORE *EATINNNNGGGG.*
HA HA
ANYONE SEEN JERRICA?

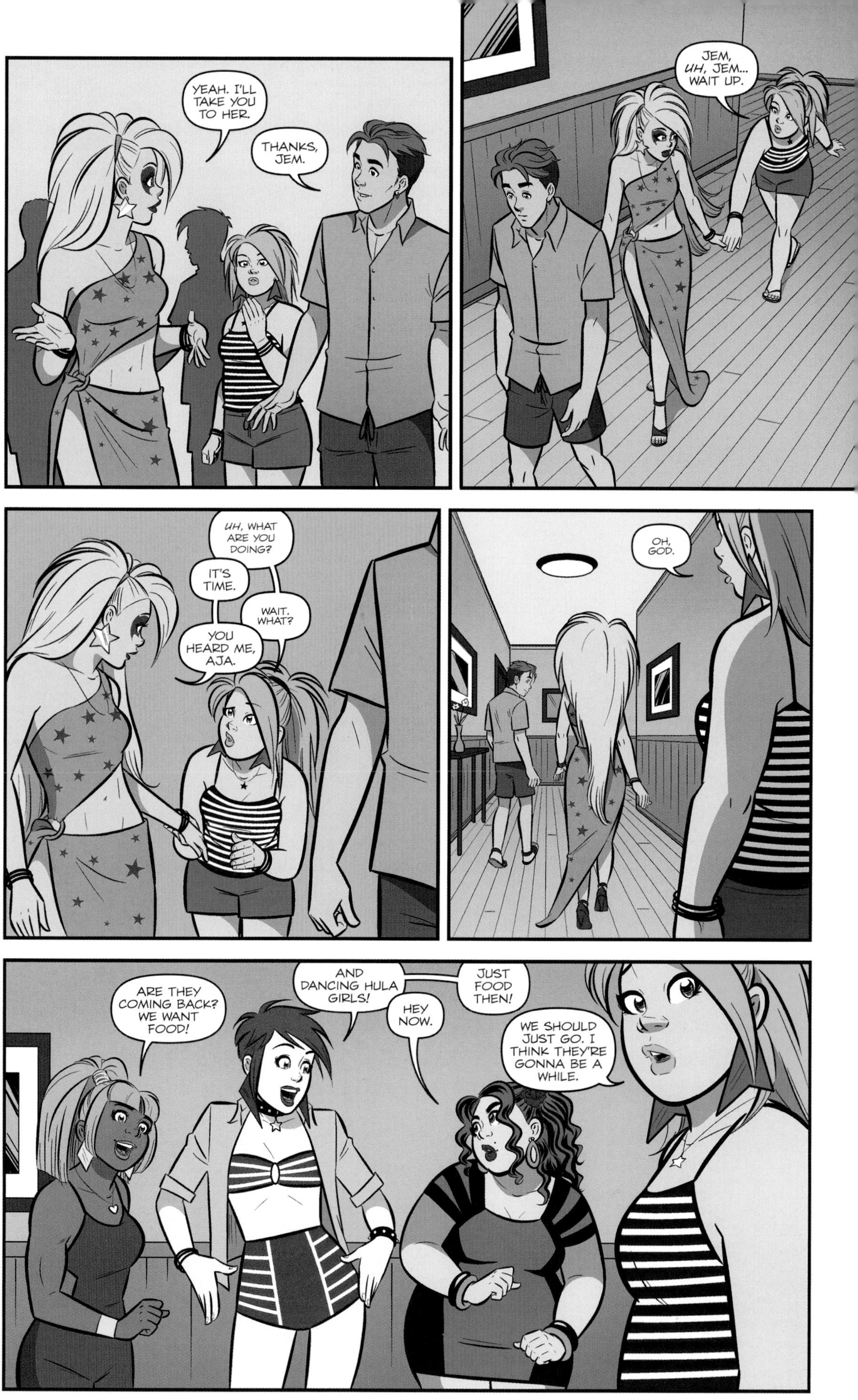
YEAH. I'LL TAKE YOU TO HER.
THANKS, JEM.
JEM, UH, JEM... WAIT UP.
UH, WHAT ARE YOU DOING?
IT'S TIME.
WAIT. WHAT?
YOU HEARD ME, AJA.
OH, GOD.
ARE THEY COMING BACK? WE WANT FOOD!
AND DANCING HULA GIRLS!
HEY NOW.
JUST FOOD THEN!
WE SHOULD JUST GO. I THINK THEY'RE GONNA BE A WHILE.

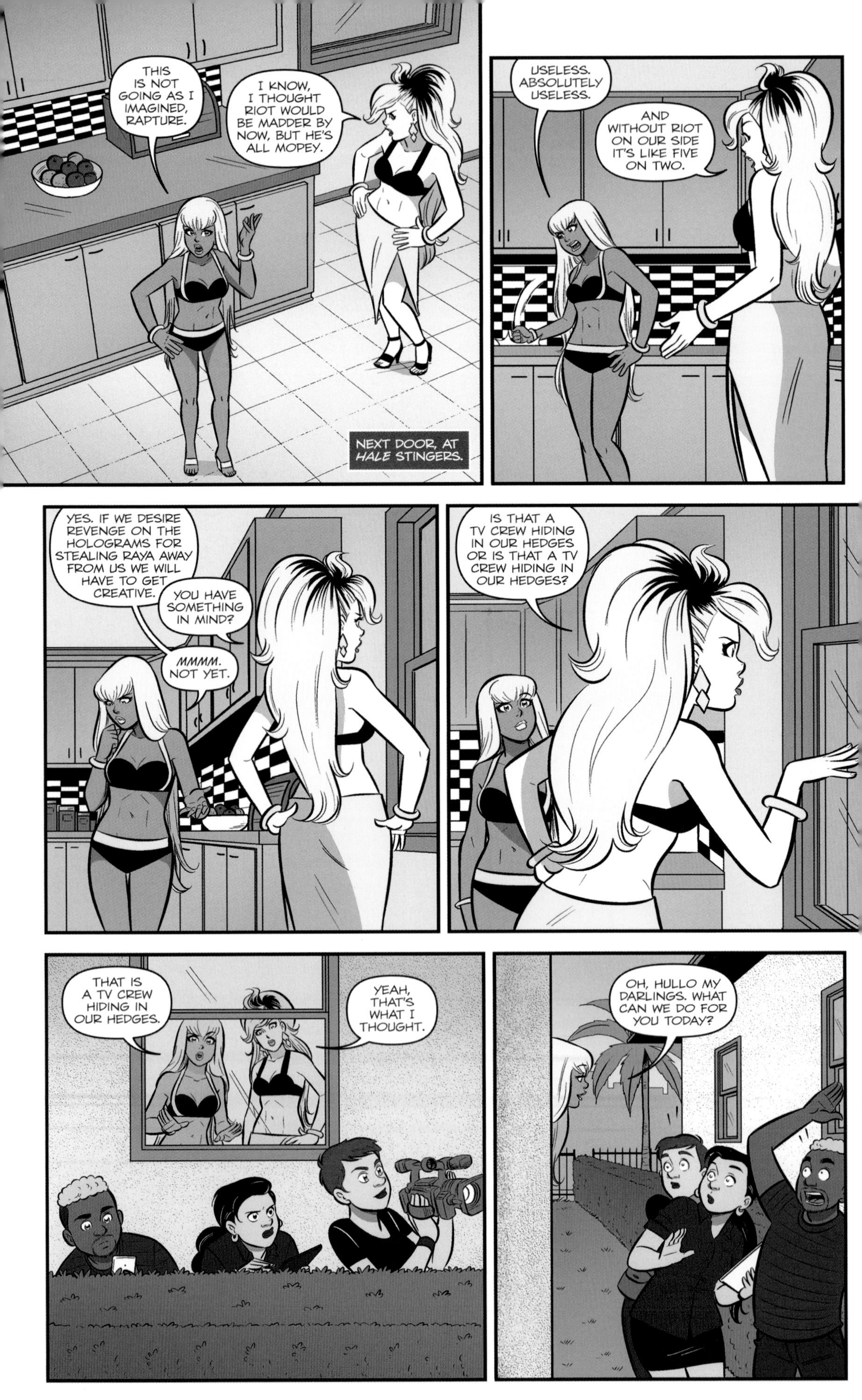
THIS IS NOT GOING AS I IMAGINED, RAPTURE.
I KNOW, I THOUGHT RIOT WOULD BE MADDER BY NOW, BUT HE'S ALL MOPEY.
NEXT DOOR, AT HALE STINGERS.
USELESS. ABSOLUTELY USELESS.
AND WITHOUT RIOT ON OUR SIDE IT'S LIKE FIVE ON TWO.
YES. IF WE DESIRE REVENGE ON THE HOLOGRAMS FOR STEALING RAYA AWAY FROM US WE WILL HAVE TO GET CREATIVE.
YOU HAVE SOMETHING IN MIND?
MMMM. NOT YET.
IS THAT A TV CREW HIDING IN OUR HEDGES OR IS THAT A TV CREW HIDING IN OUR HEDGES?
THAT IS A TV CREW HIDING IN OUR HEDGES.
YEAH, THAT'S WHAT I THOUGHT.
OH, HULLO MY DARLINGS. WHAT CAN WE DO FOR YOU TODAY?

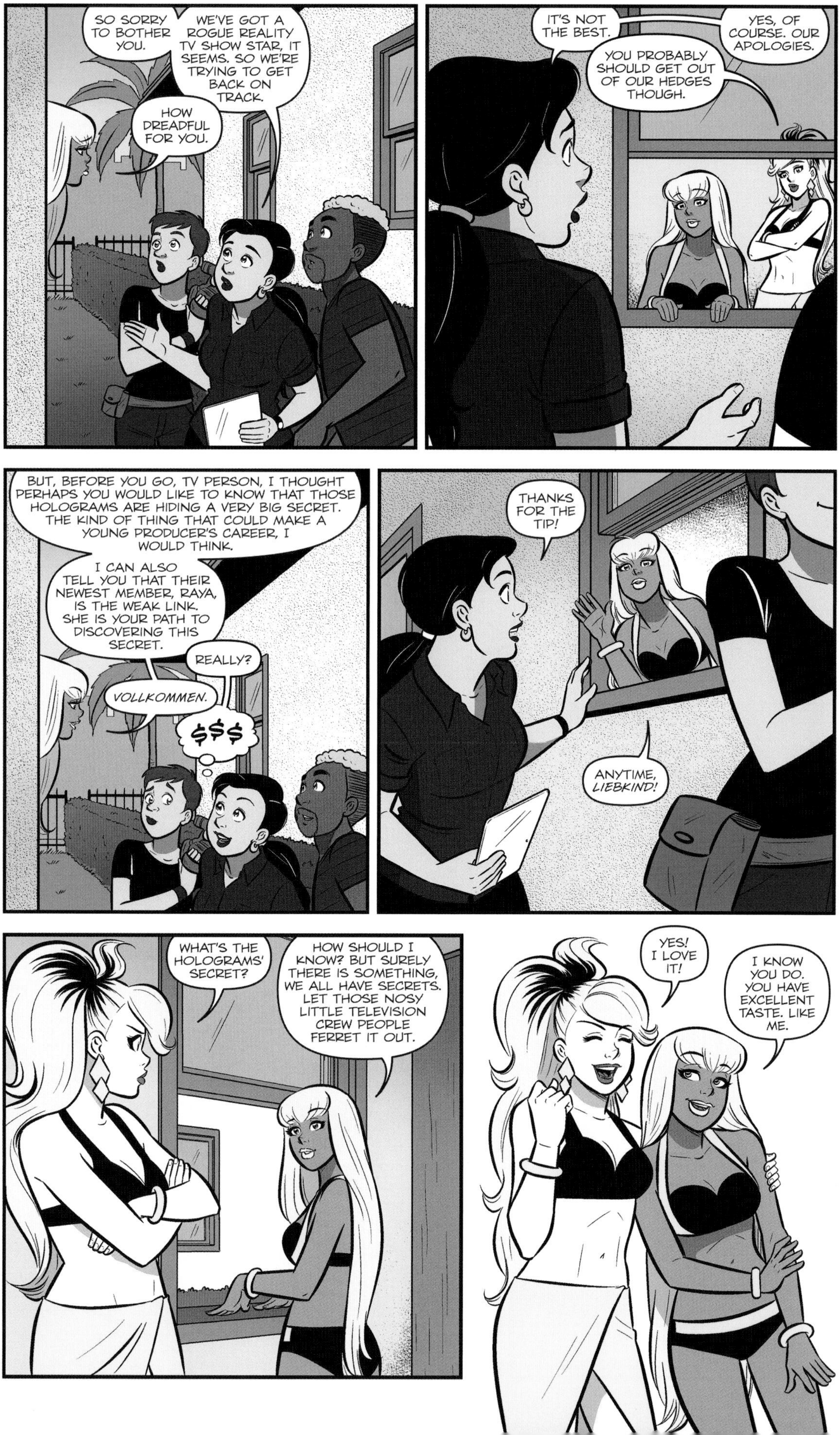
SO SORRY TO BOTHER YOU.
WE'VE GOT A ROGUE REALITY TV SHOW STAR, IT SEEMS. SO WE'RE TRYING TO GET BACK ON TRACK.
HOW DREADFUL FOR YOU.
IT'S NOT THE BEST.
YES, OF COURSE. OUR APOLOGIES.
YOU PROBABLY SHOULD GET OUT OF OUR HEDGES THOUGH.
BUT, BEFORE YOU GO, TV PERSON, I THOUGHT PERHAPS YOU WOULD LIKE TO KNOW THAT THOSE HOLOGRAMS ARE HIDING A VERY BIG SECRET. THE KIND OF THING THAT COULD MAKE A YOUNG PRODUCER'S CAREER, I WOULD THINK.
I CAN ALSO TELL YOU THAT THEIR NEWEST MEMBER, RAYA, IS THE WEAK LINK. SHE IS YOUR PATH TO DISCOVERING THIS SECRET.
REALLY?
VOLLKOMMEN.
$$$
THANKS FOR THE TIP!
ANYTIME, *LIEBKIND!*
WHAT'S THE HOLOGRAMS' SECRET?
HOW SHOULD I KNOW? BUT SURELY THERE IS SOMETHING. WE ALL HAVE SECRETS. LET THOSE NOSY LITTLE TELEVISION CREW PEOPLE FERRET IT OUT.
YES! I LOVE IT!
I KNOW YOU DO. YOU HAVE EXCELLENT TASTE. LIKE ME.

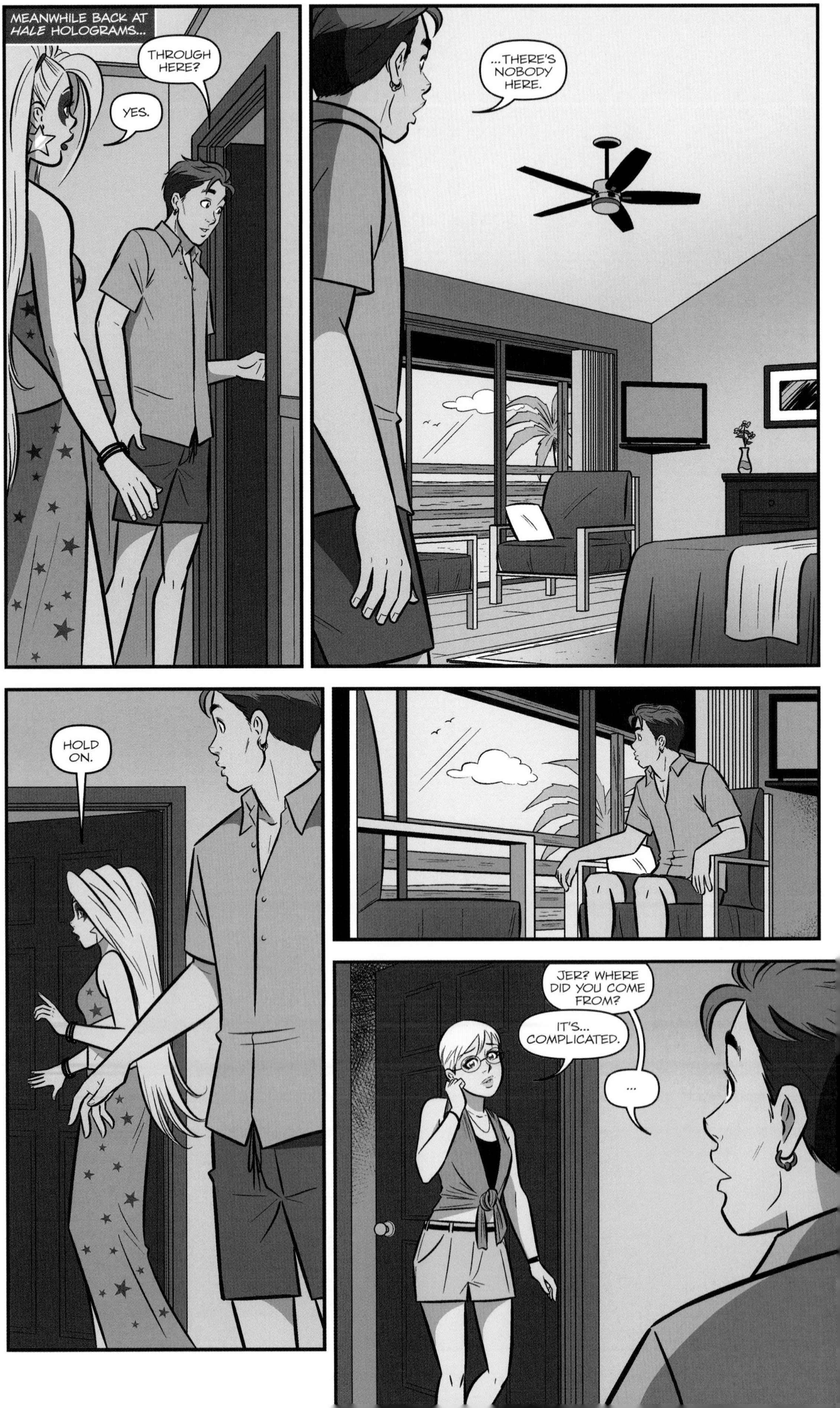

MEANWHILE BACK AT *HALE* HOLOGRAMS...
THROUGH HERE?
YES.
...THERE'S NOBODY HERE.
HOLD ON.
JER? WHERE DID YOU COME FROM?
IT'S... COMPLICATED.
...

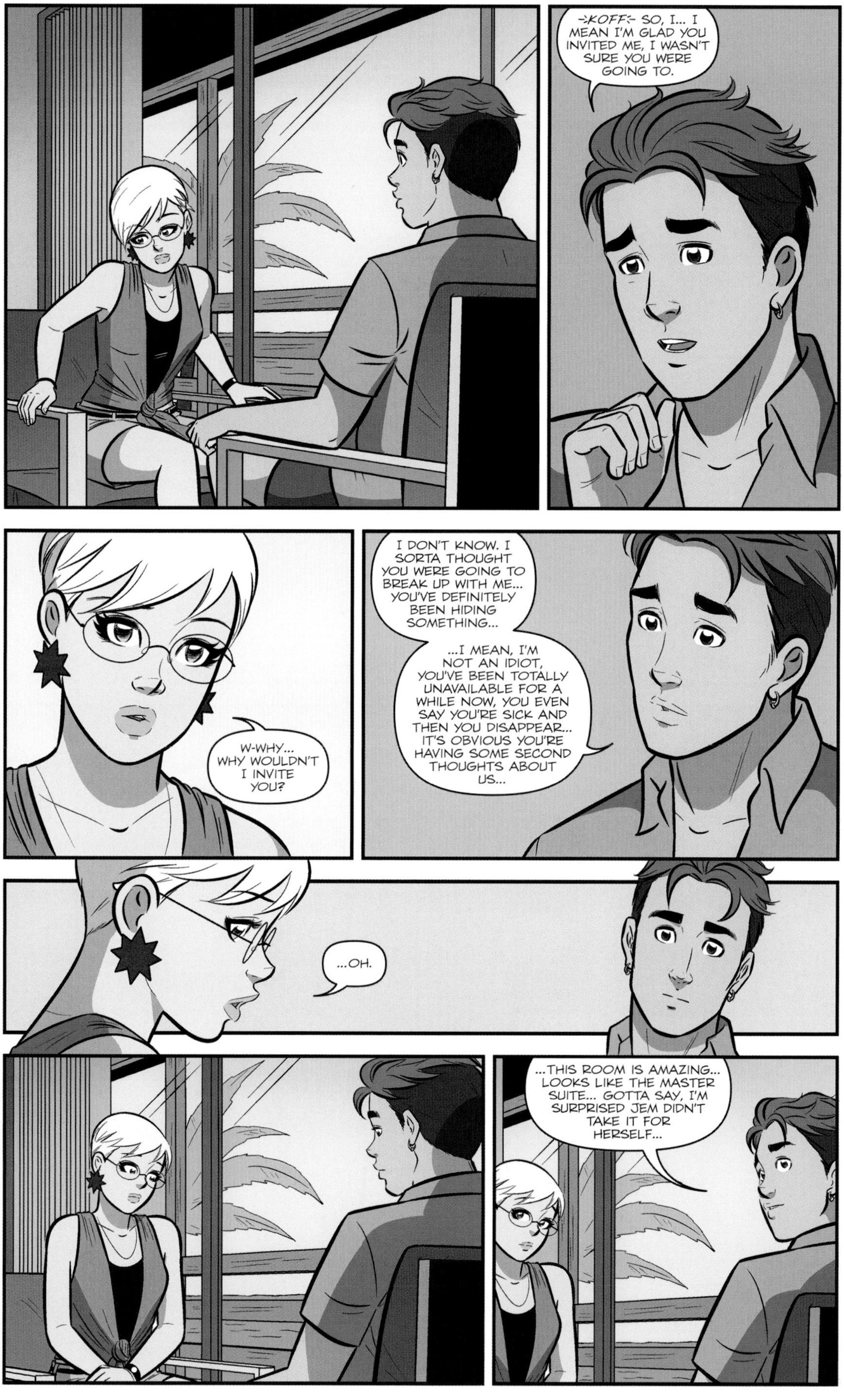
-KOFF- SO, I... I MEAN I'M GLAD YOU INVITED ME, I WASN'T SURE YOU WERE GOING TO.
W-WHY... WHY WOULDN'T I INVITE YOU?
I DON'T KNOW. I SORTA THOUGHT YOU WERE GOING TO BREAK UP WITH ME... YOU'VE DEFINITELY BEEN HIDING SOMETHING...
...I MEAN, I'M NOT AN IDIOT, YOU'VE BEEN TOTALLY UNAVAILABLE FOR A WHILE NOW, YOU EVEN SAY YOU'RE SICK AND THEN YOU DISAPPEAR... IT'S OBVIOUS YOU'RE HAVING SOME SECOND THOUGHTS ABOUT US...
...OH.
...THIS ROOM IS AMAZING... LOOKS LIKE THE MASTER SUITE... GOTTA SAY, I'M SURPRISED JEM DIDN'T TAKE IT FOR HERSELF...

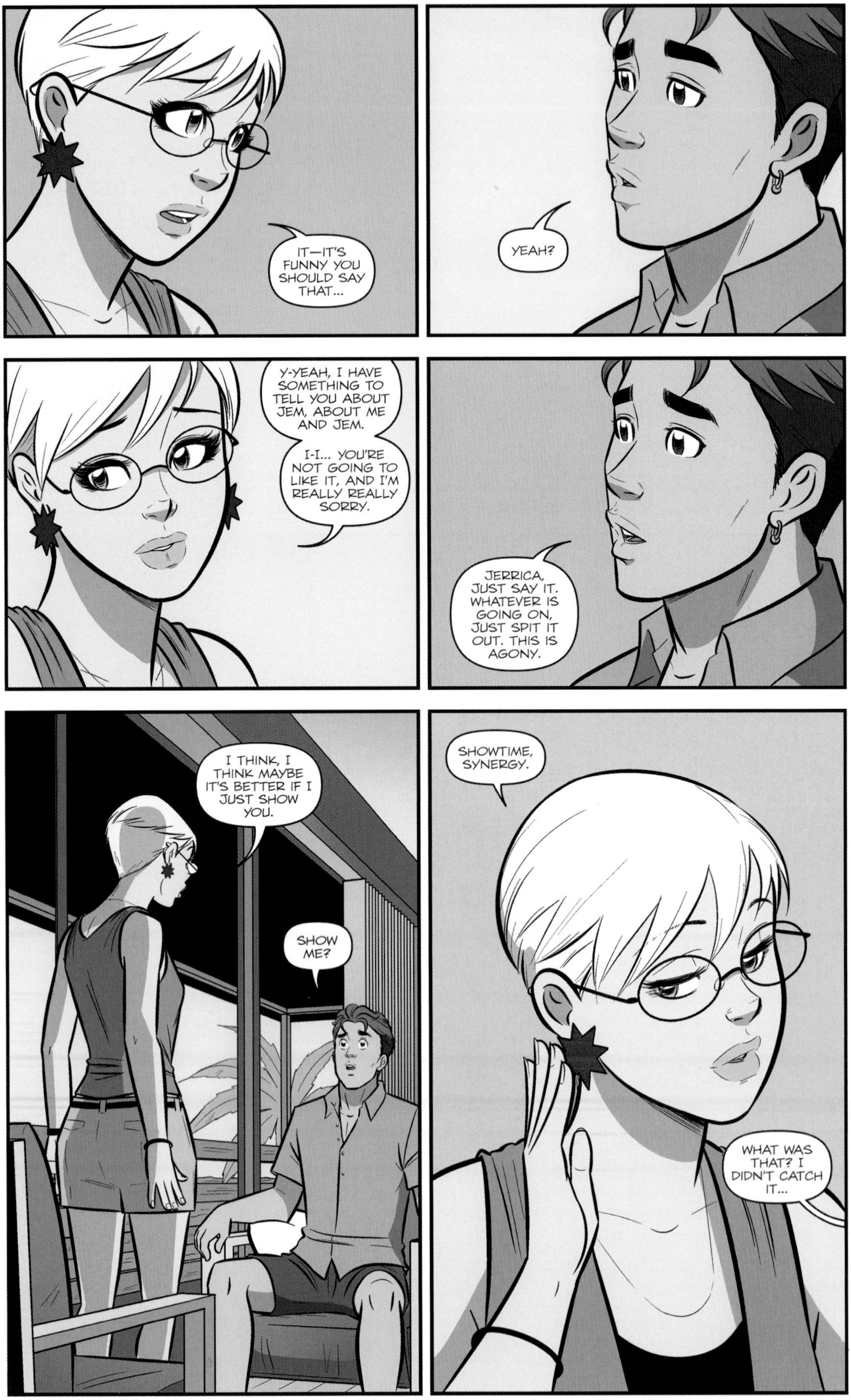
IT—IT'S FUNNY YOU SHOULD SAY THAT...
YEAH?
Y-YEAH, I HAVE SOMETHING TO TELL YOU ABOUT JEM, ABOUT ME AND JEM.
I-I... YOU'RE NOT GOING TO LIKE IT, AND I'M REALLY REALLY SORRY.
JERRICA, JUST SAY IT. WHATEVER IS GOING ON, JUST SPIT IT OUT. THIS IS AGONY.
I THINK, I THINK MAYBE IT'S BETTER IF I JUST SHOW YOU.
SHOW ME?
SHOWTIME, SYNERGY.
WHAT WAS THAT? I DIDN'T CATCH IT...

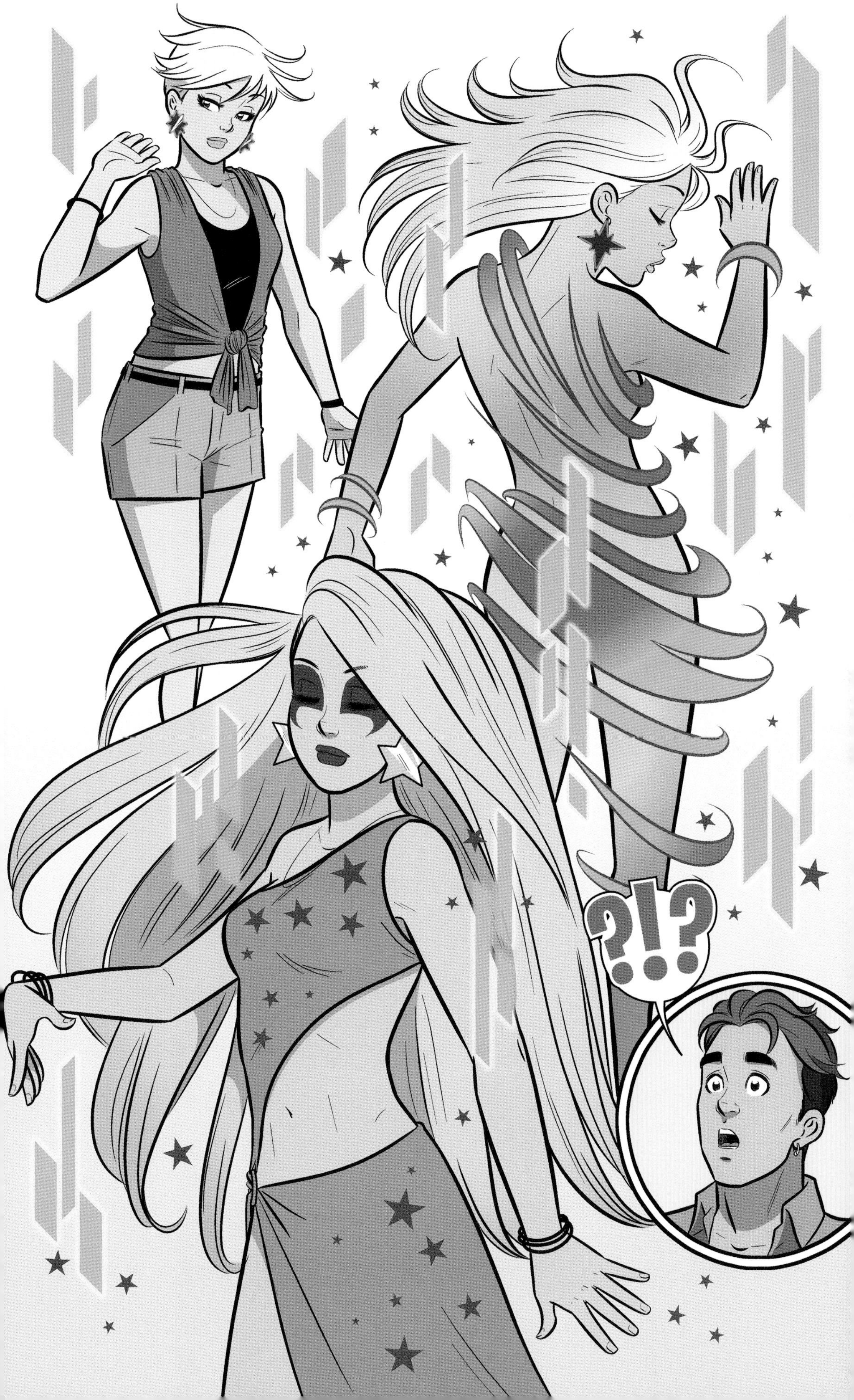
?!?

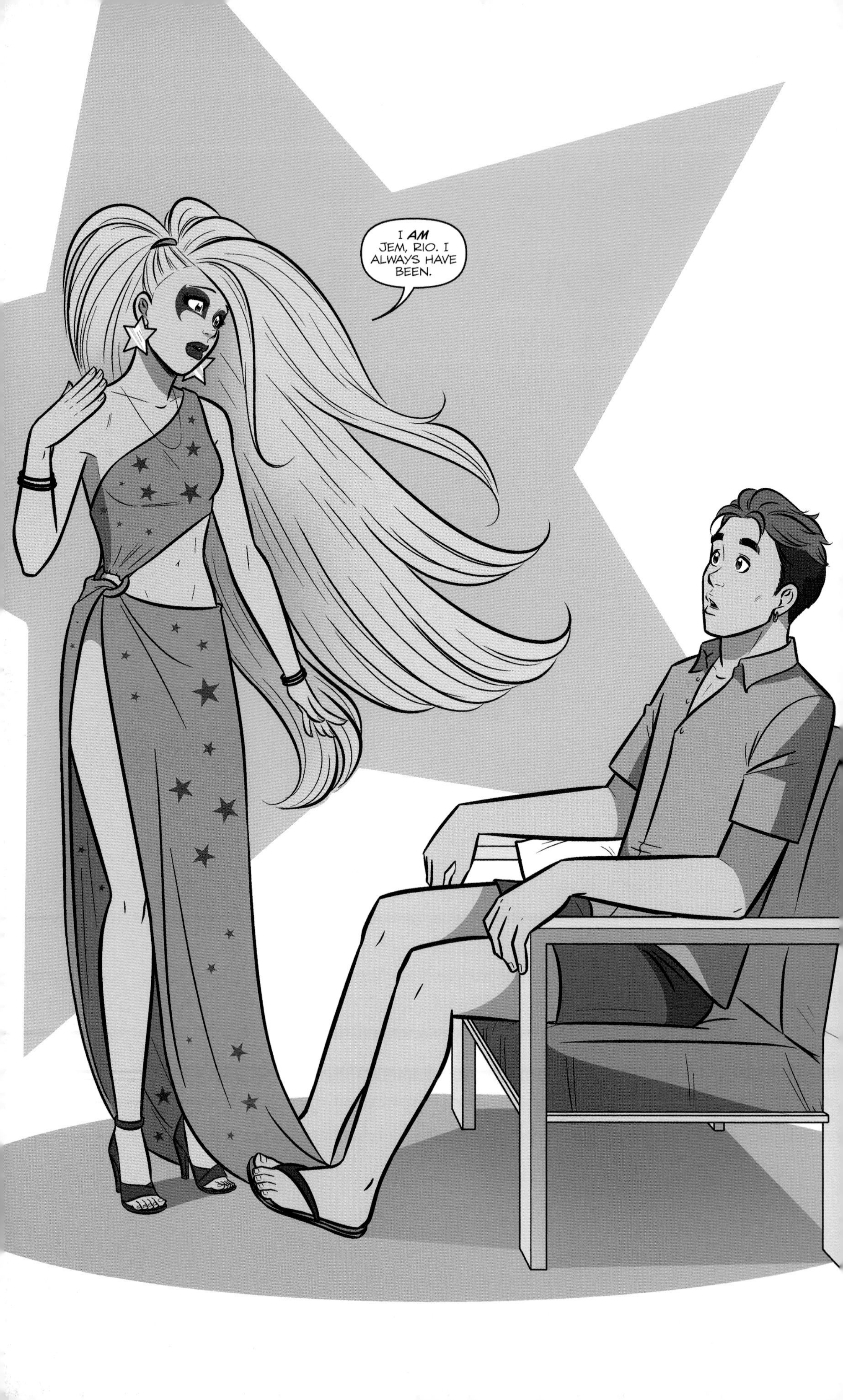
I *AM* JEM, RIO. I ALWAYS HAVE BEEN.

2 ART BY **JEN BARTEL**

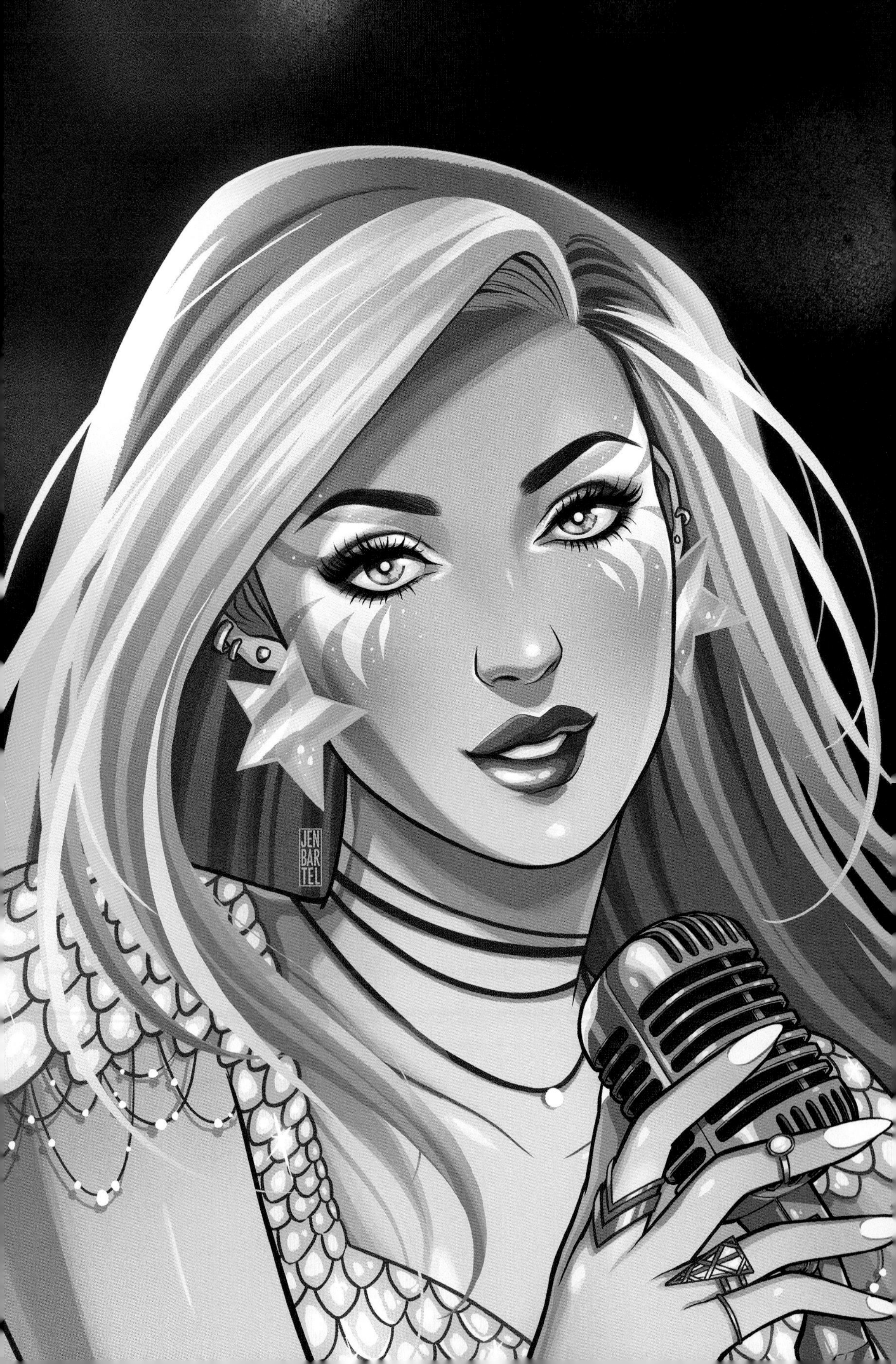
JEN BARTEL

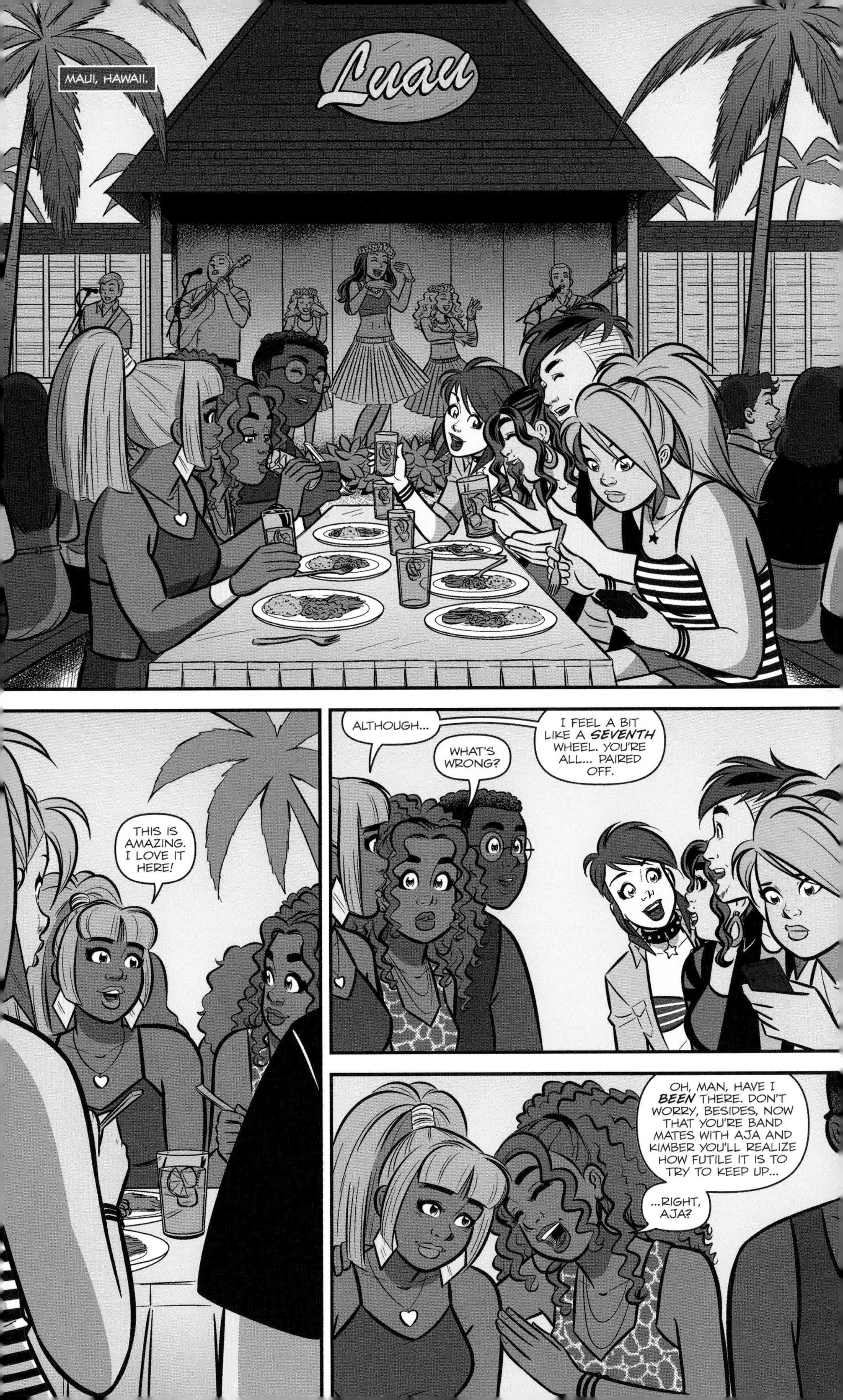

MAUI, HAWAII.
Luau
THIS IS AMAZING. I LOVE IT HERE!
ALTHOUGH...
WHAT'S WRONG?
I FEEL A BIT LIKE A SEVENTH WHEEL. YOU'RE ALL... PAIRED OFF.
OH, MAN, HAVE I BEEN THERE. DON'T WORRY, BESIDES, NOW THAT YOU'RE BAND MATES WITH AJA AND KIMBER YOU'LL REALIZE HOW FUTILE IT IS TO TRY TO KEEP UP...
...RIGHT, AJA?

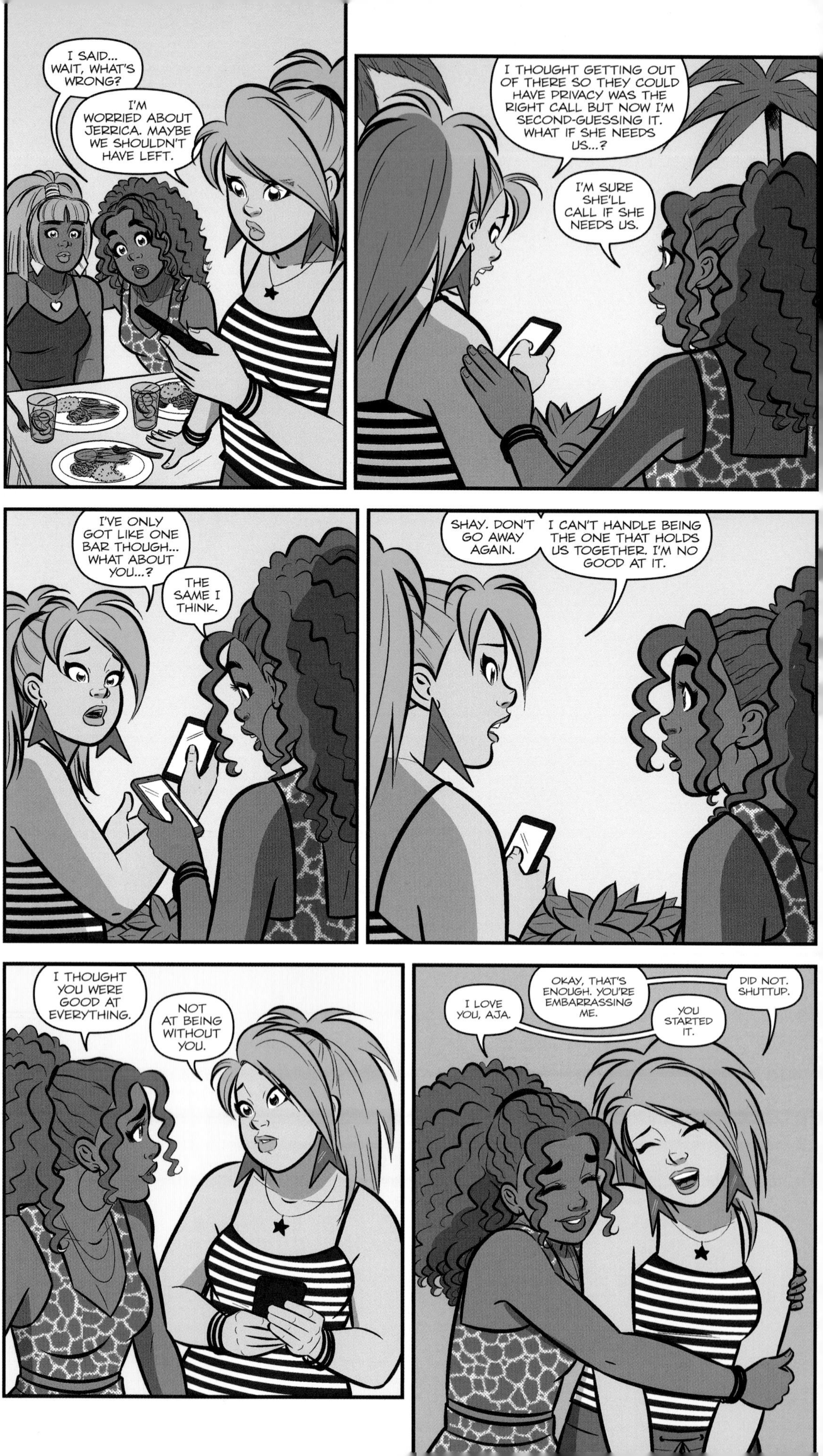
I SAID... WAIT, WHAT'S WRONG?
I'M WORRIED ABOUT JERRICA. MAYBE WE SHOULDN'T HAVE LEFT.
I THOUGHT GETTING OUT OF THERE SO THEY COULD HAVE PRIVACY WAS THE RIGHT CALL BUT NOW I'M SECOND-GUESSING IT. WHAT IF SHE NEEDS US...?
I'M SURE SHE'LL CALL IF SHE NEEDS US.
I'VE ONLY GOT LIKE ONE BAR THOUGH... WHAT ABOUT YOU...?
THE SAME I THINK.
SHAY. DON'T GO AWAY AGAIN.
I CAN'T HANDLE BEING THE ONE THAT HOLDS US TOGETHER. I'M NO GOOD AT IT.
I THOUGHT YOU WERE GOOD AT EVERYTHING.
NOT AT BEING WITHOUT YOU.
I LOVE YOU, AJA.
OKAY, THAT'S ENOUGH. YOU'RE EMBARRASSING ME.
YOU STARTED IT.
DID NOT. SHUTTUP.

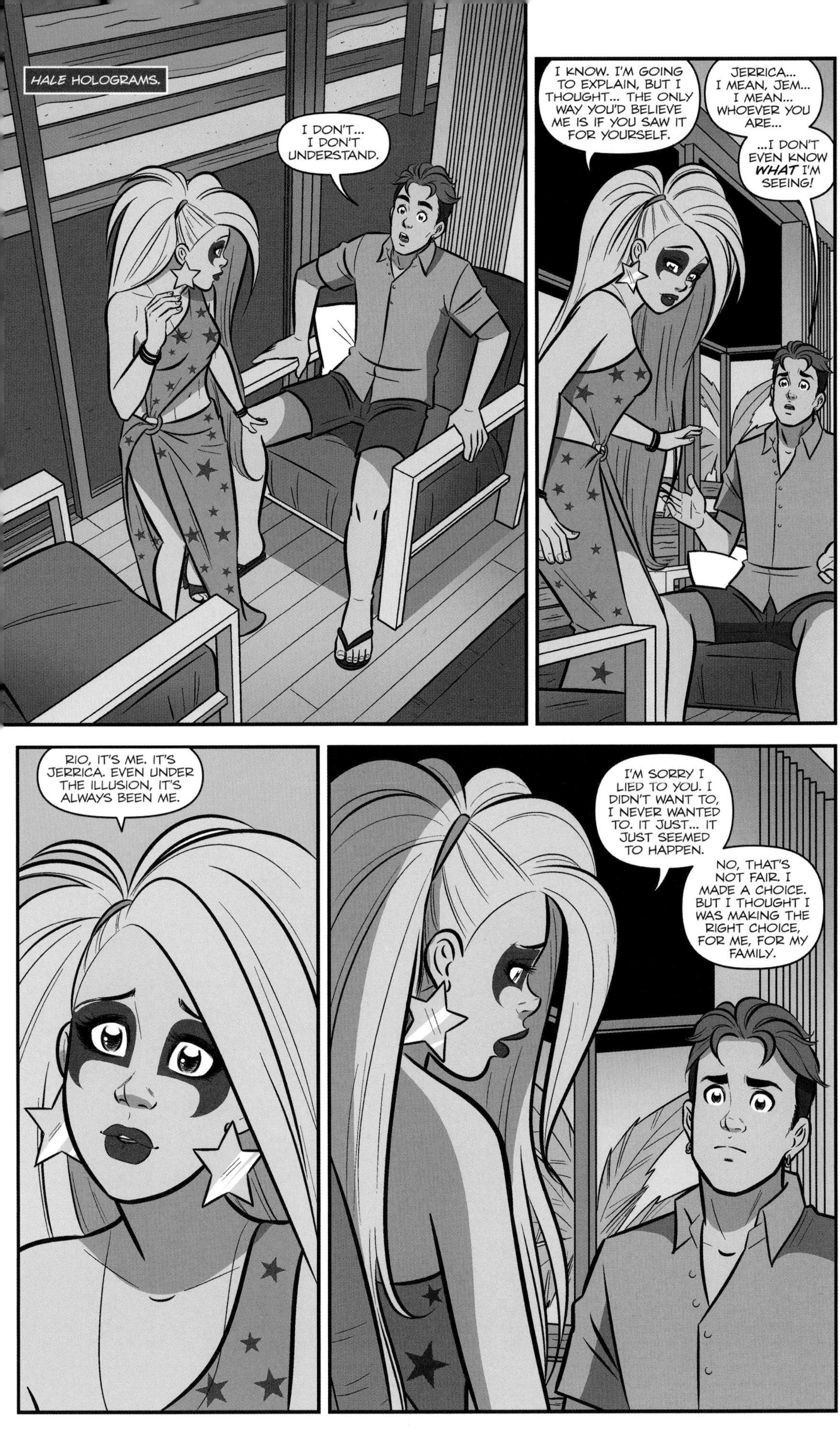
HALE HOLOGRAMS.
I DON'T... I DON'T UNDERSTAND.
I KNOW. I'M GOING TO EXPLAIN, BUT I THOUGHT... THE ONLY WAY YOU'D BELIEVE ME IS IF YOU SAW IT FOR YOURSELF.
JERRICA... I MEAN, JEM... I MEAN... WHOEVER YOU ARE...
...I DON'T EVEN KNOW *WHAT* I'M SEEING!
RIO, IT'S ME. IT'S JERRICA. EVEN UNDER THE ILLUSION, IT'S ALWAYS BEEN ME.
I'M SORRY I LIED TO YOU. I DIDN'T WANT TO, I NEVER WANTED TO. IT JUST... IT JUST SEEMED TO HAPPEN.
NO, THAT'S NOT FAIR. I MADE A CHOICE. BUT I THOUGHT I WAS MAKING THE RIGHT CHOICE, FOR ME, FOR MY FAMILY.

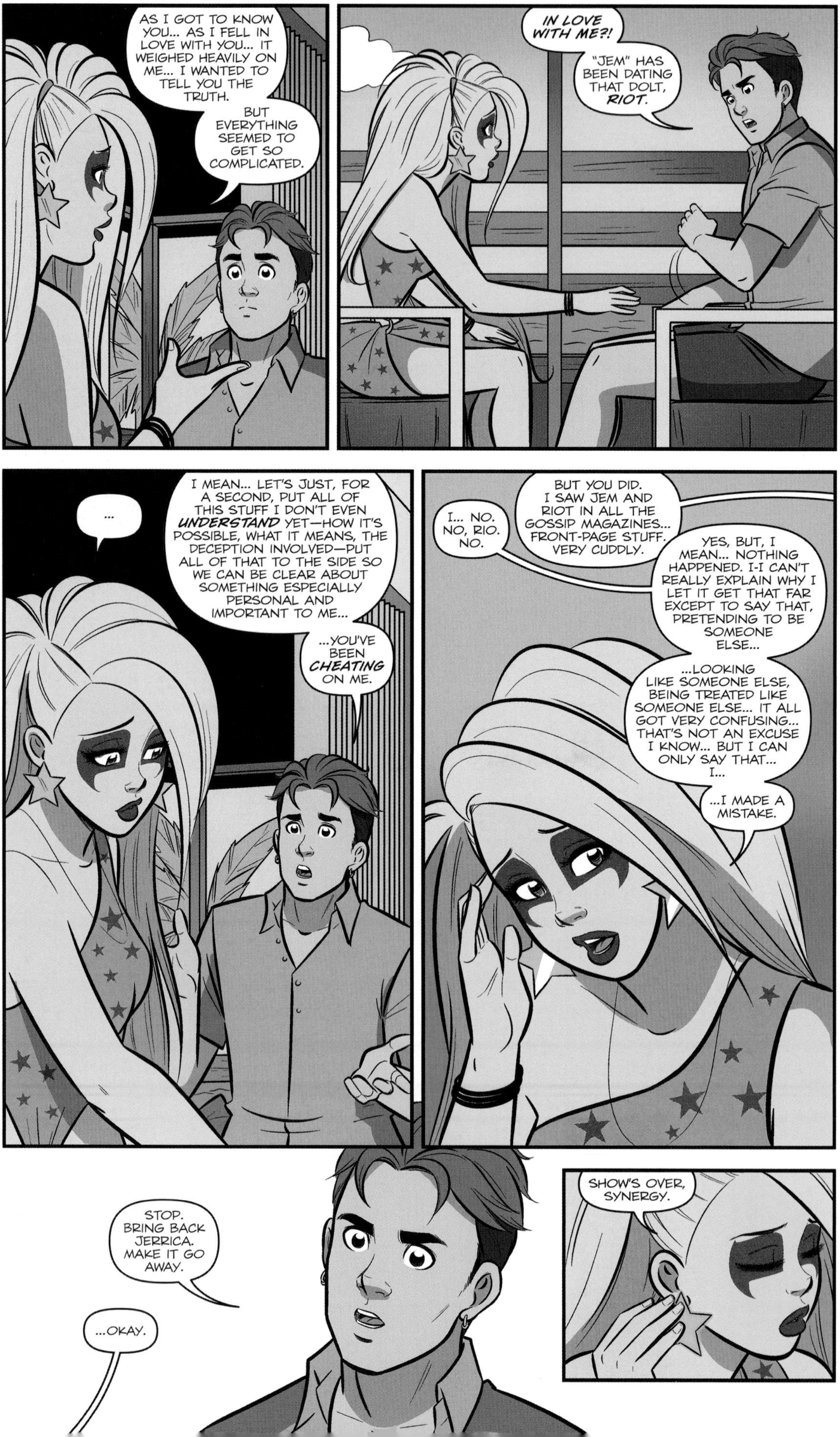

AS I GOT TO KNOW YOU... AS I FELL IN LOVE WITH YOU... IT WEIGHED HEAVILY ON ME... I WANTED TO TELL YOU THE TRUTH.
BUT EVERYTHING SEEMED TO GET SO COMPLICATED.
IN LOVE WITH ME?!
"JEM" HAS BEEN DATING THAT DOLT, RIOT.
...
I MEAN... LET'S JUST, FOR A SECOND, PUT ALL OF THIS STUFF I DON'T EVEN UNDERSTAND YET—HOW IT'S POSSIBLE, WHAT IT MEANS, THE DECEPTION INVOLVED—PUT ALL OF THAT TO THE SIDE SO WE CAN BE CLEAR ABOUT SOMETHING ESPECIALLY PERSONAL AND IMPORTANT TO ME...
...YOU'VE BEEN CHEATING ON ME.
I... NO. NO, RIO. NO.
BUT YOU DID. I SAW JEM AND RIOT IN ALL THE GOSSIP MAGAZINES... FRONT-PAGE STUFF. VERY CUDDLY.
YES, BUT, I MEAN... NOTHING HAPPENED. I-I CAN'T REALLY EXPLAIN WHY I LET IT GET THAT FAR EXCEPT TO SAY THAT, PRETENDING TO BE SOMEONE ELSE...
...LOOKING LIKE SOMEONE ELSE, BEING TREATED LIKE SOMEONE ELSE... IT ALL GOT VERY CONFUSING... THAT'S NOT AN EXCUSE I KNOW... BUT I CAN ONLY SAY THAT... I...
...I MADE A MISTAKE.
STOP. BRING BACK JERRICA. MAKE IT GO AWAY.
...OKAY.
SHOW'S OVER, SYNERGY.

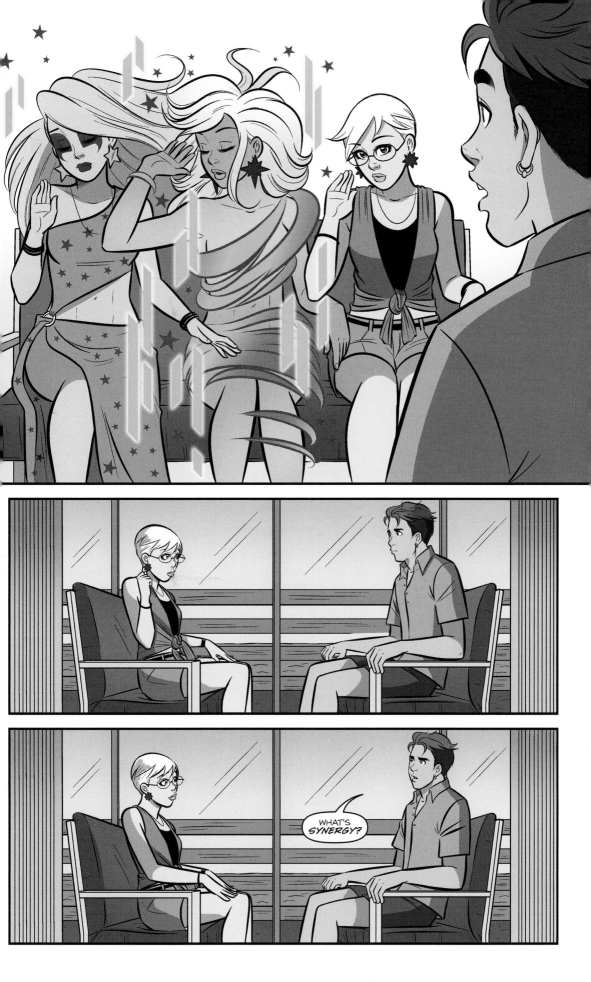

WHAT'S SYNERGY?

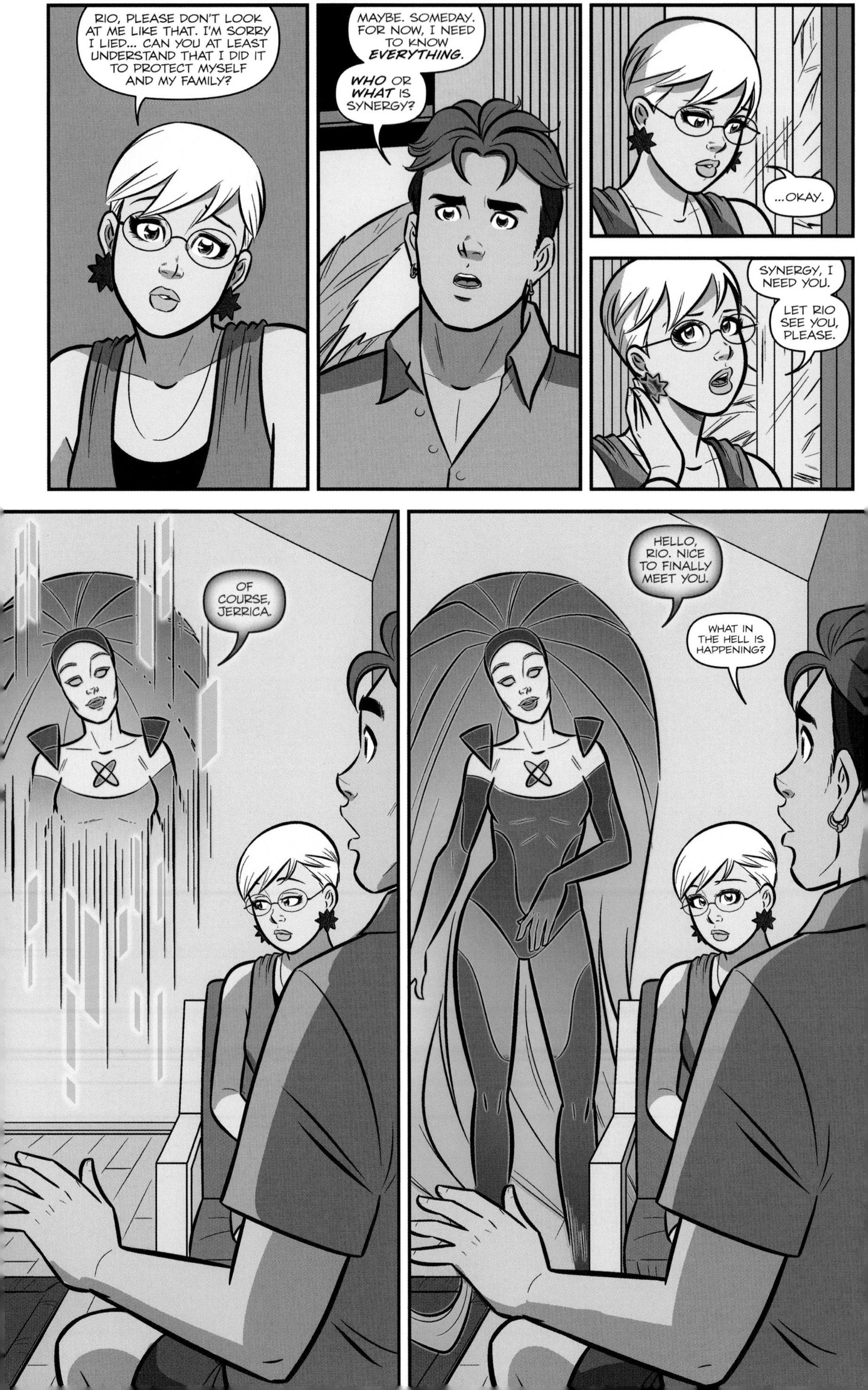
RIO, PLEASE DON'T LOOK AT ME LIKE THAT. I'M SORRY I LIED... CAN YOU AT LEAST UNDERSTAND THAT I DID IT TO PROTECT MYSELF AND MY FAMILY?
MAYBE. SOMEDAY. FOR NOW, I NEED TO KNOW EVERYTHING.
WHO OR WHAT IS SYNERGY?
...OKAY.
SYNERGY, I NEED YOU.
LET RIO SEE YOU, PLEASE.
OF COURSE, JERRICA.
HELLO, RIO. NICE TO FINALLY MEET YOU.
WHAT IN THE HELL IS HAPPENING?

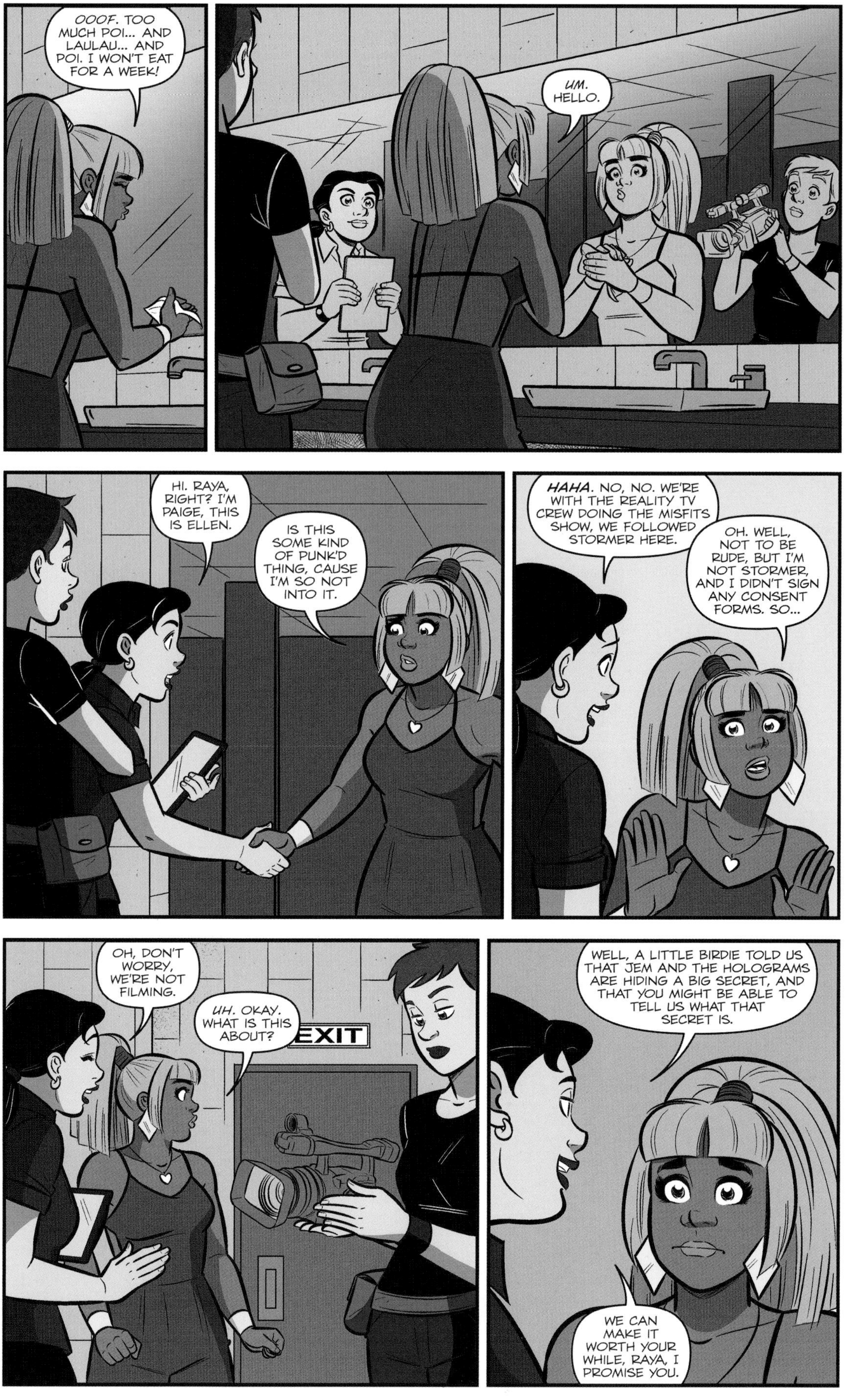

OOOF. TOO MUCH POI... AND LAULAU... AND POI. I WON'T EAT FOR A WEEK!
UM. HELLO.
HI. RAYA, RIGHT? I'M PAIGE, THIS IS ELLEN.
IS THIS SOME KIND OF PUNK'D THING, CAUSE I'M SO NOT INTO IT.
HAHA. NO, NO. WE'RE WITH THE REALITY TV CREW DOING THE MISFITS SHOW, WE FOLLOWED STORMER HERE.
OH. WELL, NOT TO BE RUDE, BUT I'M NOT STORMER, AND I DIDN'T SIGN ANY CONSENT FORMS. SO...
OH, DON'T WORRY, WE'RE NOT FILMING.
UH. OKAY. WHAT IS THIS ABOUT?
EXIT
WELL, A LITTLE BIRDIE TOLD US THAT JEM AND THE HOLOGRAMS ARE HIDING A BIG SECRET, AND THAT YOU MIGHT BE ABLE TO TELL US WHAT THAT SECRET IS.
WE CAN MAKE IT WORTH YOUR WHILE, RAYA, I PROMISE YOU.

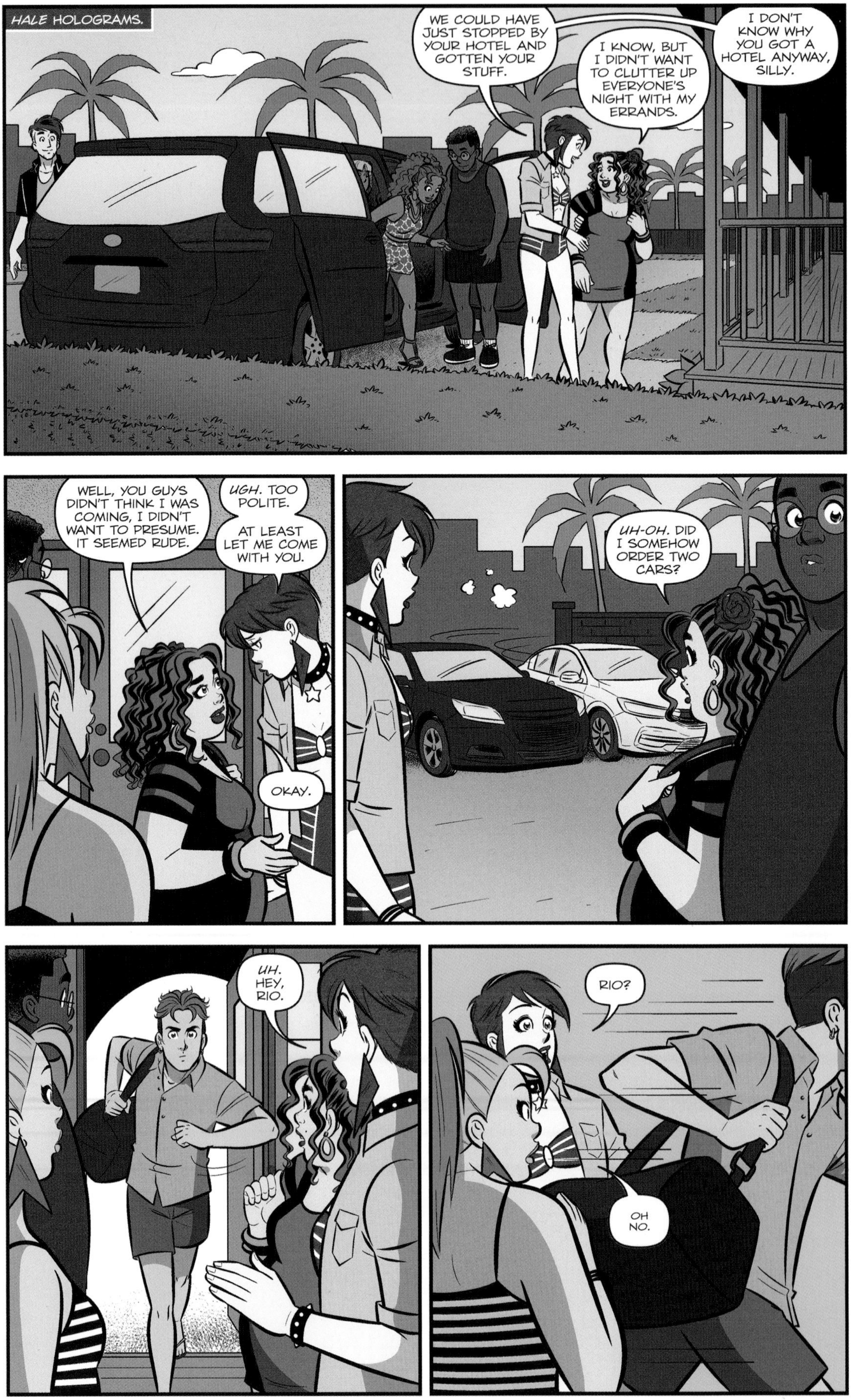
HALE HOLOGRAMS.
WE COULD HAVE JUST STOPPED BY YOUR HOTEL AND GOTTEN YOUR STUFF.
I DON'T KNOW WHY YOU GOT A HOTEL ANYWAY, SILLY.
I KNOW, BUT I DIDN'T WANT TO CLUTTER UP EVERYONE'S NIGHT WITH MY ERRANDS.
WELL, YOU GUYS DIDN'T THINK I WAS COMING, I DIDN'T WANT TO PRESUME. IT SEEMED RUDE.
UGH. TOO POLITE.
AT LEAST LET ME COME WITH YOU.
OKAY.
UH-OH. DID I SOMEHOW ORDER TWO CARS?
UH. HEY, RIO.
RIO?
OH NO.

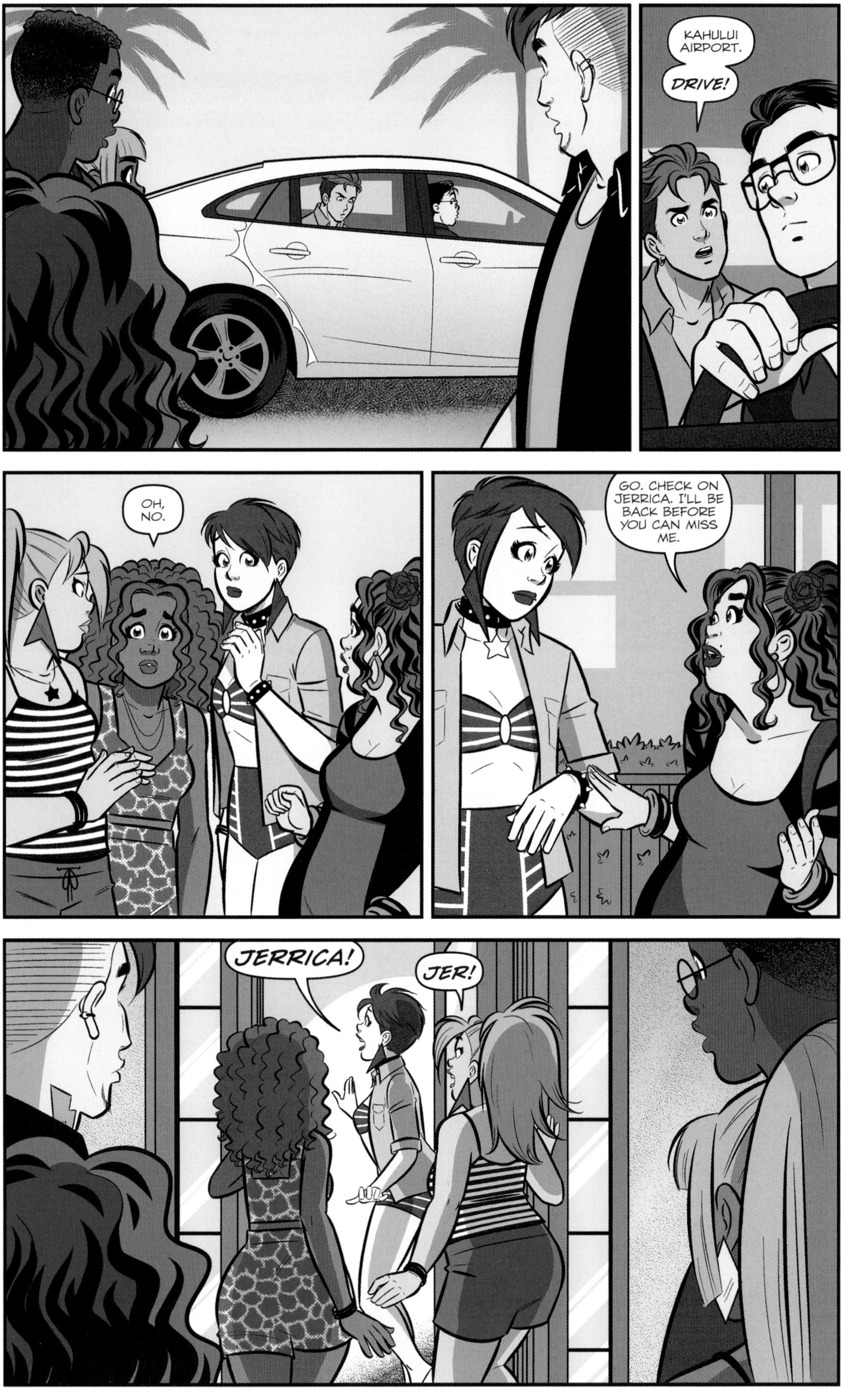
KAHULUI AIRPORT.
DRIVE!
OH, NO.
GO. CHECK ON JERRICA. I'LL BE BACK BEFORE YOU CAN MISS ME.
JERRICA!
JER!

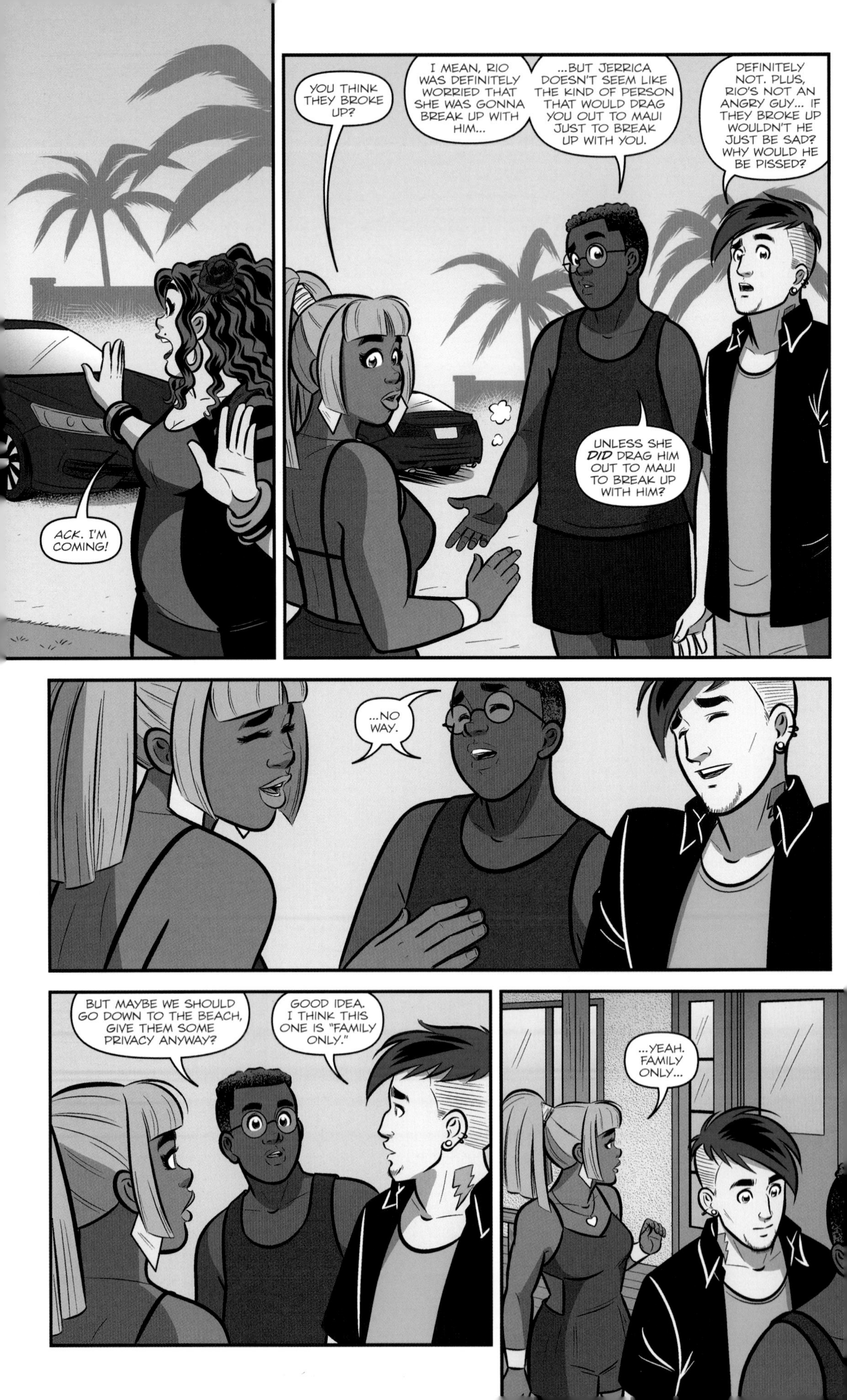
ACK. I'M COMING!
YOU THINK THEY BROKE UP?
I MEAN, RIO WAS DEFINITELY WORRIED THAT SHE WAS GONNA BREAK UP WITH HIM...
...BUT JERRICA DOESN'T SEEM LIKE THE KIND OF PERSON THAT WOULD DRAG YOU OUT TO MAUI JUST TO BREAK UP WITH YOU.
DEFINITELY NOT. PLUS, RIO'S NOT AN ANGRY GUY... IF THEY BROKE UP WOULDN'T HE JUST BE SAD? WHY WOULD HE BE PISSED?
UNLESS SHE DID DRAG HIM OUT TO MAUI TO BREAK UP WITH HIM?
...NO WAY.
BUT MAYBE WE SHOULD GO DOWN TO THE BEACH, GIVE THEM SOME PRIVACY ANYWAY?
GOOD IDEA. I THINK THIS ONE IS "FAMILY ONLY."
...YEAH. FAMILY ONLY...

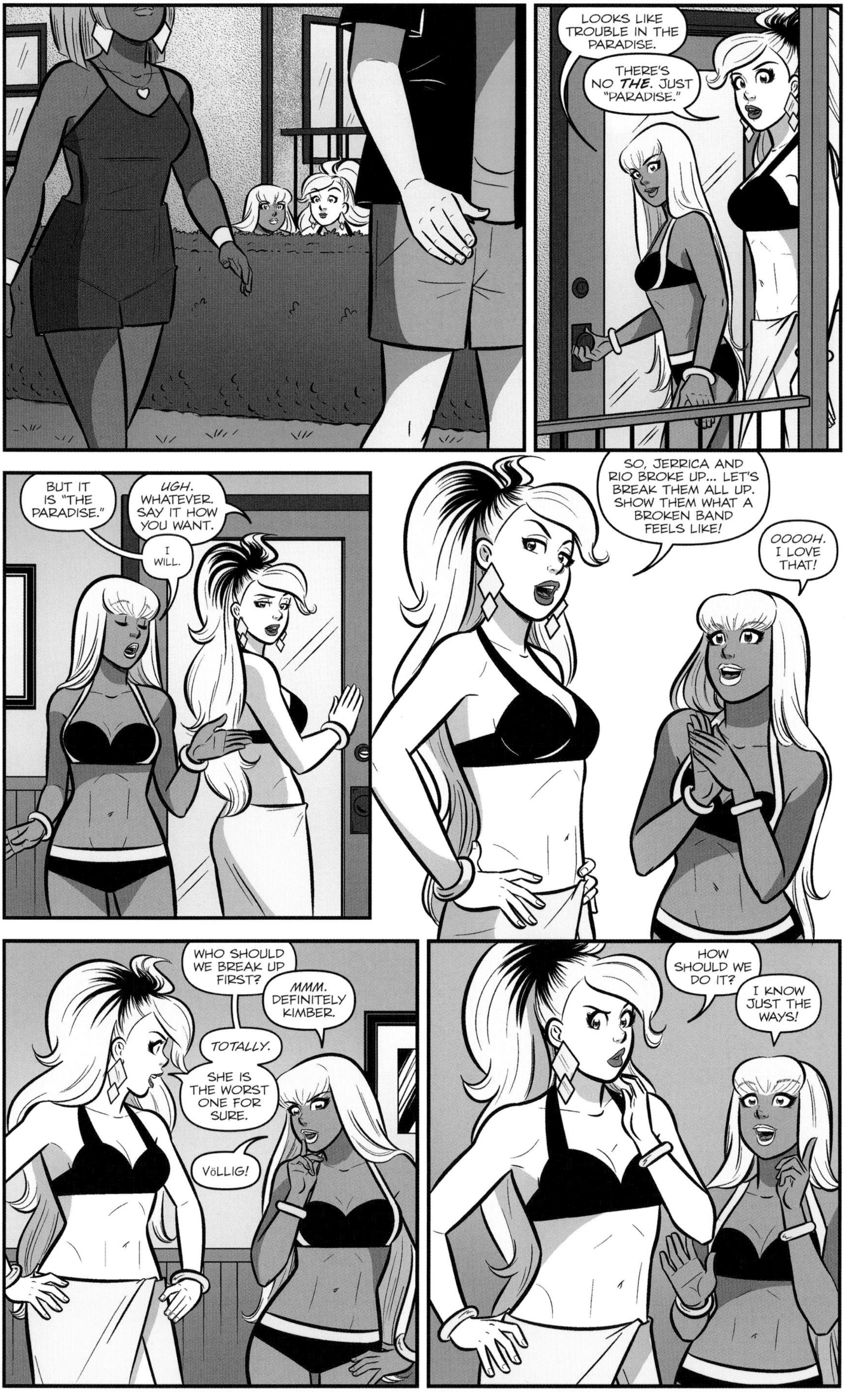
LOOKS LIKE TROUBLE IN THE PARADISE.
THERE'S NO *THE*. JUST "PARADISE."
BUT IT IS "THE PARADISE."
UGH. WHATEVER. SAY IT HOW YOU WANT.
I WILL.
SO, JERRICA AND RIO BROKE UP... LET'S BREAK THEM ALL UP. SHOW THEM WHAT A BROKEN BAND FEELS LIKE!
OOOOH. I LOVE THAT!
WHO SHOULD WE BREAK UP FIRST?
MMM. DEFINITELY KIMBER.
TOTALLY.
SHE IS THE WORST ONE FOR SURE.
VöLLIG!
HOW SHOULD WE DO IT?
I KNOW JUST THE WAYS!

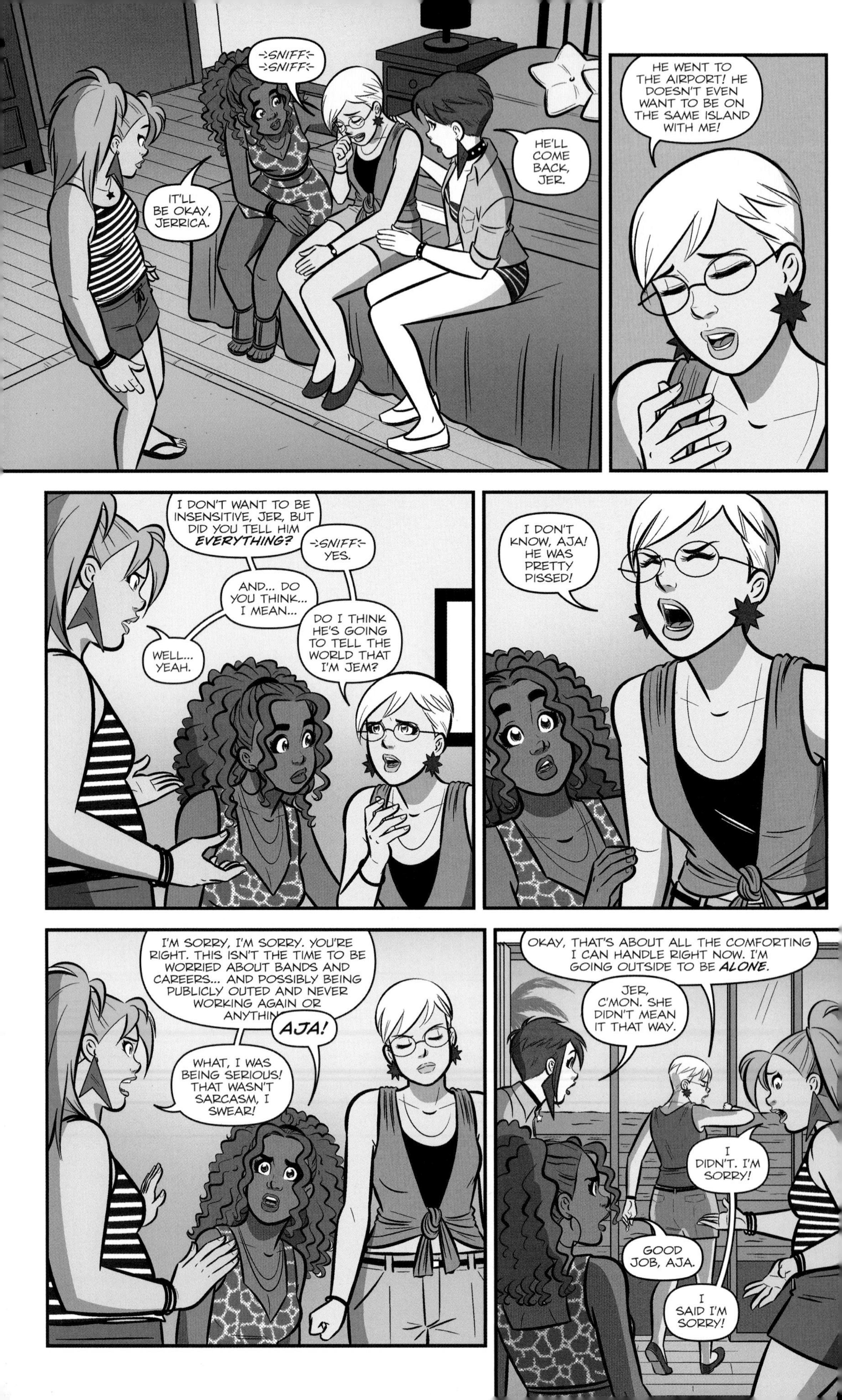

-SNIFF- -SNIFF-
IT'LL BE OKAY, JERRICA.
HE'LL COME BACK, JER.
HE WENT TO THE AIRPORT! HE DOESN'T EVEN WANT TO BE ON THE SAME ISLAND WITH ME!
I DON'T WANT TO BE INSENSITIVE, JER, BUT DID YOU TELL HIM EVERYTHING?
-SNIFF- YES.
AND... DO YOU THINK... I MEAN...
WELL... YEAH.
DO I THINK HE'S GOING TO TELL THE WORLD THAT I'M JEM?
I DON'T KNOW, AJA! HE WAS PRETTY PISSED!
I'M SORRY, I'M SORRY. YOU'RE RIGHT. THIS ISN'T THE TIME TO BE WORRIED ABOUT BANDS AND CAREERS... AND POSSIBLY BEING PUBLICLY OUTED AND NEVER WORKING AGAIN OR ANYTHIN
AJA!
WHAT, I WAS BEING SERIOUS! THAT WASN'T SARCASM, I SWEAR!
OKAY, THAT'S ABOUT ALL THE COMFORTING I CAN HANDLE RIGHT NOW. I'M GOING OUTSIDE TO BE ALONE.
JER, C'MON. SHE DIDN'T MEAN IT THAT WAY.
I DIDN'T. I'M SORRY!
GOOD JOB, AJA.
I SAID I'M SORRY!

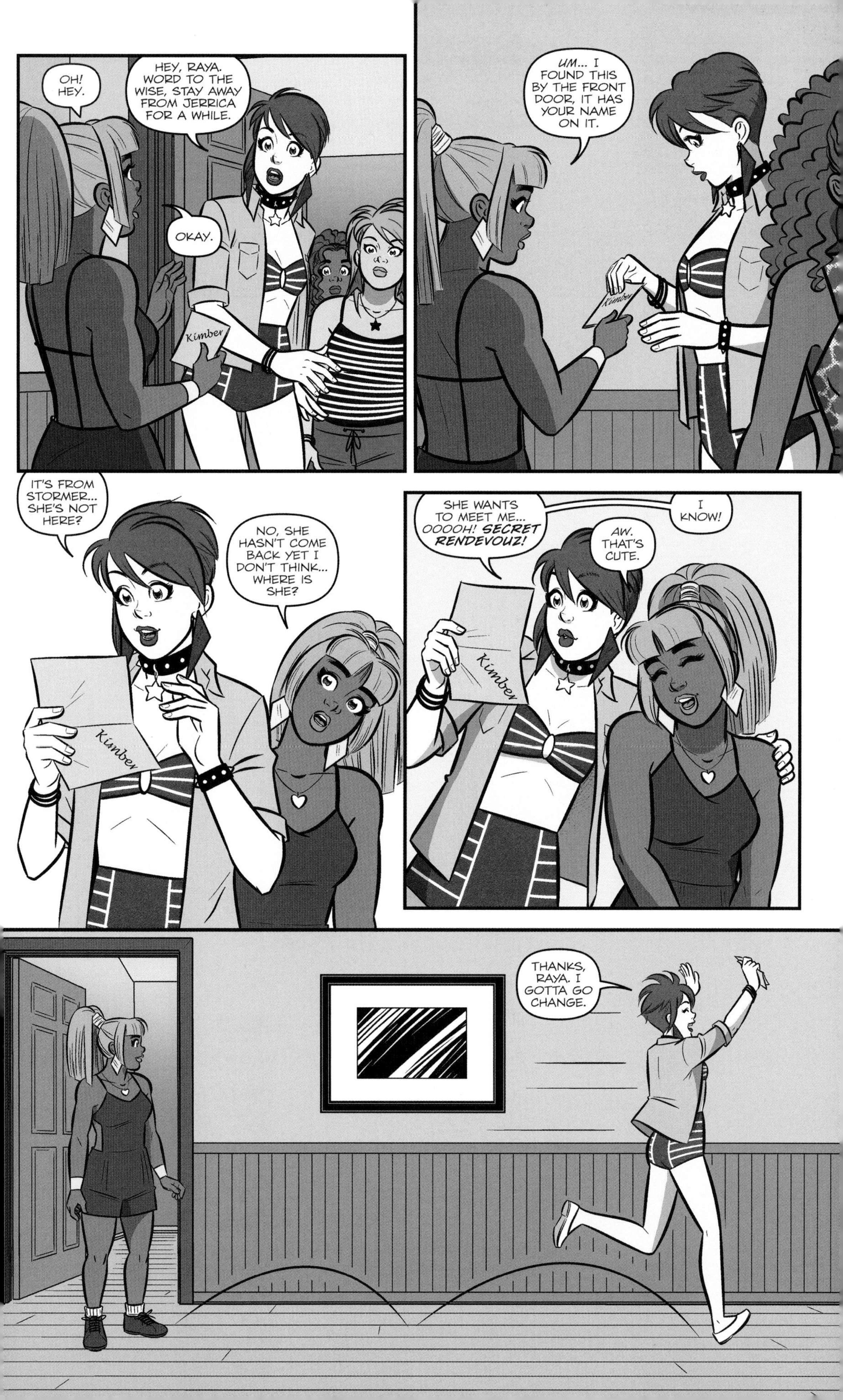
OH! HEY.
HEY, RAYA. WORD TO THE WISE, STAY AWAY FROM JERRICA FOR A WHILE.
OKAY.
Kimber
UM... I FOUND THIS BY THE FRONT DOOR, IT HAS YOUR NAME ON IT.
Kimber
IT'S FROM STORMER... SHE'S NOT HERE?
NO, SHE HASN'T COME BACK YET I DON'T THINK... WHERE IS SHE?
Kimber
SHE WANTS TO MEET ME... OOOOH! SECRET RENDEVOUZ!
I KNOW!
AW. THAT'S CUTE.
Kimber
THANKS, RAYA. I GOTTA GO CHANGE.

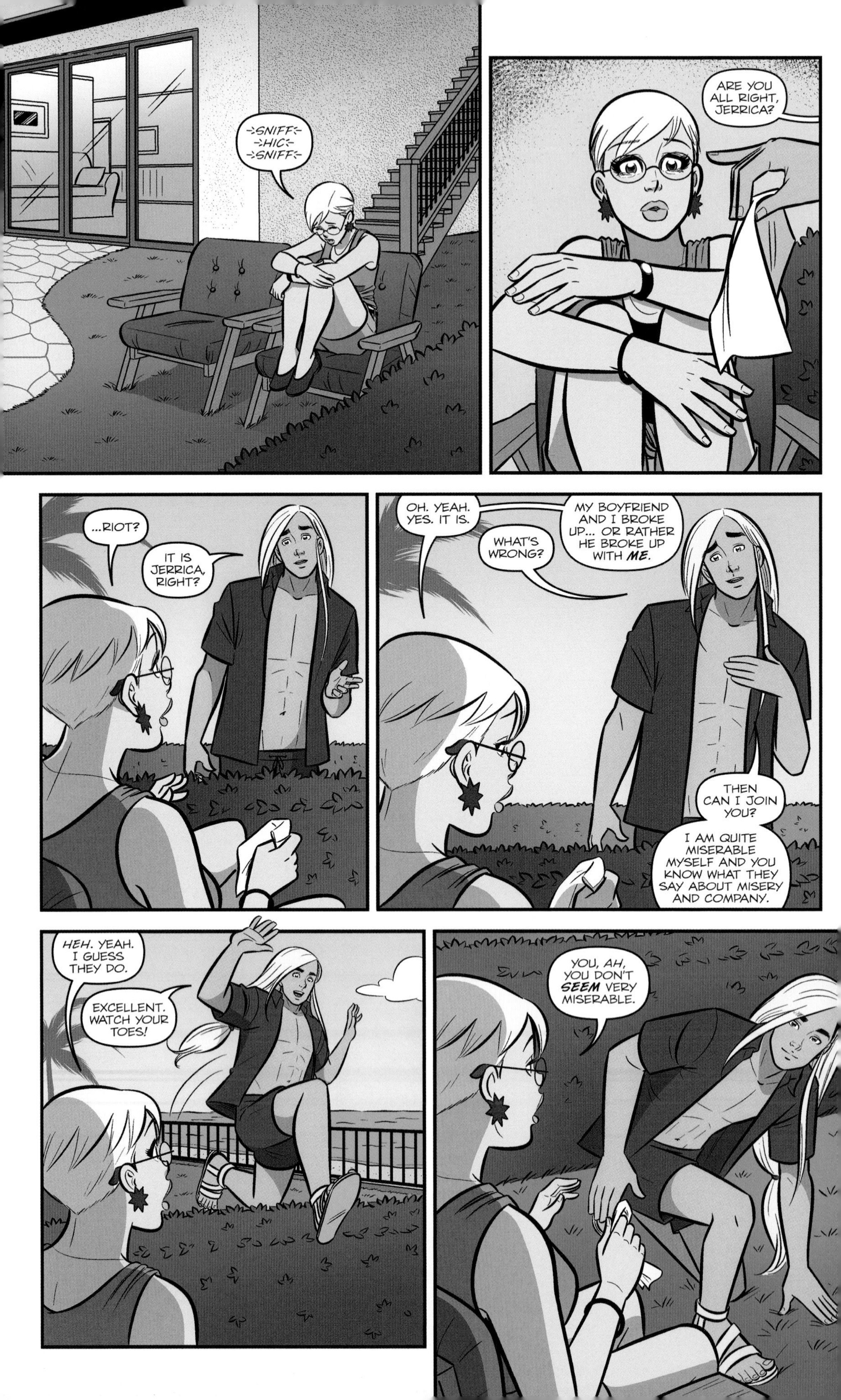
-SNIFF-
-HIC-
-SNIFF-
ARE YOU ALL RIGHT, JERRICA?
...RIOT?
IT IS JERRICA, RIGHT?
OH. YEAH. YES. IT IS.
WHAT'S WRONG?
MY BOYFRIEND AND I BROKE UP... OR RATHER HE BROKE UP WITH *ME*.
THEN CAN I JOIN YOU?
I AM QUITE MISERABLE MYSELF AND YOU KNOW WHAT THEY SAY ABOUT MISERY AND COMPANY.
HEH. YEAH. I GUESS THEY DO.
EXCELLENT. WATCH YOUR TOES!
YOU, AH, YOU DON'T *SEEM* VERY MISERABLE.

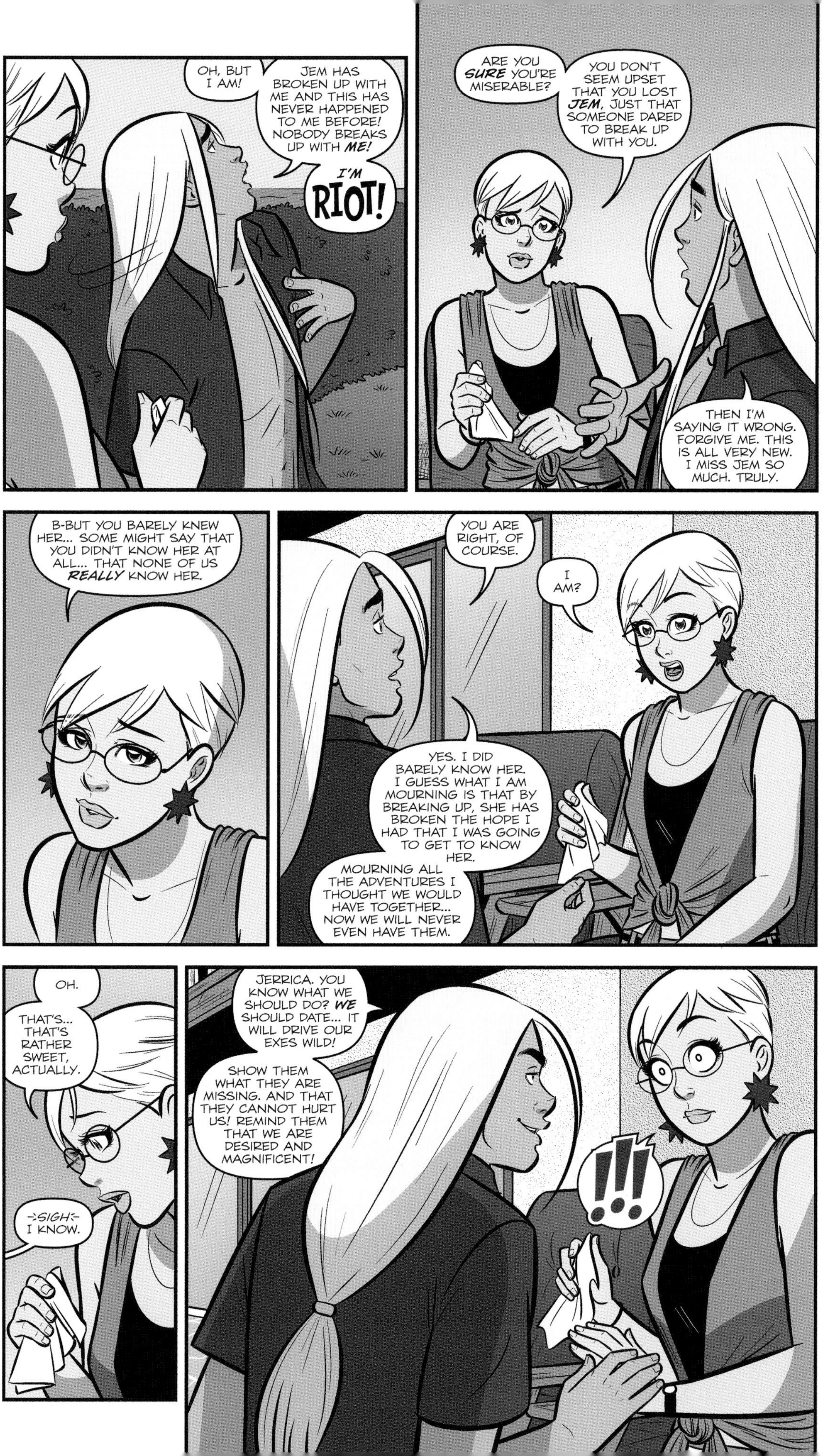
OH, BUT I AM!
JEM HAS BROKEN UP WITH ME AND THIS HAS NEVER HAPPENED TO ME BEFORE! NOBODY BREAKS UP WITH *ME!*
I'M RIOT!
ARE YOU *SURE* YOU'RE MISERABLE?
YOU DON'T SEEM UPSET THAT YOU LOST *JEM*, JUST THAT SOMEONE DARED TO BREAK UP WITH YOU.
THEN I'M SAYING IT WRONG. FORGIVE ME. THIS IS ALL VERY NEW. I MISS JEM SO MUCH. TRULY.
B-BUT YOU BARELY KNEW HER... SOME MIGHT SAY THAT YOU DIDN'T KNOW HER AT ALL... THAT NONE OF US *REALLY* KNOW HER.
YOU ARE RIGHT, OF COURSE.
I AM?
YES. I DID BARELY KNOW HER. I GUESS WHAT I AM MOURNING IS THAT BY BREAKING UP, SHE HAS BROKEN THE HOPE I HAD THAT I WAS GOING TO GET TO KNOW HER.
MOURNING ALL THE ADVENTURES I THOUGHT WE WOULD HAVE TOGETHER... NOW WE WILL NEVER EVEN HAVE THEM.
OH.
THAT'S... THAT'S RATHER SWEET, ACTUALLY.
-SIGH- I KNOW.
JERRICA. YOU KNOW WHAT WE SHOULD DO? *WE* SHOULD DATE... IT WILL DRIVE OUR EXES WILD!
SHOW THEM WHAT THEY ARE MISSING. AND THAT THEY CANNOT HURT US! REMIND THEM THAT WE ARE DESIRED AND MAGNIFICENT!
!!!

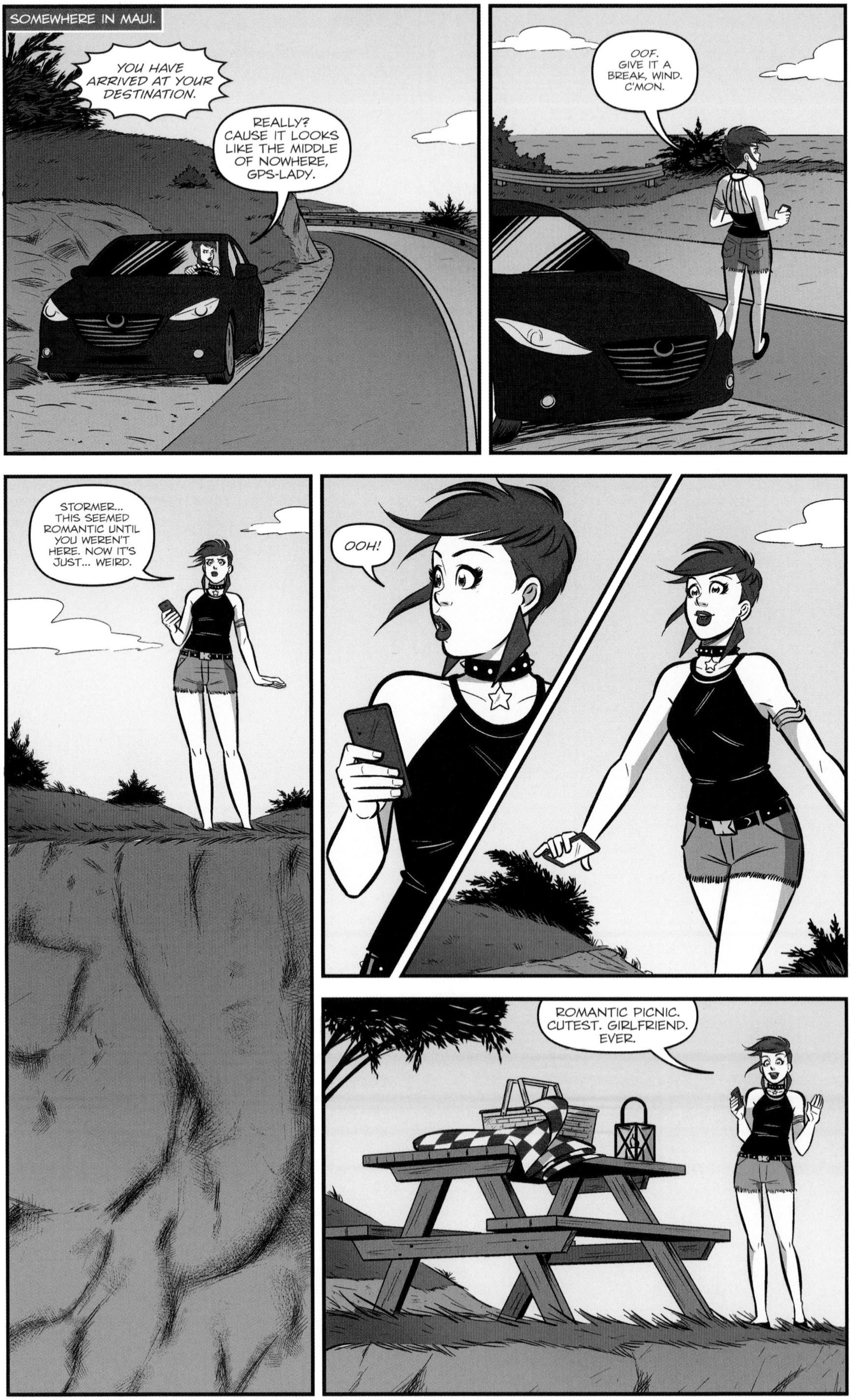
SOMEWHERE IN MAUI.
YOU HAVE ARRIVED AT YOUR DESTINATION.
REALLY? CAUSE IT LOOKS LIKE THE MIDDLE OF NOWHERE, GPS-LADY.
OOF. GIVE IT A BREAK, WIND. C'MON.
STORMER... THIS SEEMED ROMANTIC UNTIL YOU WEREN'T HERE. NOW IT'S JUST... WEIRD.
OOH!
ROMANTIC PICNIC. CUTEST. GIRLFRIEND. EVER.

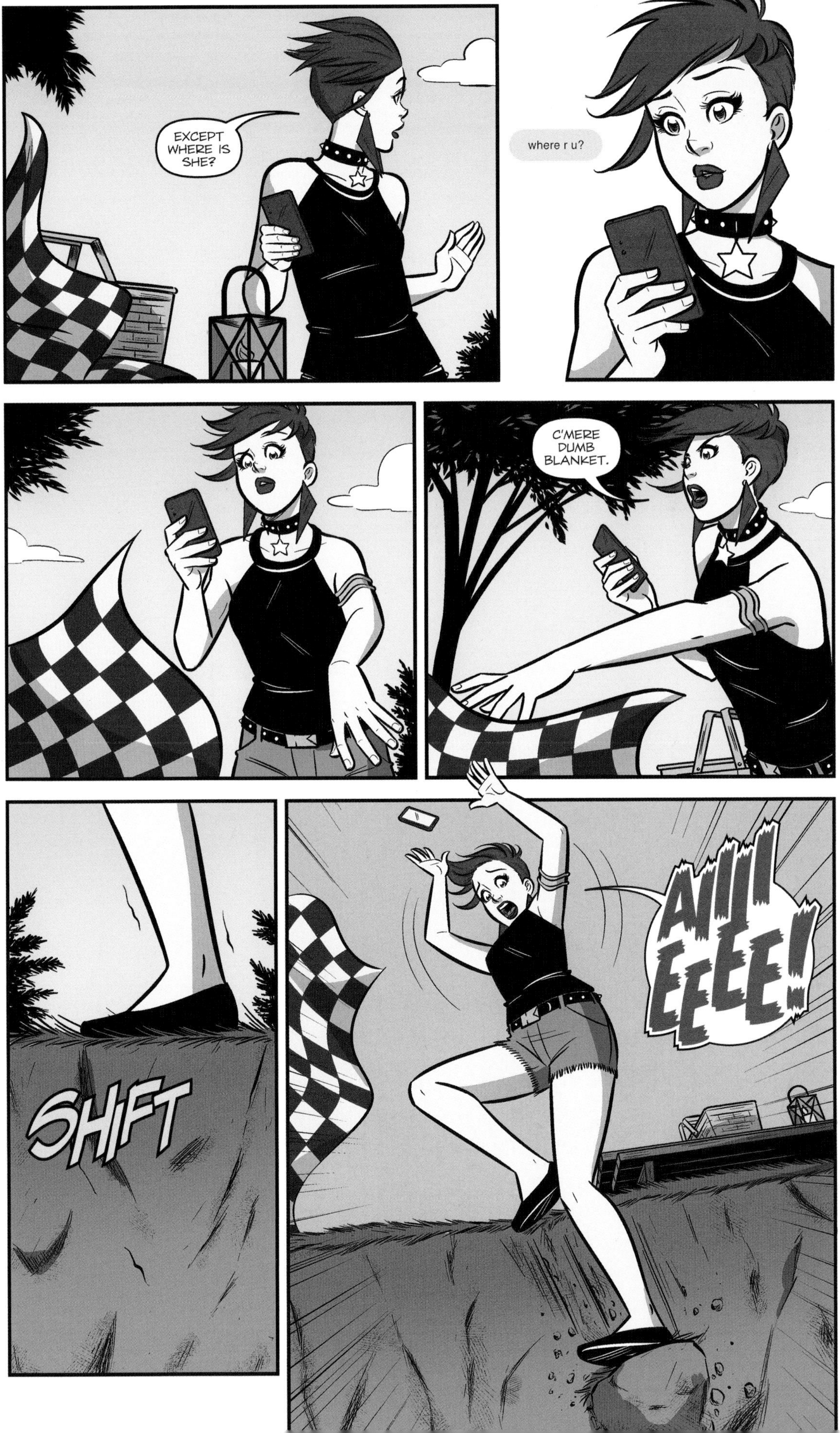

EXCEPT WHERE IS SHE?
where r u?
C'MERE DUMB BLANKET.
SHIFT
AIIIII EEEE!

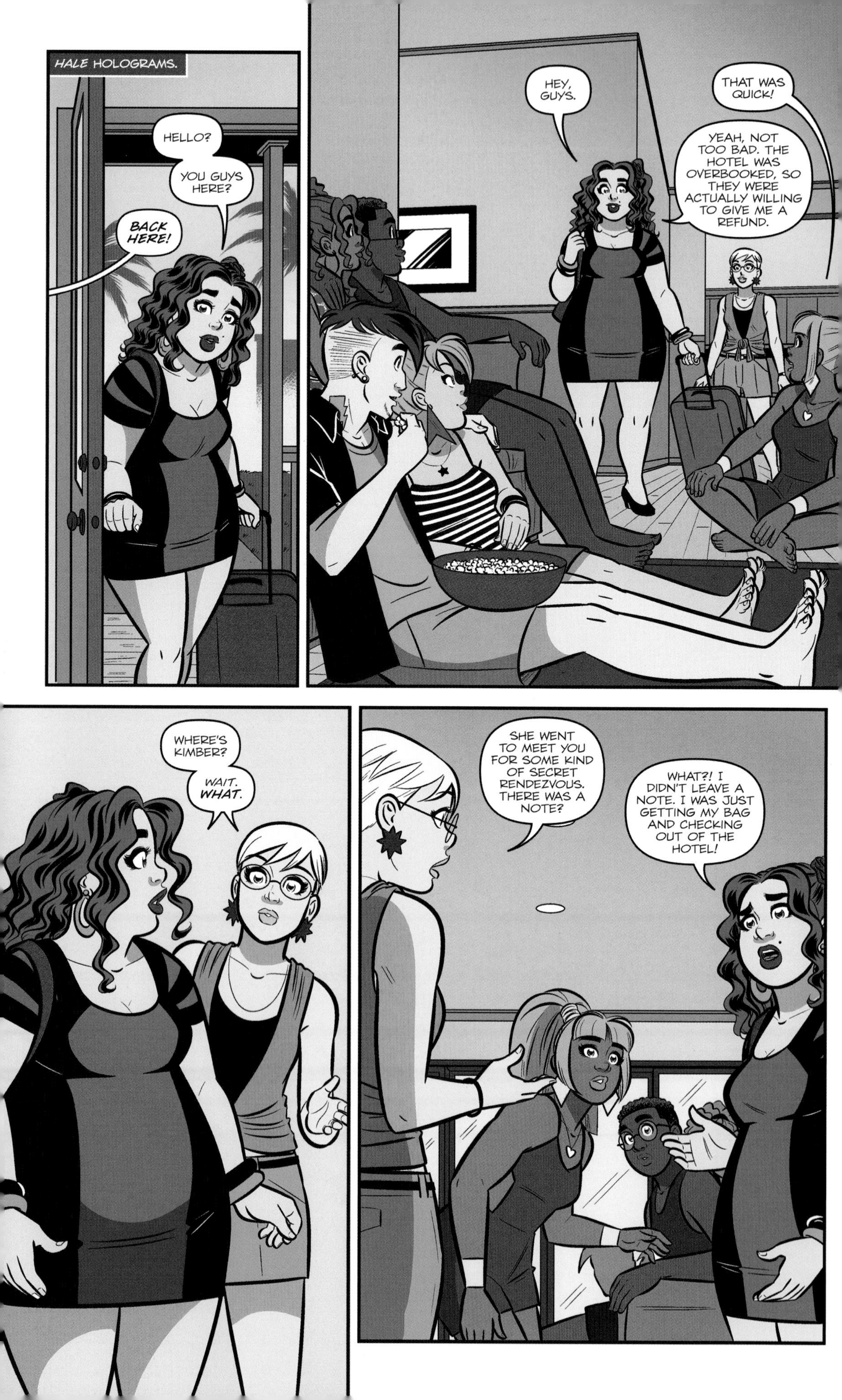
HALE HOLOGRAMS.
HELLO?
YOU GUYS HERE?
BACK HERE!
HEY, GUYS.
THAT WAS QUICK!
YEAH, NOT TOO BAD. THE HOTEL WAS OVERBOOKED, SO THEY WERE ACTUALLY WILLING TO GIVE ME A REFUND.
WHERE'S KIMBER?
WAIT. WHAT.
SHE WENT TO MEET YOU FOR SOME KIND OF SECRET RENDEZVOUS. THERE WAS A NOTE?
WHAT?! I DIDN'T LEAVE A NOTE. I WAS JUST GETTING MY BAG AND CHECKING OUT OF THE HOTEL!

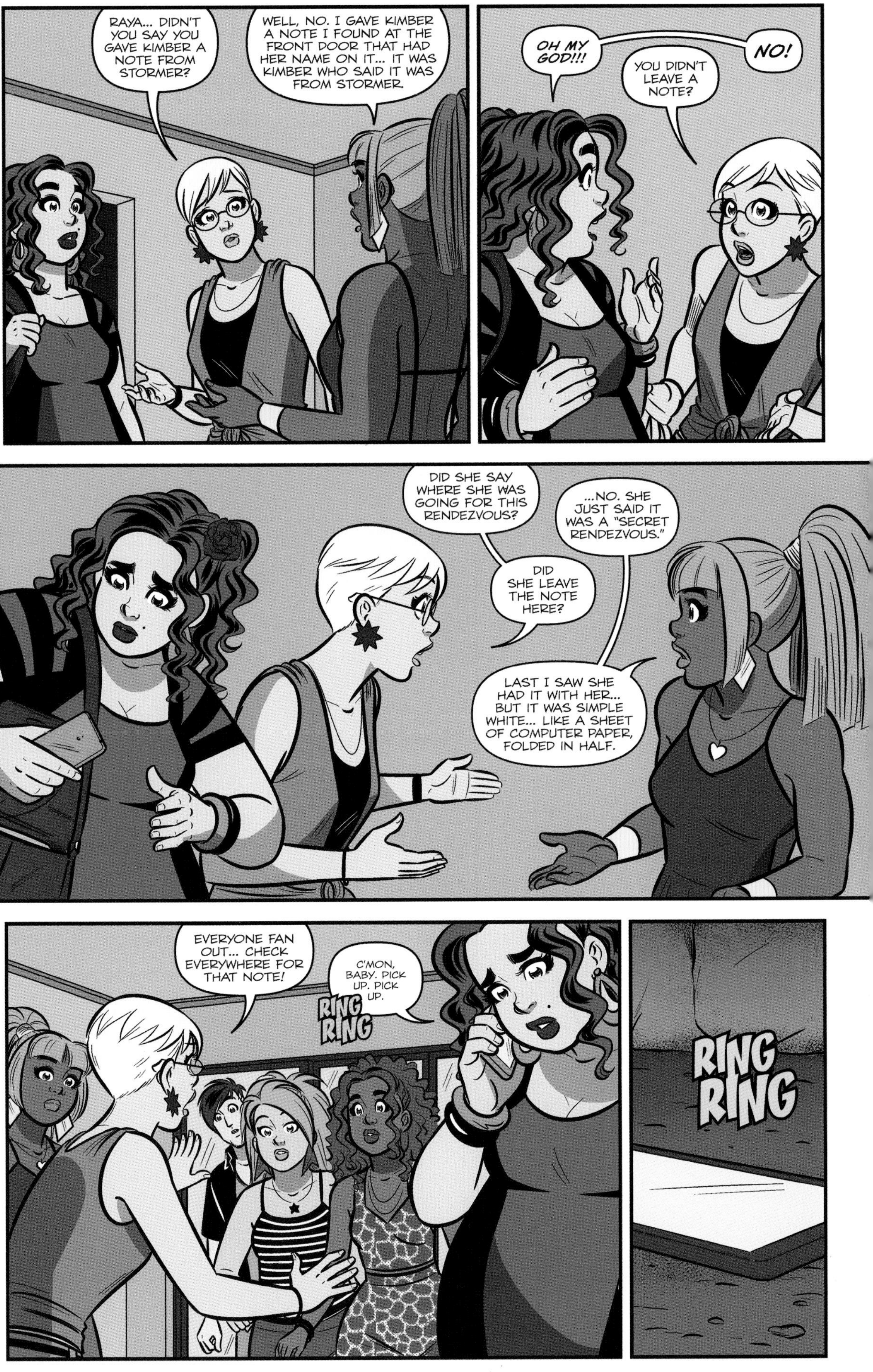
RAYA... DIDN'T YOU SAY YOU GAVE KIMBER A NOTE FROM STORMER?
WELL, NO. I GAVE KIMBER A NOTE I FOUND AT THE FRONT DOOR THAT HAD HER NAME ON IT... IT WAS KIMBER WHO SAID IT WAS FROM STORMER.
OH MY GOD!!!
NO!
YOU DIDN'T LEAVE A NOTE?
DID SHE SAY WHERE SHE WAS GOING FOR THIS RENDEZVOUS?
...NO. SHE JUST SAID IT WAS A "SECRET RENDEZVOUS."
DID SHE LEAVE THE NOTE HERE?
LAST I SAW SHE HAD IT WITH HER... BUT IT WAS SIMPLE WHITE... LIKE A SHEET OF COMPUTER PAPER, FOLDED IN HALF.
EVERYONE FAN OUT... CHECK EVERYWHERE FOR THAT NOTE!
RING RING
C'MON, BABY. PICK UP. PICK UP.
RING RING

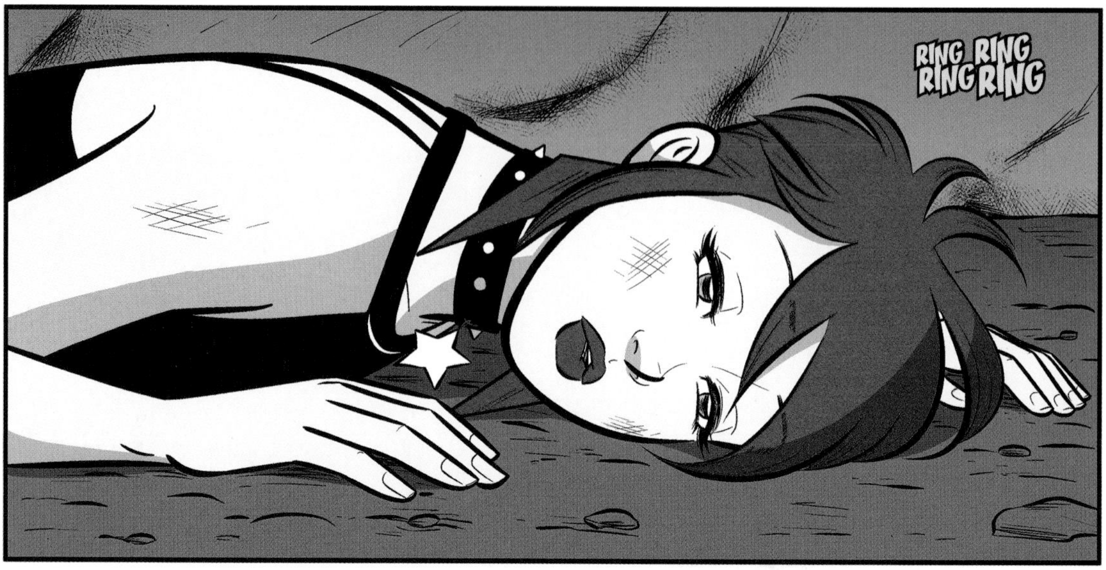
RING RING
RING RING

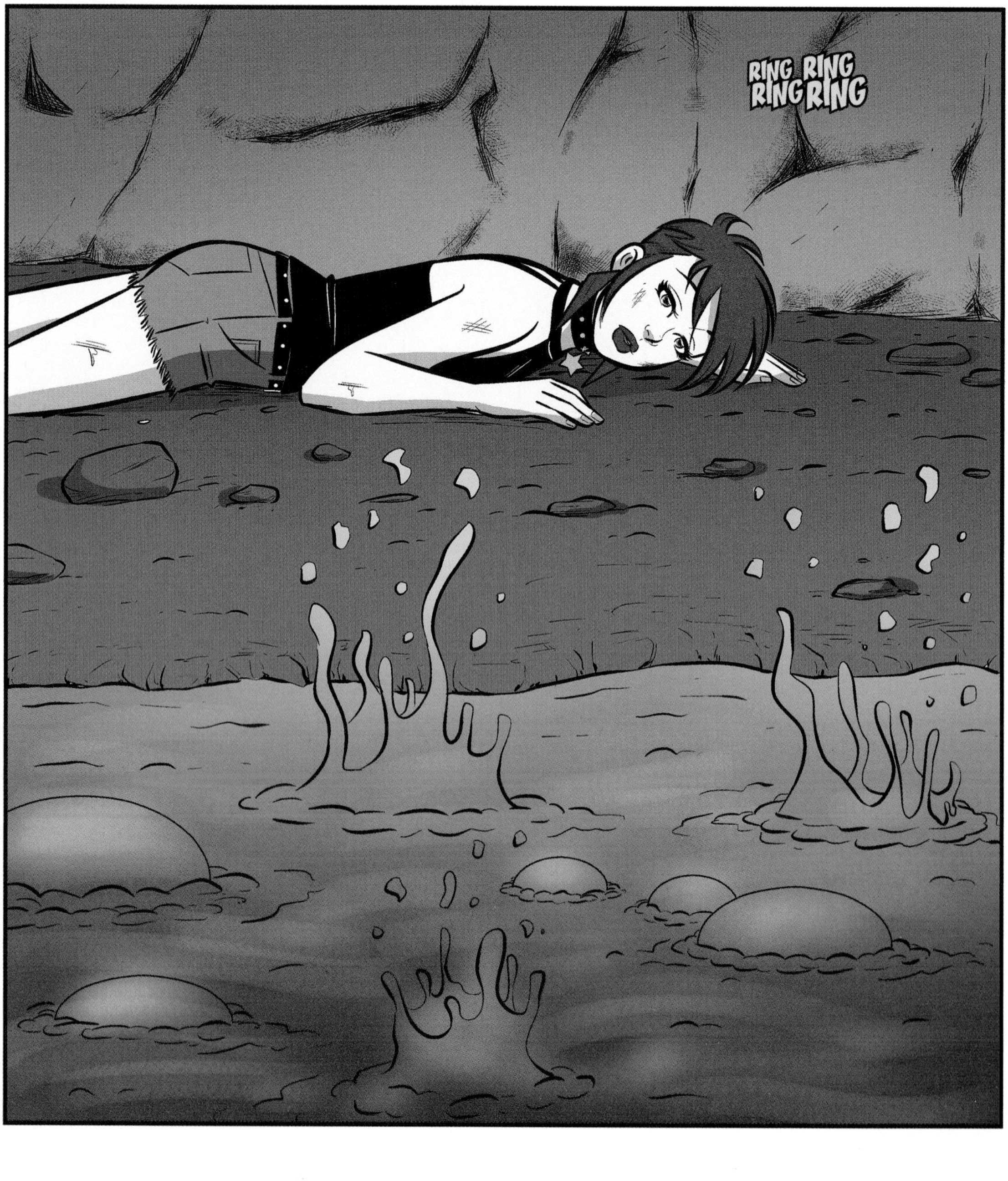
RING RING
RING RING

3 ART BY **JEN BARTEL**

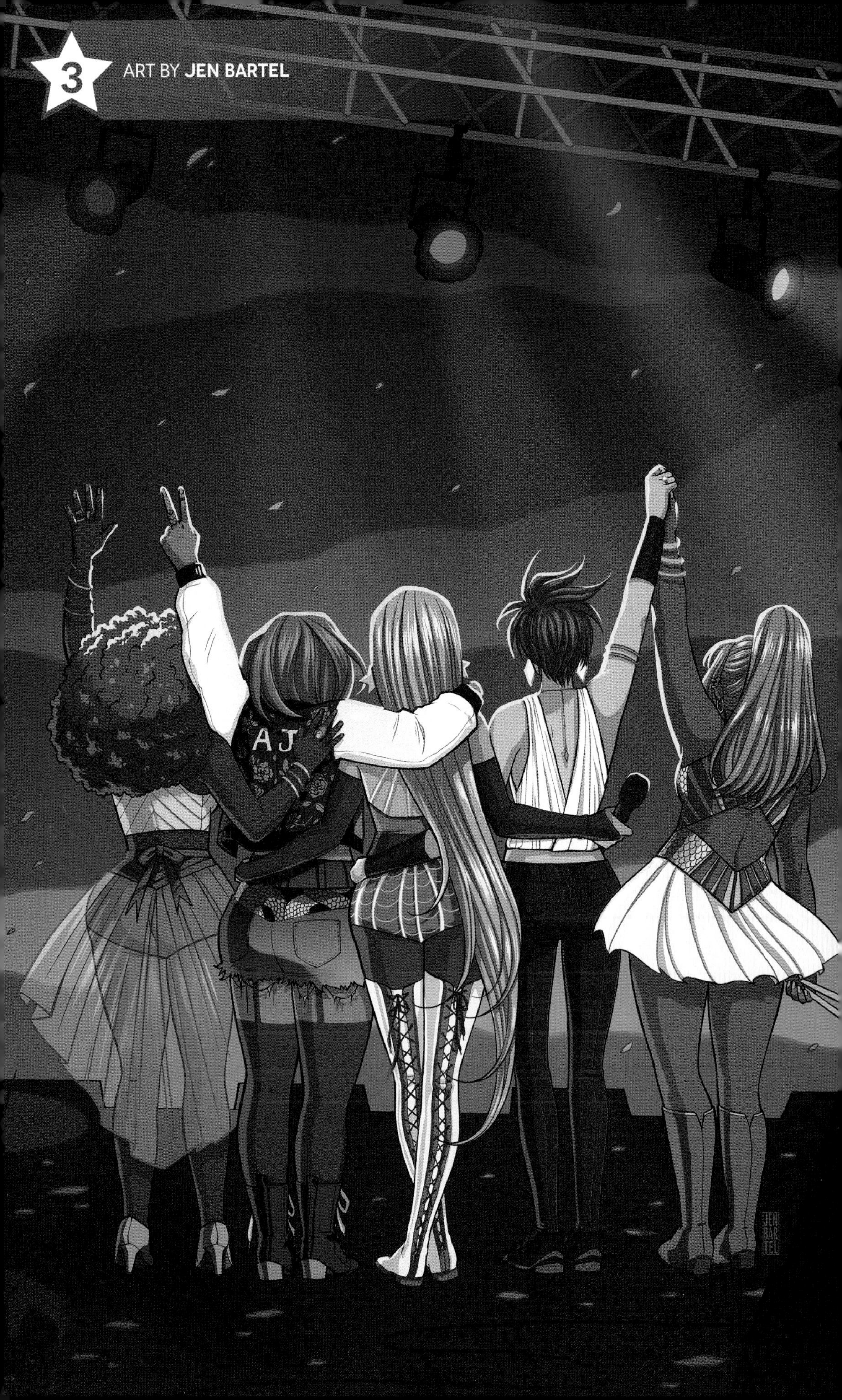
AJ
JEN BARTEL

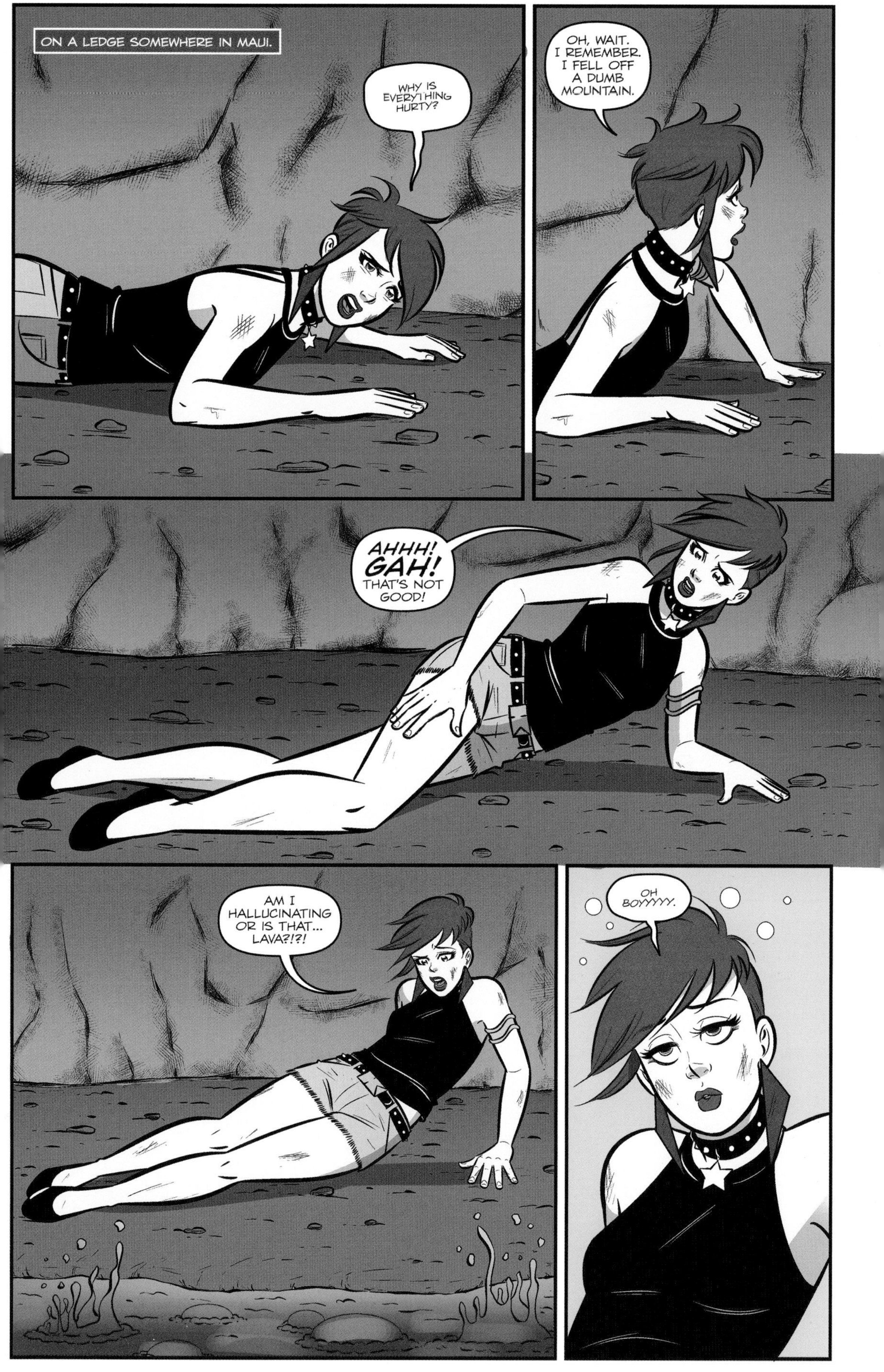
ON A LEDGE SOMEWHERE IN MAUI.
WHY IS EVERYTHING HURTY?
OH, WAIT. I REMEMBER. I FELL OFF A DUMB MOUNTAIN.
AHHH! GAH! THAT'S NOT GOOD!
AM I HALLUCINATING OR IS THAT... LAVA?!?!
OH BOYYYYY.

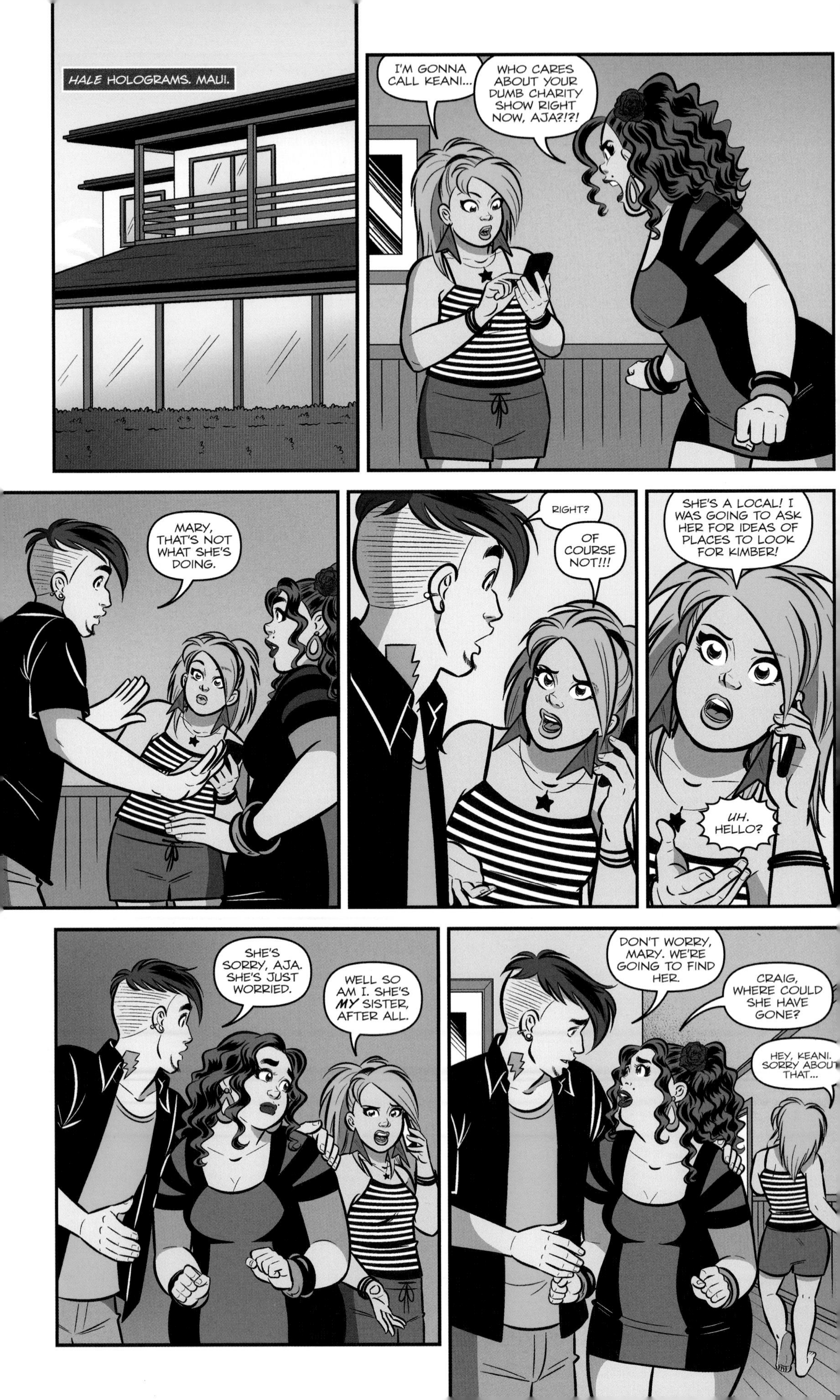
HALE HOLOGRAMS. MAUI.
I'M GONNA CALL KEANI...
WHO CARES ABOUT YOUR DUMB CHARITY SHOW RIGHT NOW, AJA?!?!
MARY, THAT'S NOT WHAT SHE'S DOING.
RIGHT?
OF COURSE NOT!!!
SHE'S A LOCAL! I WAS GOING TO ASK HER FOR IDEAS OF PLACES TO LOOK FOR KIMBER!
UH. HELLO?
SHE'S SORRY, AJA. SHE'S JUST WORRIED.
WELL SO AM I. SHE'S MY SISTER, AFTER ALL.
DON'T WORRY, MARY. WE'RE GOING TO FIND HER.
CRAIG, WHERE COULD SHE HAVE GONE?
HEY, KEANI. SORRY ABOUT THAT...

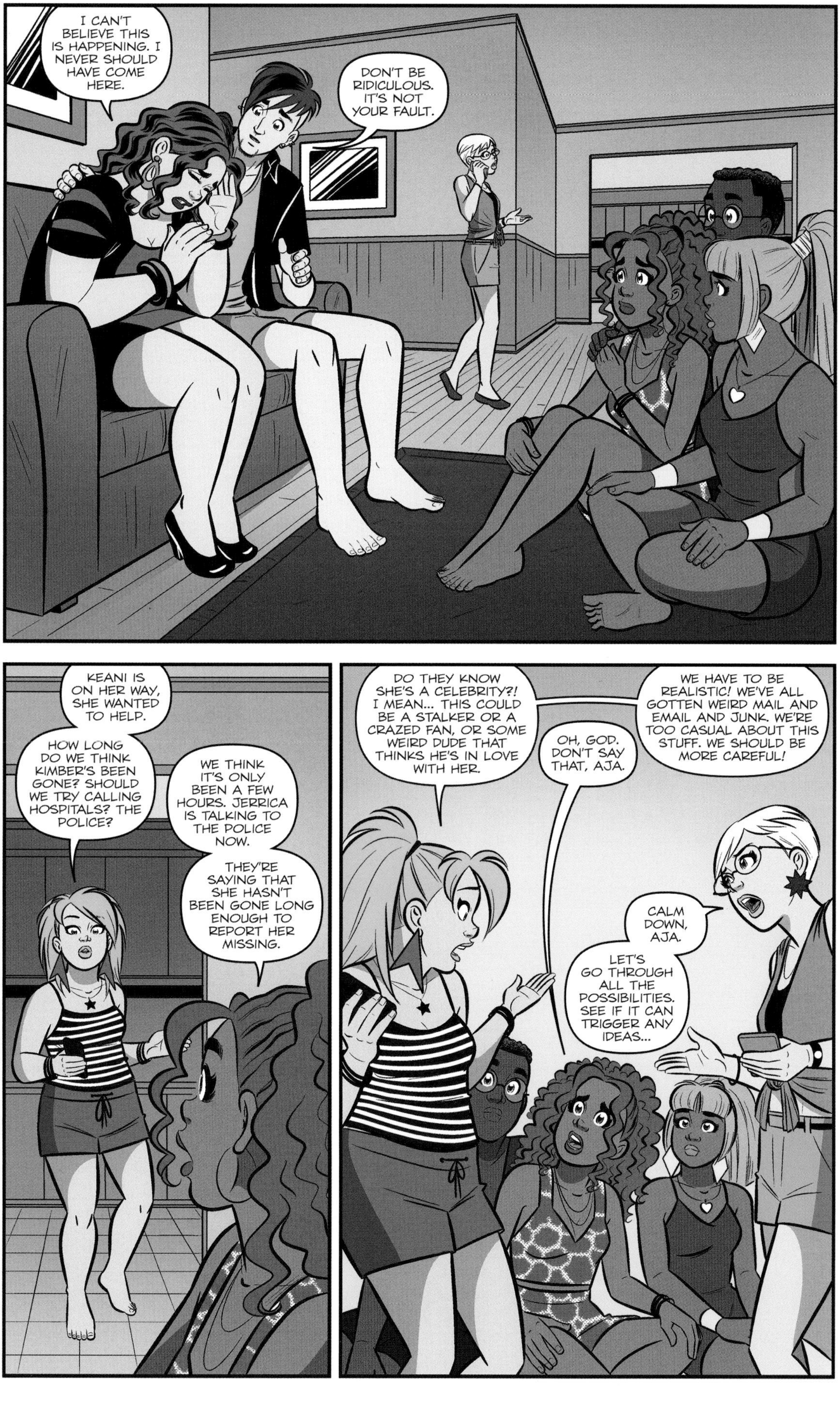
I CAN'T BELIEVE THIS IS HAPPENING. I NEVER SHOULD HAVE COME HERE.
DON'T BE RIDICULOUS. IT'S NOT YOUR FAULT.
KEANI IS ON HER WAY, SHE WANTED TO HELP.
HOW LONG DO WE THINK KIMBER'S BEEN GONE? SHOULD WE TRY CALLING HOSPITALS? THE POLICE?
WE THINK IT'S ONLY BEEN A FEW HOURS. JERRICA IS TALKING TO THE POLICE NOW.
THEY'RE SAYING THAT SHE HASN'T BEEN GONE LONG ENOUGH TO REPORT HER MISSING.
DO THEY KNOW SHE'S A CELEBRITY?! I MEAN... THIS COULD BE A STALKER OR A CRAZED FAN, OR SOME WEIRD DUDE THAT THINKS HE'S IN LOVE WITH HER.
OH, GOD. DON'T SAY THAT, AJA.
WE HAVE TO BE REALISTIC! WE'VE ALL GOTTEN WEIRD MAIL AND EMAIL AND JUNK. WE'RE TOO CASUAL ABOUT THIS STUFF. WE SHOULD BE MORE CAREFUL!
CALM DOWN, AJA.
LET'S GO THROUGH ALL THE POSSIBILITIES. SEE IF IT CAN TRIGGER ANY IDEAS...

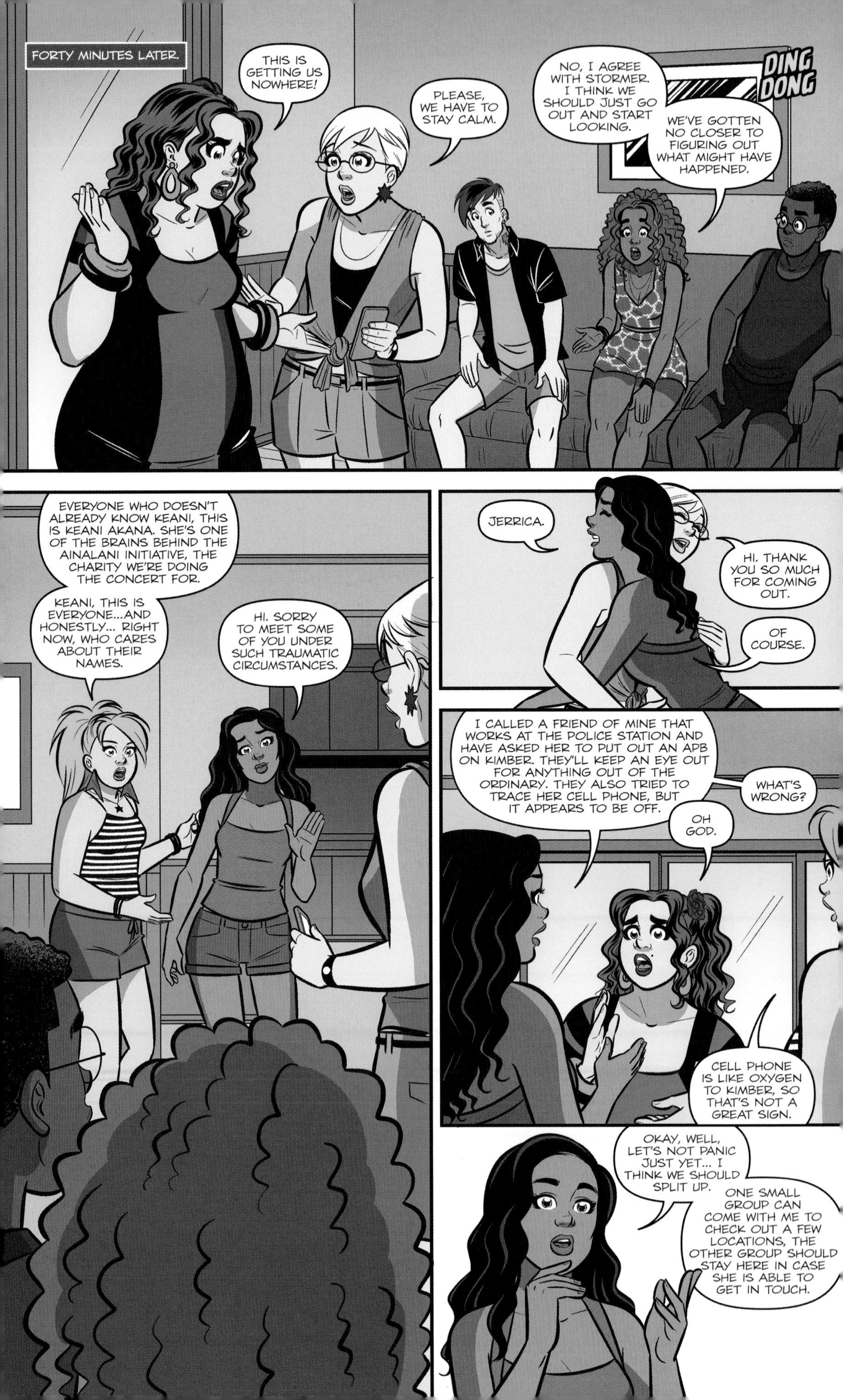
FORTY MINUTES LATER.
THIS IS GETTING US NOWHERE!
PLEASE, WE HAVE TO STAY CALM.
NO, I AGREE WITH STORMER. I THINK WE SHOULD JUST GO OUT AND START LOOKING.
WE'VE GOTTEN NO CLOSER TO FIGURING OUT WHAT MIGHT HAVE HAPPENED.
DING DONG
EVERYONE WHO DOESN'T ALREADY KNOW KEANI, THIS IS KEANI AKANA. SHE'S ONE OF THE BRAINS BEHIND THE AINALANI INITIATIVE, THE CHARITY WE'RE DOING THE CONCERT FOR.
KEANI, THIS IS EVERYONE...AND HONESTLY... RIGHT NOW, WHO CARES ABOUT THEIR NAMES.
HI. SORRY TO MEET SOME OF YOU UNDER SUCH TRAUMATIC CIRCUMSTANCES.
JERRICA.
HI. THANK YOU SO MUCH FOR COMING OUT.
OF COURSE.
I CALLED A FRIEND OF MINE THAT WORKS AT THE POLICE STATION AND HAVE ASKED HER TO PUT OUT AN APB ON KIMBER. THEY'LL KEEP AN EYE OUT FOR ANYTHING OUT OF THE ORDINARY. THEY ALSO TRIED TO TRACE HER CELL PHONE, BUT IT APPEARS TO BE OFF.
WHAT'S WRONG?
OH GOD.
CELL PHONE IS LIKE OXYGEN TO KIMBER, SO THAT'S NOT A GREAT SIGN.
OKAY, WELL, LET'S NOT PANIC JUST YET... I THINK WE SHOULD SPLIT UP.
ONE SMALL GROUP CAN COME WITH ME TO CHECK OUT A FEW LOCATIONS, THE OTHER GROUP SHOULD STAY HERE IN CASE SHE IS ABLE TO GET IN TOUCH.

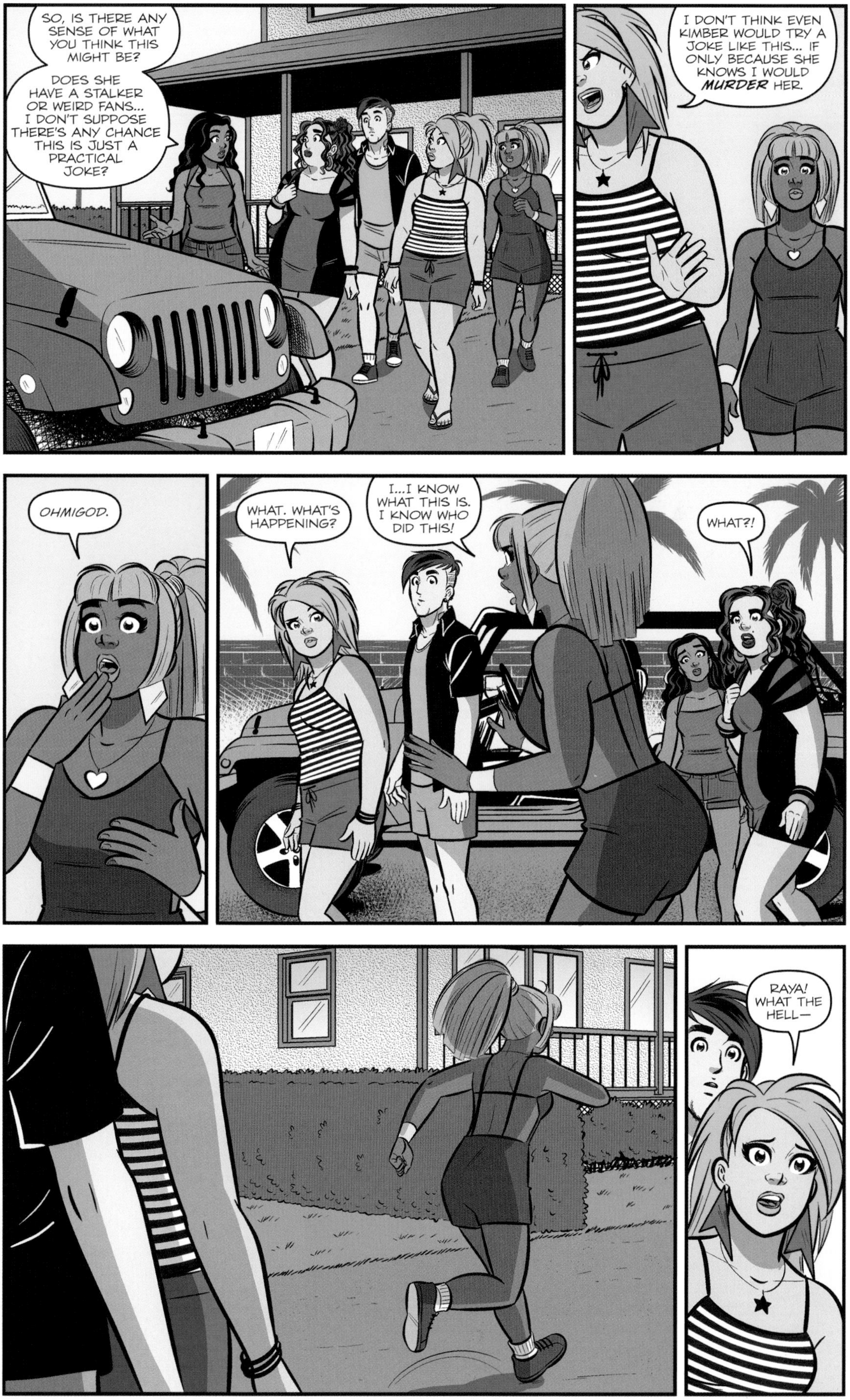
SO, IS THERE ANY SENSE OF WHAT YOU THINK THIS MIGHT BE?
DOES SHE HAVE A STALKER OR WEIRD FANS... I DON'T SUPPOSE THERE'S ANY CHANCE THIS IS JUST A PRACTICAL JOKE?
I DON'T THINK EVEN KIMBER WOULD TRY A JOKE LIKE THIS... IF ONLY BECAUSE SHE KNOWS I WOULD ***MURDER*** HER.
OHMIGOD.
WHAT. WHAT'S HAPPENING?
I...I KNOW WHAT THIS IS. I KNOW WHO DID THIS!
WHAT?!
RAYA! WHAT THE HELL—

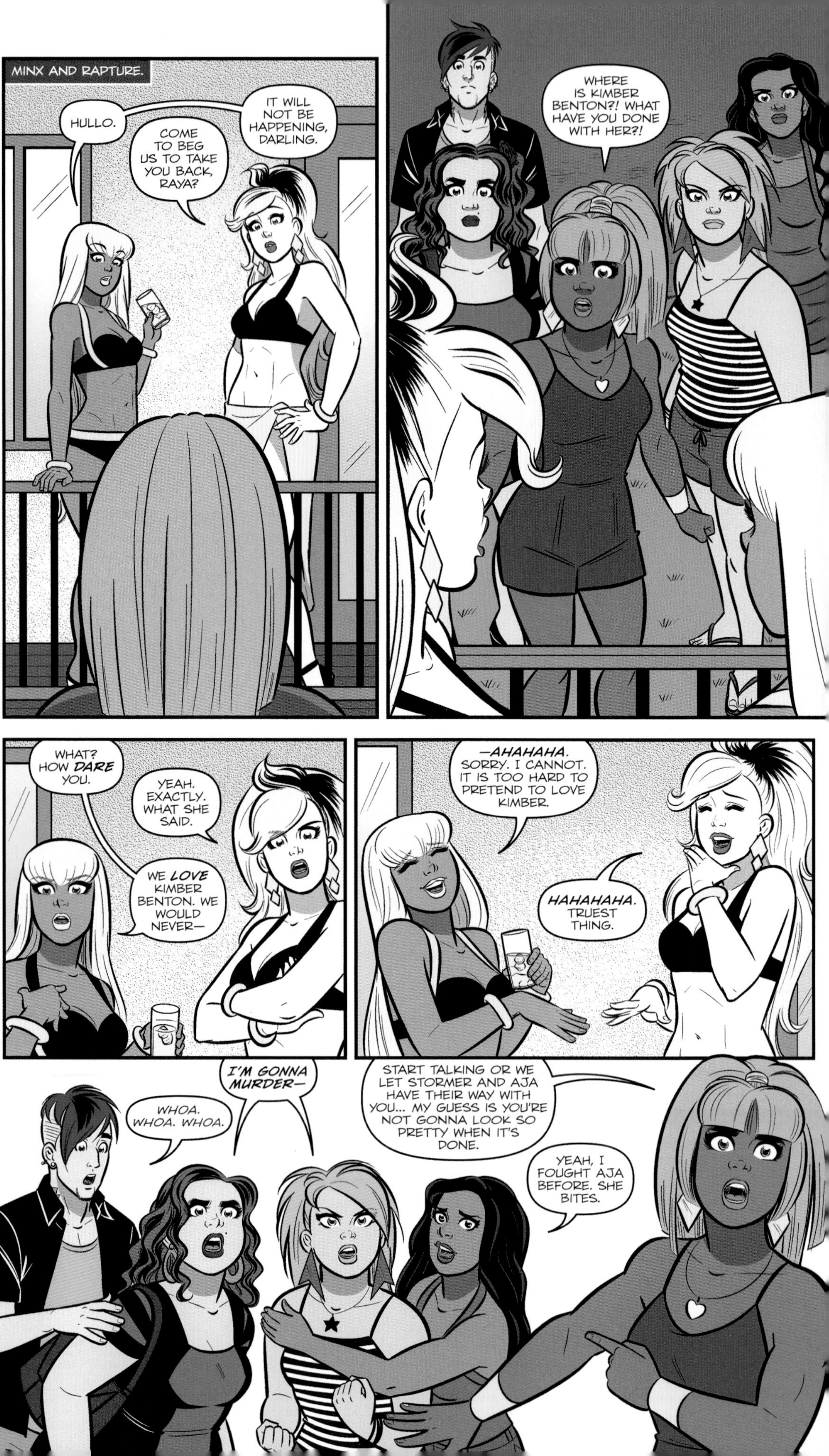
MINX AND RAPTURE.
HULLO.
IT WILL NOT BE HAPPENING, DARLING.
COME TO BEG US TO TAKE YOU BACK, RAYA?
WHERE IS KIMBER BENTON?! WHAT HAVE YOU DONE WITH HER?!
WHAT? HOW DARE YOU.
YEAH. EXACTLY. WHAT SHE SAID.
WE LOVE KIMBER BENTON. WE WOULD NEVER—
—AHAHAHA. SORRY. I CANNOT. IT IS TOO HARD TO PRETEND TO LOVE KIMBER.
HAHAHAHA. TRUEST THING.
WHOA. WHOA. WHOA.
I'M GONNA MURDER—
START TALKING OR WE LET STORMER AND AJA HAVE THEIR WAY WITH YOU... MY GUESS IS YOU'RE NOT GONNA LOOK SO PRETTY WHEN IT'S DONE.
YEAH, I FOUGHT AJA BEFORE. SHE BITES.

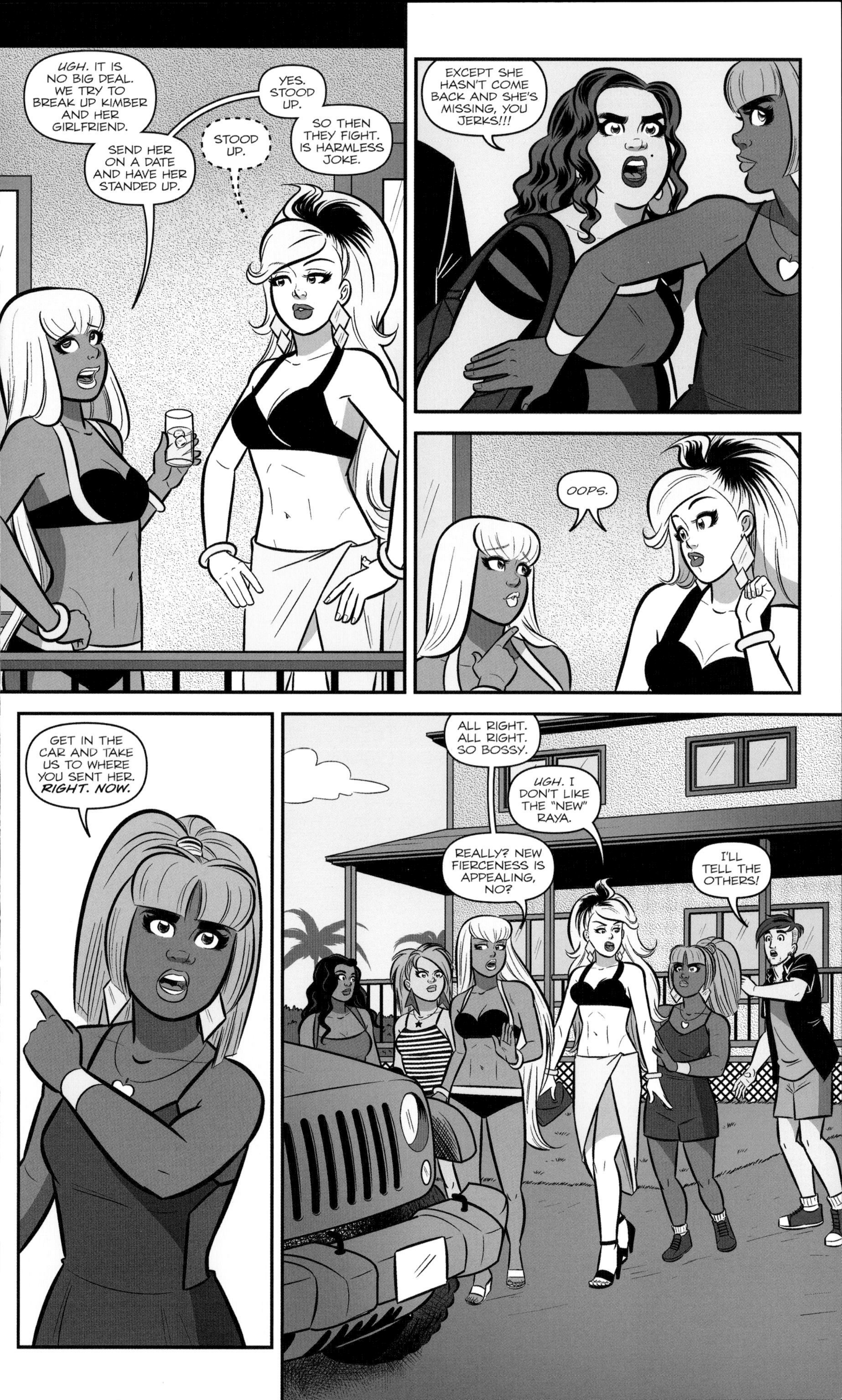
UGH. IT IS NO BIG DEAL. WE TRY TO BREAK UP KIMBER AND HER GIRLFRIEND.
SEND HER ON A DATE AND HAVE HER STANDED UP.
STOOD UP.
YES. STOOD UP.
SO THEN THEY FIGHT. IS HARMLESS JOKE.
EXCEPT SHE HASN'T COME BACK AND SHE'S MISSING, YOU JERKS!!!
OOPS.
GET IN THE CAR AND TAKE US TO WHERE YOU SENT HER. RIGHT. NOW.
ALL RIGHT. ALL RIGHT. SO BOSSY.
UGH. I DON'T LIKE THE "NEW" RAYA.
REALLY? NEW FIERCENESS IS APPEALING, NO?
I'LL TELL THE OTHERS!

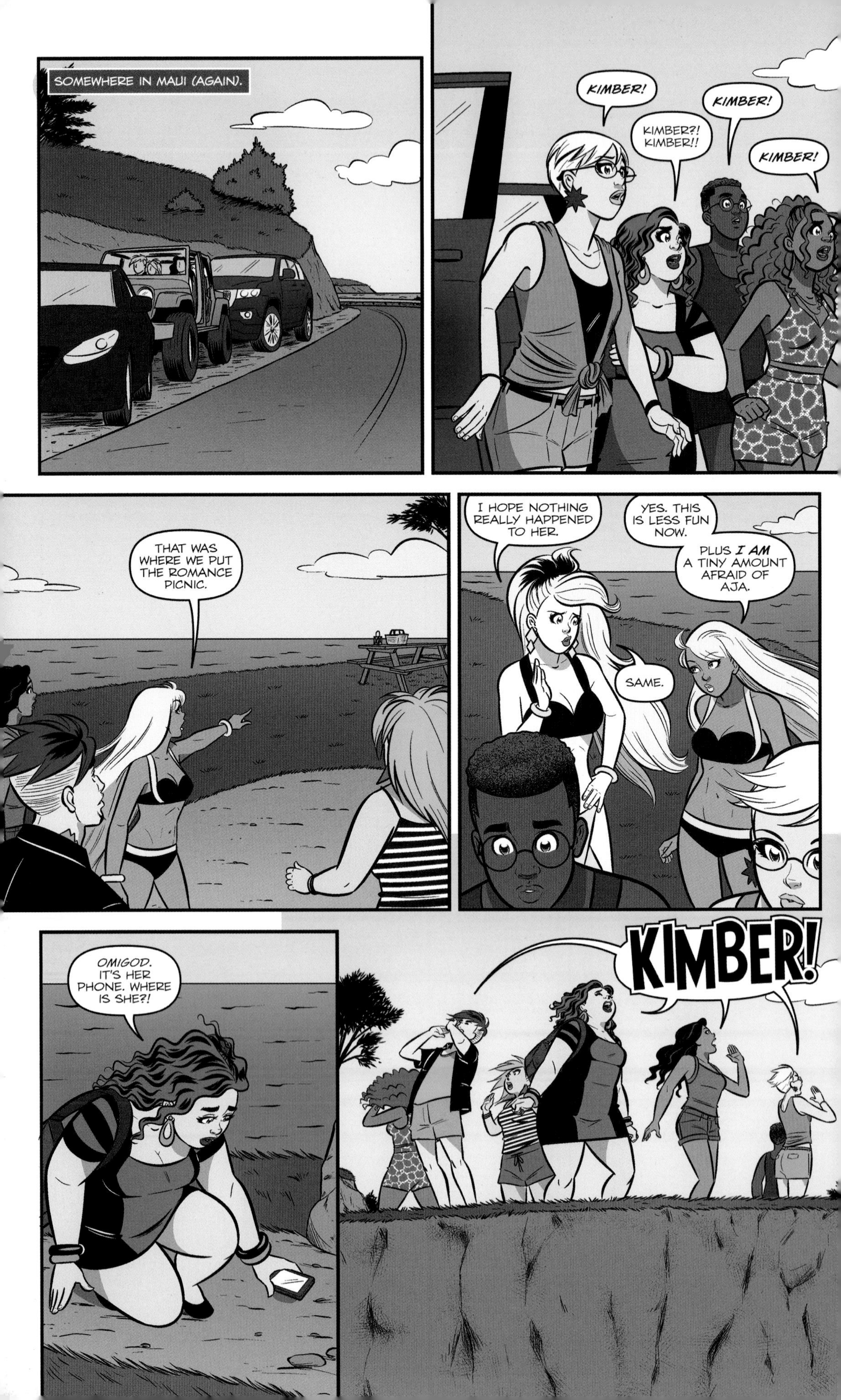

SOMEWHERE IN MAUI (AGAIN).
KIMBER!
KIMBER?! KIMBER!!
KIMBER!
KIMBER!
THAT WAS WHERE WE PUT THE ROMANCE PICNIC.
I HOPE NOTHING REALLY HAPPENED TO HER.
YES. THIS IS LESS FUN NOW.
PLUS *I AM* A TINY AMOUNT AFRAID OF AJA.
SAME.
OMIGOD. IT'S HER PHONE. WHERE IS SHE?!
KIMBER!

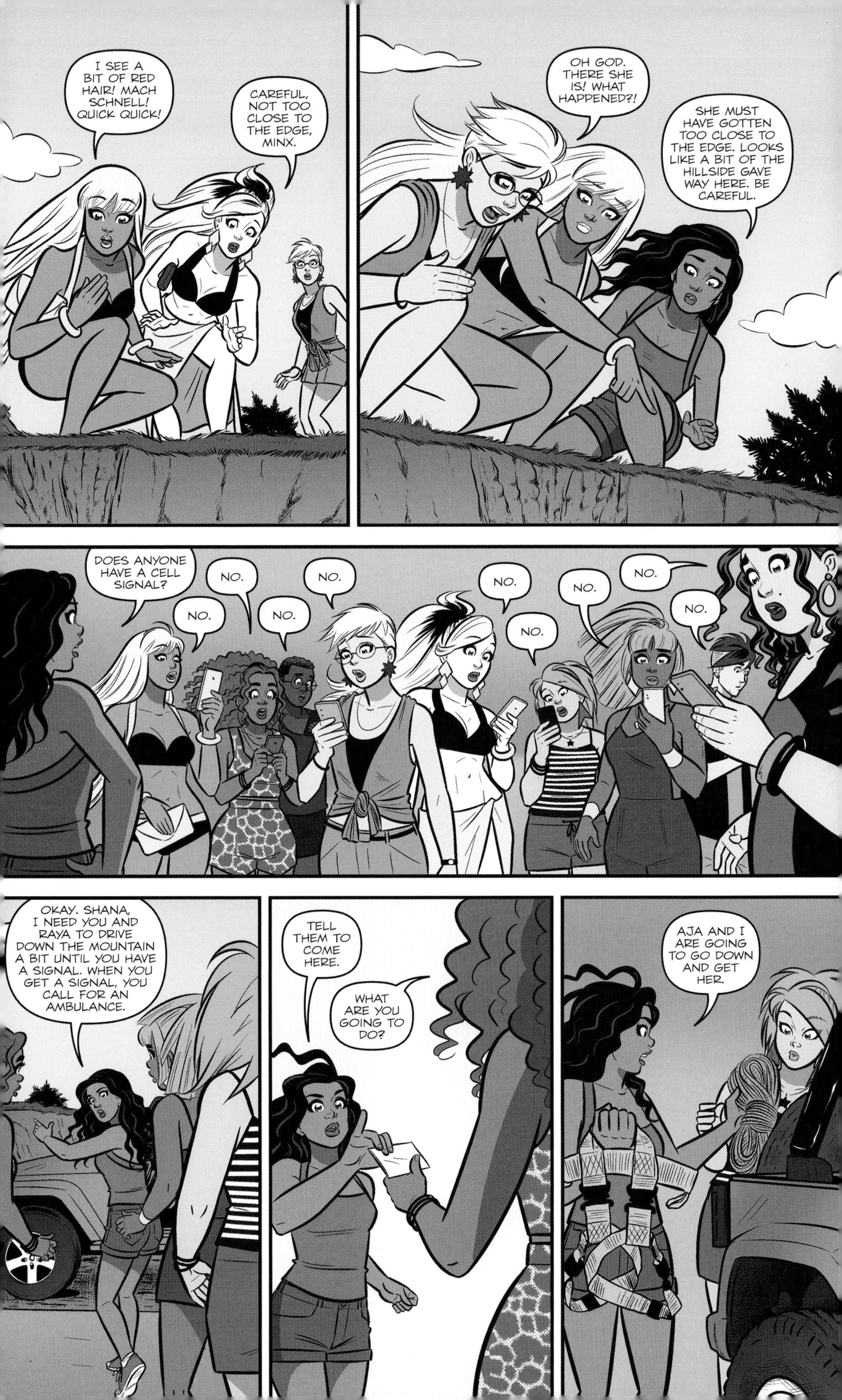
I SEE A BIT OF RED HAIR! MACH SCHNELL! QUICK QUICK!
CAREFUL, NOT TOO CLOSE TO THE EDGE, MINX.
OH GOD. THERE SHE IS! WHAT HAPPENED?!
SHE MUST HAVE GOTTEN TOO CLOSE TO THE EDGE. LOOKS LIKE A BIT OF THE HILLSIDE GAVE WAY HERE. BE CAREFUL.
DOES ANYONE HAVE A CELL SIGNAL?
NO.
NO.
NO.
NO.
NO.
NO.
NO.
NO.
NO.
OKAY. SHANA, I NEED YOU AND RAYA TO DRIVE DOWN THE MOUNTAIN A BIT UNTIL YOU HAVE A SIGNAL. WHEN YOU GET A SIGNAL, YOU CALL FOR AN AMBULANCE.
TELL THEM TO COME HERE.
WHAT ARE YOU GOING TO DO?
AJA AND I ARE GOING TO GO DOWN AND GET HER.

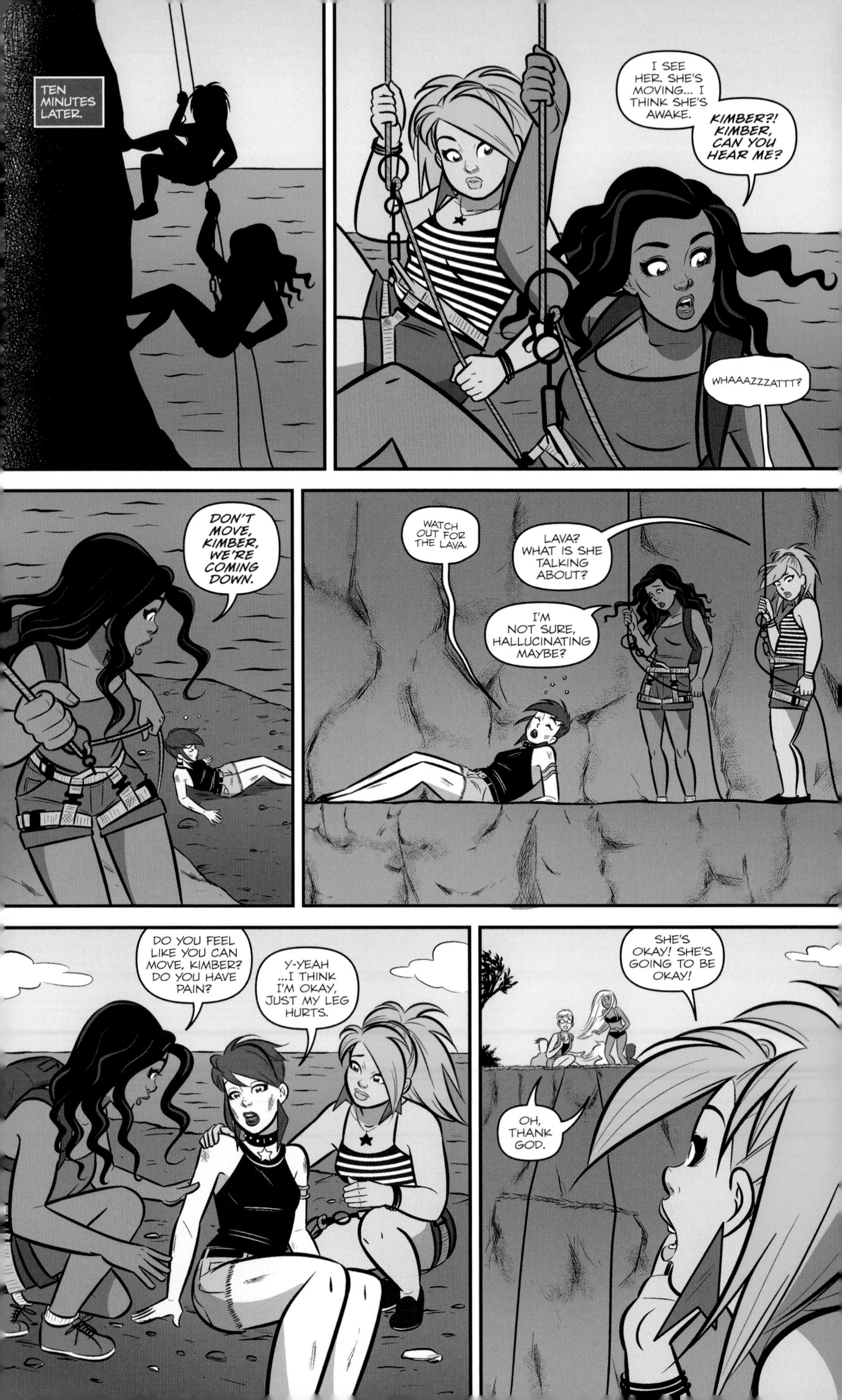
TEN MINUTES LATER.
I SEE HER. SHE'S MOVING... I THINK SHE'S AWAKE.
KIMBER?! KIMBER, CAN YOU HEAR ME?
WHAAAZZZATTT?
DON'T MOVE, KIMBER, WE'RE COMING DOWN.
WATCH OUT FOR THE LAVA.
LAVA? WHAT IS SHE TALKING ABOUT?
I'M NOT SURE, HALLUCINATING MAYBE?
DO YOU FEEL LIKE YOU CAN MOVE, KIMBER? DO YOU HAVE PAIN?
Y-YEAH ...I THINK I'M OKAY, JUST MY LEG HURTS.
SHE'S OKAY! SHE'S GOING TO BE OKAY!
OH, THANK GOD.

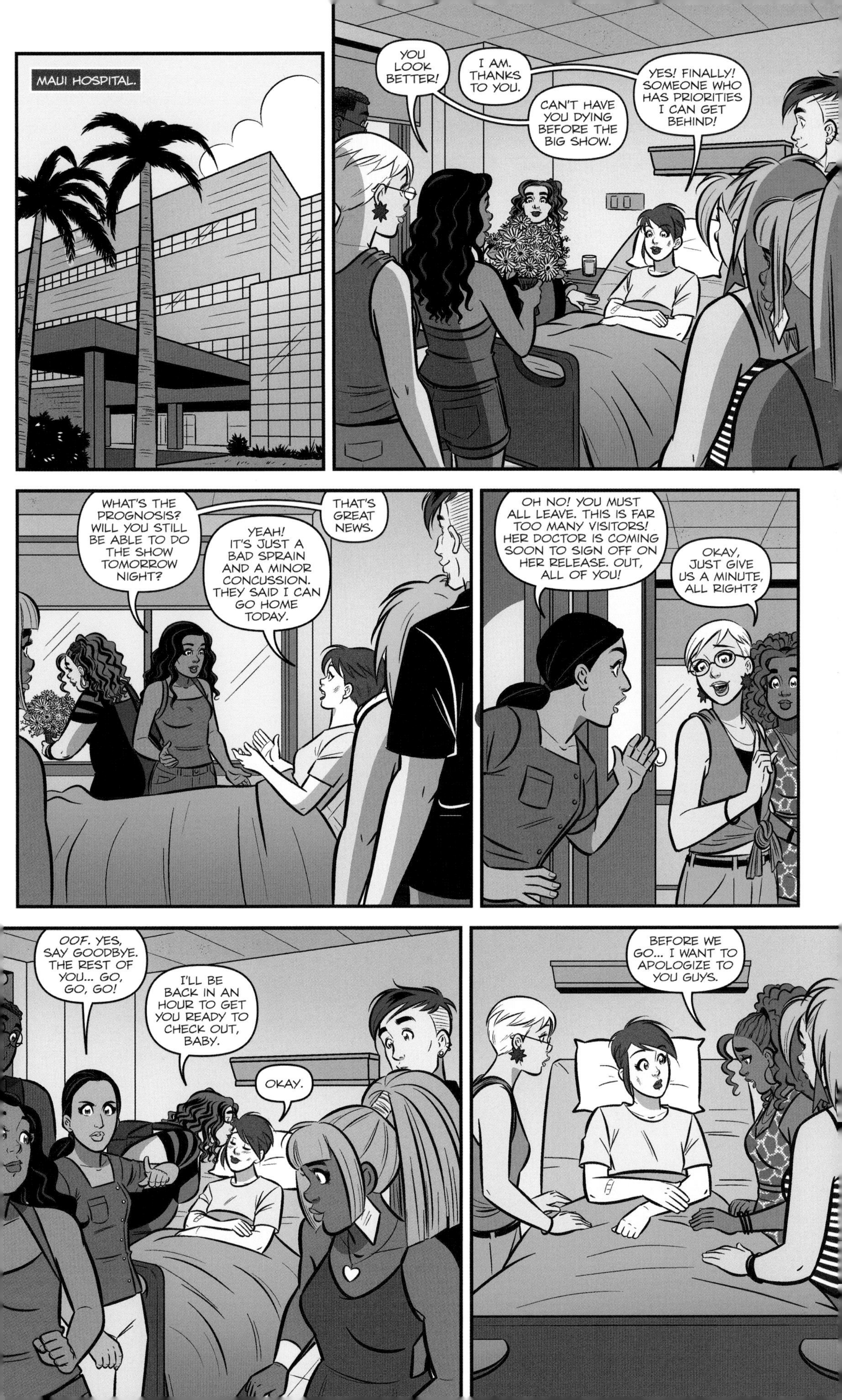
MAUI HOSPITAL.
YOU LOOK BETTER!
I AM. THANKS TO YOU.
CAN'T HAVE YOU DYING BEFORE THE BIG SHOW.
YES! FINALLY! SOMEONE WHO HAS PRIORITIES I CAN GET BEHIND!
WHAT'S THE PROGNOSIS? WILL YOU STILL BE ABLE TO DO THE SHOW TOMORROW NIGHT?
YEAH! IT'S JUST A BAD SPRAIN AND A MINOR CONCUSSION. THEY SAID I CAN GO HOME TODAY.
THAT'S GREAT NEWS.
OH NO! YOU MUST ALL LEAVE. THIS IS FAR TOO MANY VISITORS! HER DOCTOR IS COMING SOON TO SIGN OFF ON HER RELEASE. OUT, ALL OF YOU!
OKAY, JUST GIVE US A MINUTE, ALL RIGHT?
OOF. YES, SAY GOODBYE. THE REST OF YOU... GO, GO, GO!
I'LL BE BACK IN AN HOUR TO GET YOU READY TO CHECK OUT, BABY.
OKAY.
BEFORE WE GO... I WANT TO APOLOGIZE TO YOU GUYS.

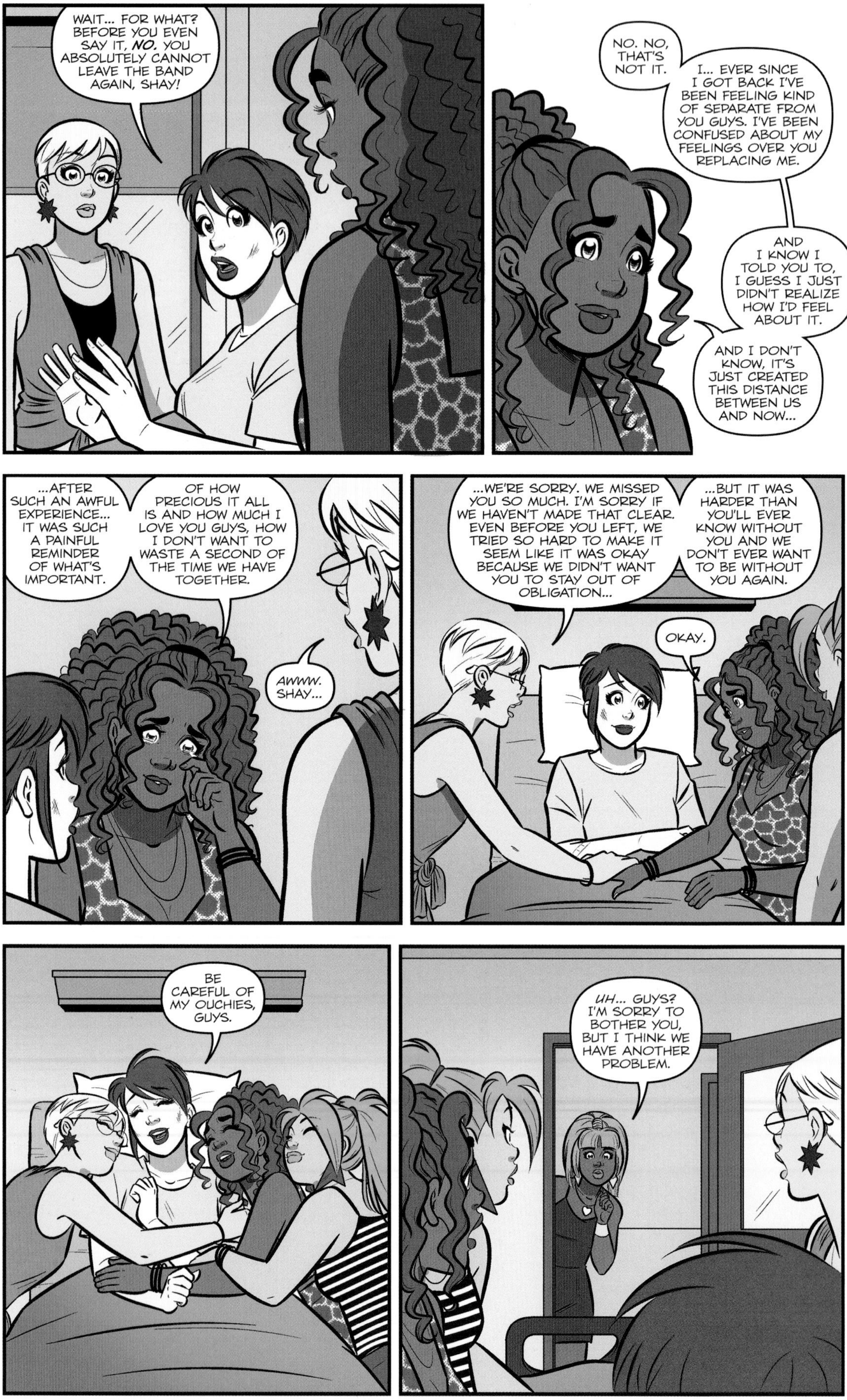
WAIT... FOR WHAT? BEFORE YOU EVEN SAY IT, NO. YOU ABSOLUTELY CANNOT LEAVE THE BAND AGAIN, SHAY!
NO. NO, THAT'S NOT IT.
I... EVER SINCE I GOT BACK I'VE BEEN FEELING KIND OF SEPARATE FROM YOU GUYS. I'VE BEEN CONFUSED ABOUT MY FEELINGS OVER YOU REPLACING ME.
AND I KNOW I TOLD YOU TO, I GUESS I JUST DIDN'T REALIZE HOW I'D FEEL ABOUT IT.
AND I DON'T KNOW, IT'S JUST CREATED THIS DISTANCE BETWEEN US AND NOW...
...AFTER SUCH AN AWFUL EXPERIENCE... IT WAS SUCH A PAINFUL REMINDER OF WHAT'S IMPORTANT.
OF HOW PRECIOUS IT ALL IS AND HOW MUCH I LOVE YOU GUYS, HOW I DON'T WANT TO WASTE A SECOND OF THE TIME WE HAVE TOGETHER.
AWWW. SHAY...
...WE'RE SORRY. WE MISSED YOU SO MUCH. I'M SORRY IF WE HAVEN'T MADE THAT CLEAR. EVEN BEFORE YOU LEFT, WE TRIED SO HARD TO MAKE IT SEEM LIKE IT WAS OKAY BECAUSE WE DIDN'T WANT YOU TO STAY OUT OF OBLIGATION...
...BUT IT WAS HARDER THAN YOU'LL EVER KNOW WITHOUT YOU AND WE DON'T EVER WANT TO BE WITHOUT YOU AGAIN.
OKAY.
BE CAREFUL OF MY OUCHIES, GUYS.
UH... GUYS? I'M SORRY TO BOTHER YOU, BUT I THINK WE HAVE ANOTHER PROBLEM.

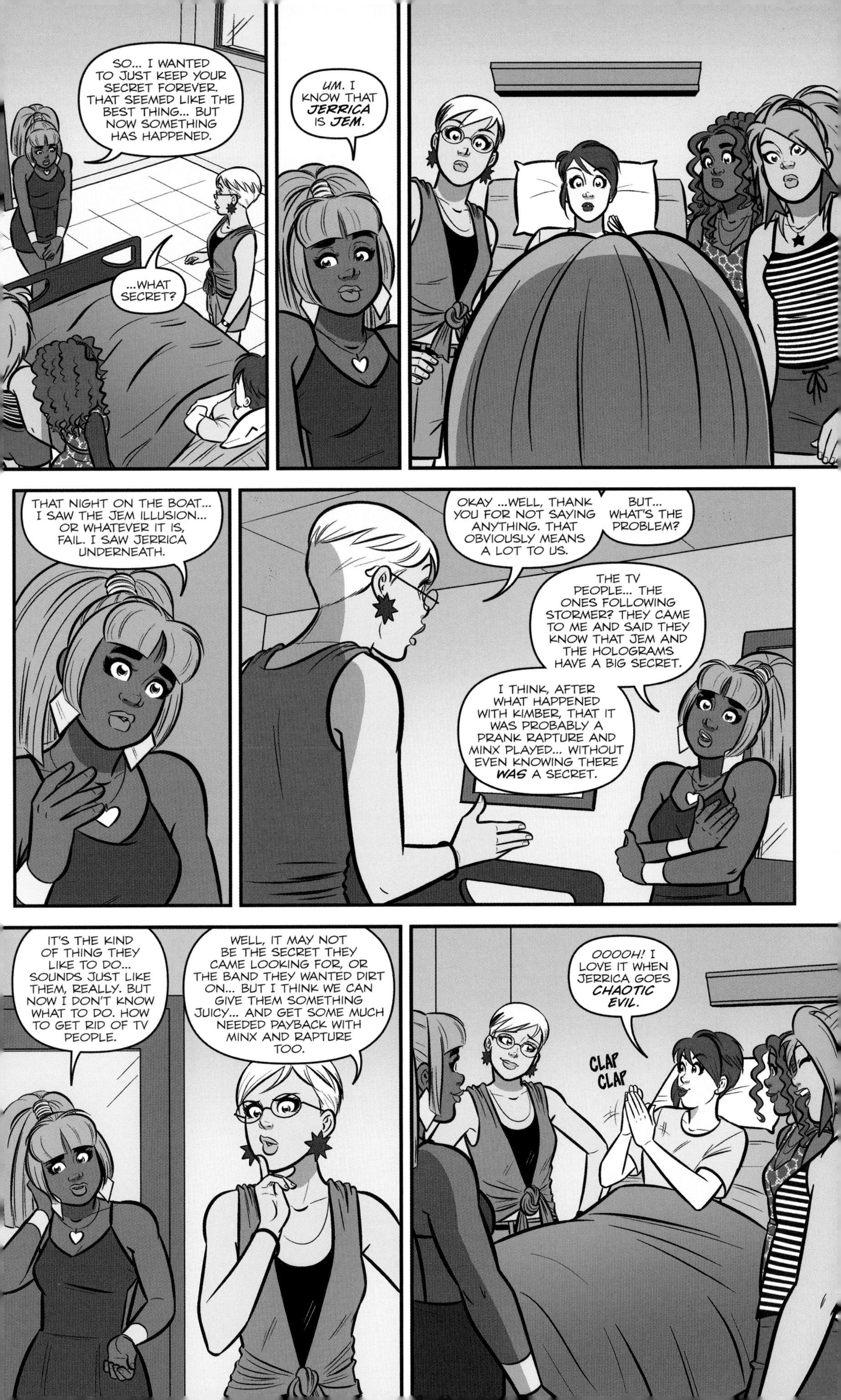

SO... I WANTED TO JUST KEEP YOUR SECRET FOREVER. THAT SEEMED LIKE THE BEST THING... BUT NOW SOMETHING HAS HAPPENED.
...WHAT SECRET?
UM. I KNOW THAT JERRICA IS JEM.
THAT NIGHT ON THE BOAT... I SAW THE JEM ILLUSION... OR WHATEVER IT IS, FAIL. I SAW JERRICA UNDERNEATH.
OKAY ...WELL, THANK YOU FOR NOT SAYING ANYTHING. THAT OBVIOUSLY MEANS A LOT TO US.
BUT... WHAT'S THE PROBLEM?
THE TV PEOPLE... THE ONES FOLLOWING STORMER? THEY CAME TO ME AND SAID THEY KNOW THAT JEM AND THE HOLOGRAMS HAVE A BIG SECRET.
I THINK, AFTER WHAT HAPPENED WITH KIMBER, THAT IT WAS PROBABLY A PRANK RAPTURE AND MINX PLAYED... WITHOUT EVEN KNOWING THERE WAS A SECRET.
IT'S THE KIND OF THING THEY LIKE TO DO... SOUNDS JUST LIKE THEM, REALLY. BUT NOW I DON'T KNOW WHAT TO DO. HOW TO GET RID OF TV PEOPLE.
WELL, IT MAY NOT BE THE SECRET THEY CAME LOOKING FOR, OR THE BAND THEY WANTED DIRT ON... BUT I THINK WE CAN GIVE THEM SOMETHING JUICY... AND GET SOME MUCH NEEDED PAYBACK WITH MINX AND RAPTURE TOO.
OOOOH! I LOVE IT WHEN JERRICA GOES CHAOTIC EVIL.
CLAP CLAP

I DO FEEL BAD ABOUT KIMBER. DO YOU THINK WE WENT TOO FAR?

PERHAPS.

BUT SHE IS FINE. IT IS FINE, DARLING.

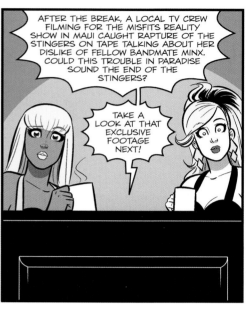

AFTER THE BREAK, A LOCAL TV CREW FILMING FOR THE MISFITS REALITY SHOW IN MAUI CAUGHT RAPTURE OF THE STINGERS ON TAPE TALKING ABOUT HER DISLIKE OF FELLOW BANDMATE MINX. COULD THIS TROUBLE IN PARADISE SOUND THE END OF THE STINGERS?

TAKE A LOOK AT THAT EXCLUSIVE FOOTAGE NEXT!

WELL, I MEAN FOR STARTERS, SHE'S JUST A TERRIBLE MUSICIAN. BUT THAT DOESN'T EVEN BEGIN TO DEAL WITH HER PERSONALITY. SUCH A NIGHTMARE.

AND SHE'S ALWAYS SAYING WORDS WRONG, IT'S LIKE, YOU'RE A WORLD TRAVELER... LEARN AMERICAN ALREADY... AND SHE THINKS SHE'S SO SMART AT...

MINX! NO! I WOULD NEVER! YOU KNOW I ADORE YOU! I-I DON'T KNOW WHAT THAT IS! IT CAN'T BE REAL!

Y-YEAH, IT'S GOTTA BE FAKE SOMEHOW.

EEEP!

AHHHHHH!

ICH WERDE DICH TOTEN!

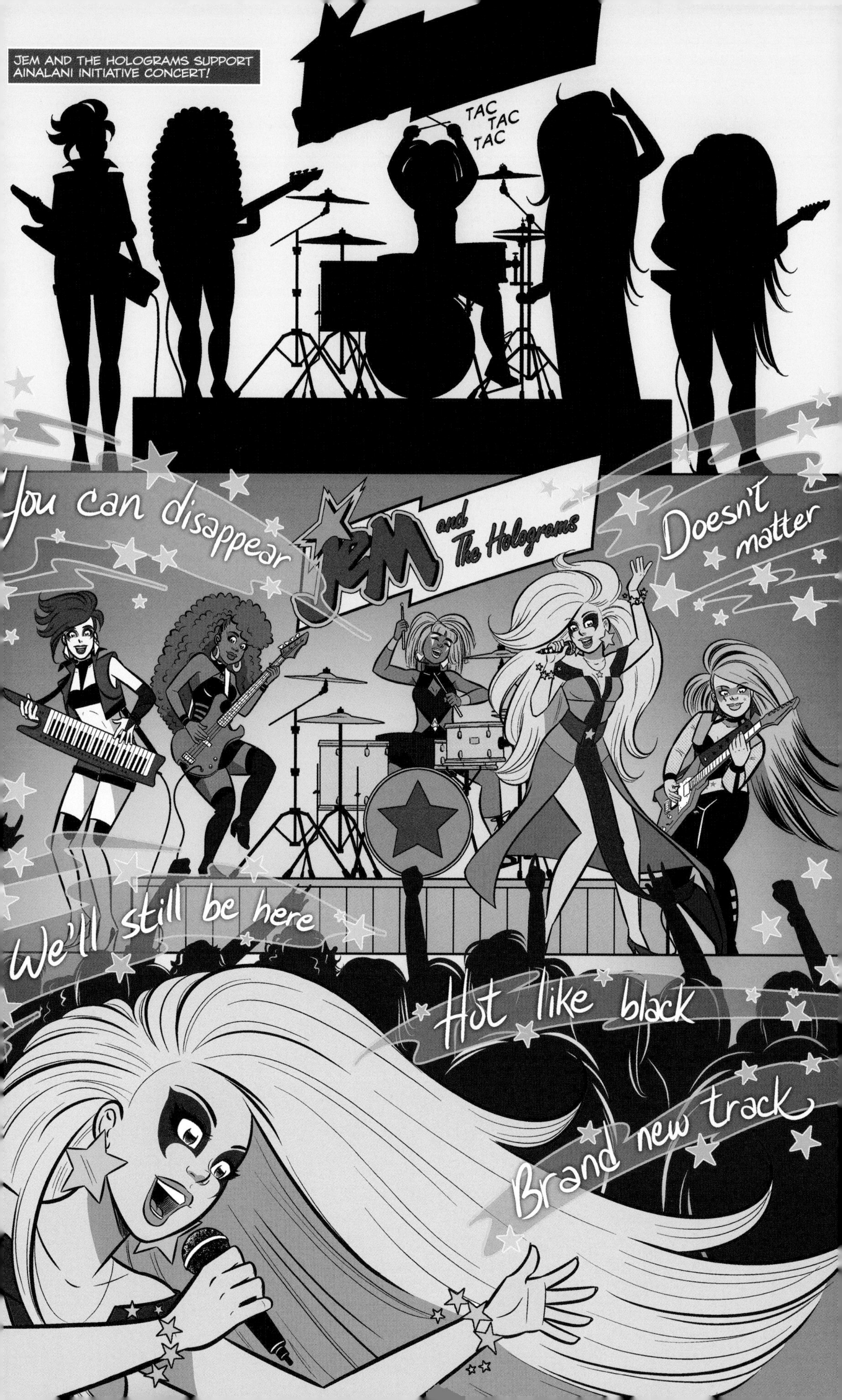
JEM AND THE HOLOGRAMS SUPPORT AINALANI INITIATIVE CONCERT!
TAC TAC TAC
You can disappear
JEM and The Holograms
Doesn't matter
We'll still be here
Hot like black
Brand new track

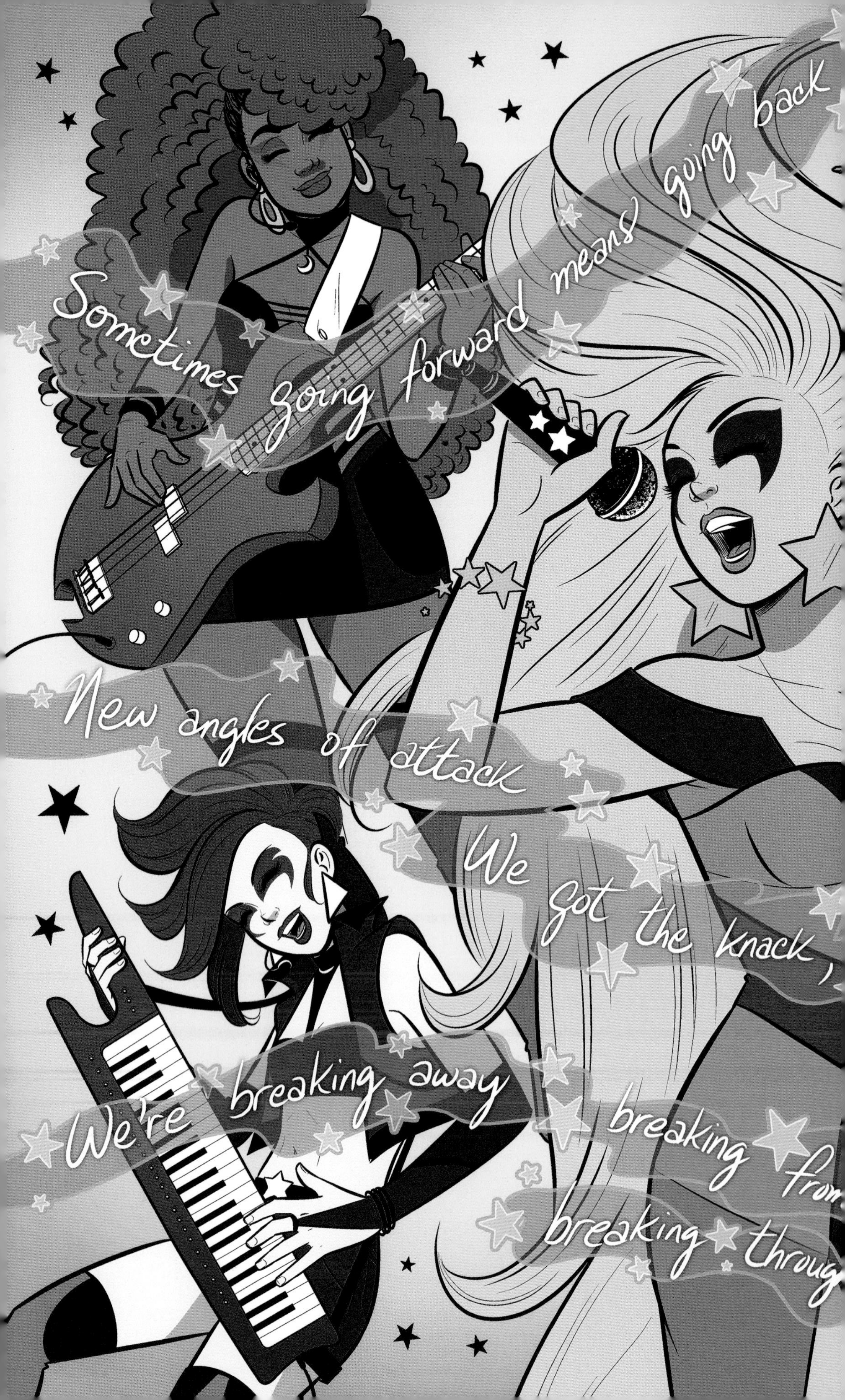
Sometimes going forward means going back
New angles of attack
We got the knack,
We're breaking away
breaking from
breaking through

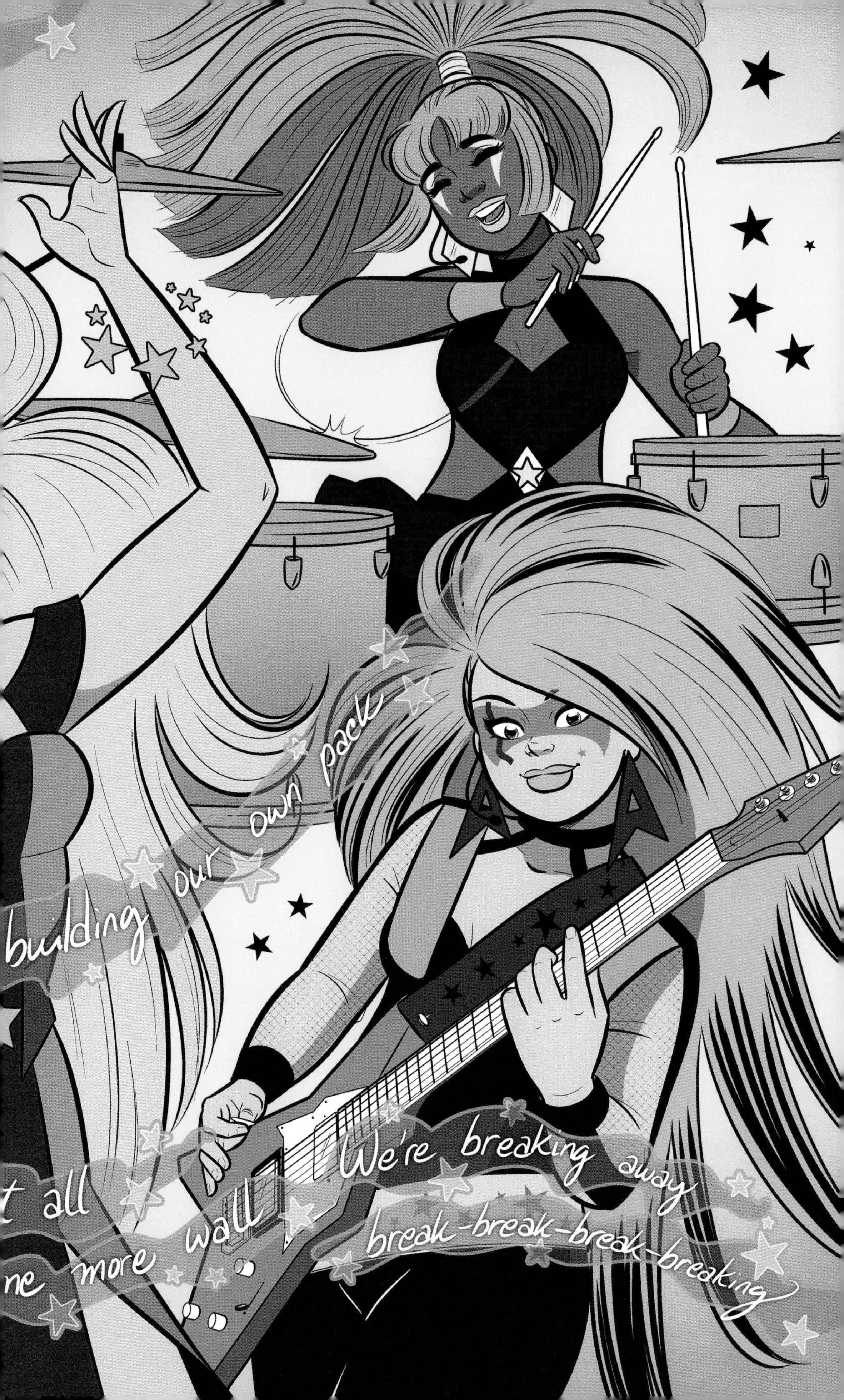
building our own pack
t all
ne more wall
We're breaking away
break-break-break-breaking

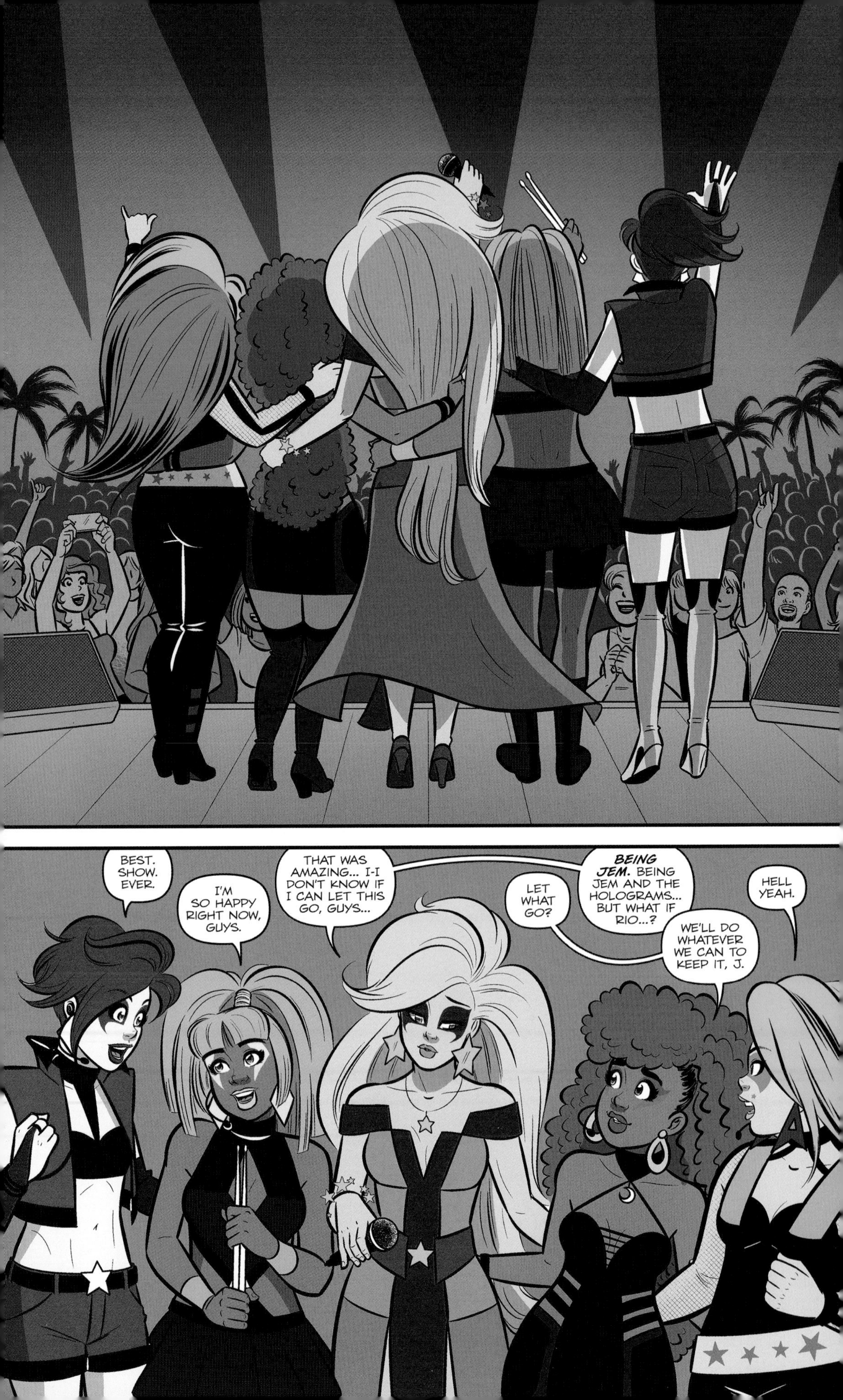
BEST. SHOW. EVER.
I'M SO HAPPY RIGHT NOW, GUYS.
THAT WAS AMAZING... I-I DON'T KNOW IF I CAN LET THIS GO, GUYS...
LET WHAT GO?
BEING JEM. BEING JEM AND THE HOLOGRAMS... BUT WHAT IF RIO...?
WE'LL DO WHATEVER WE CAN TO KEEP IT, J.
HELL YEAH.

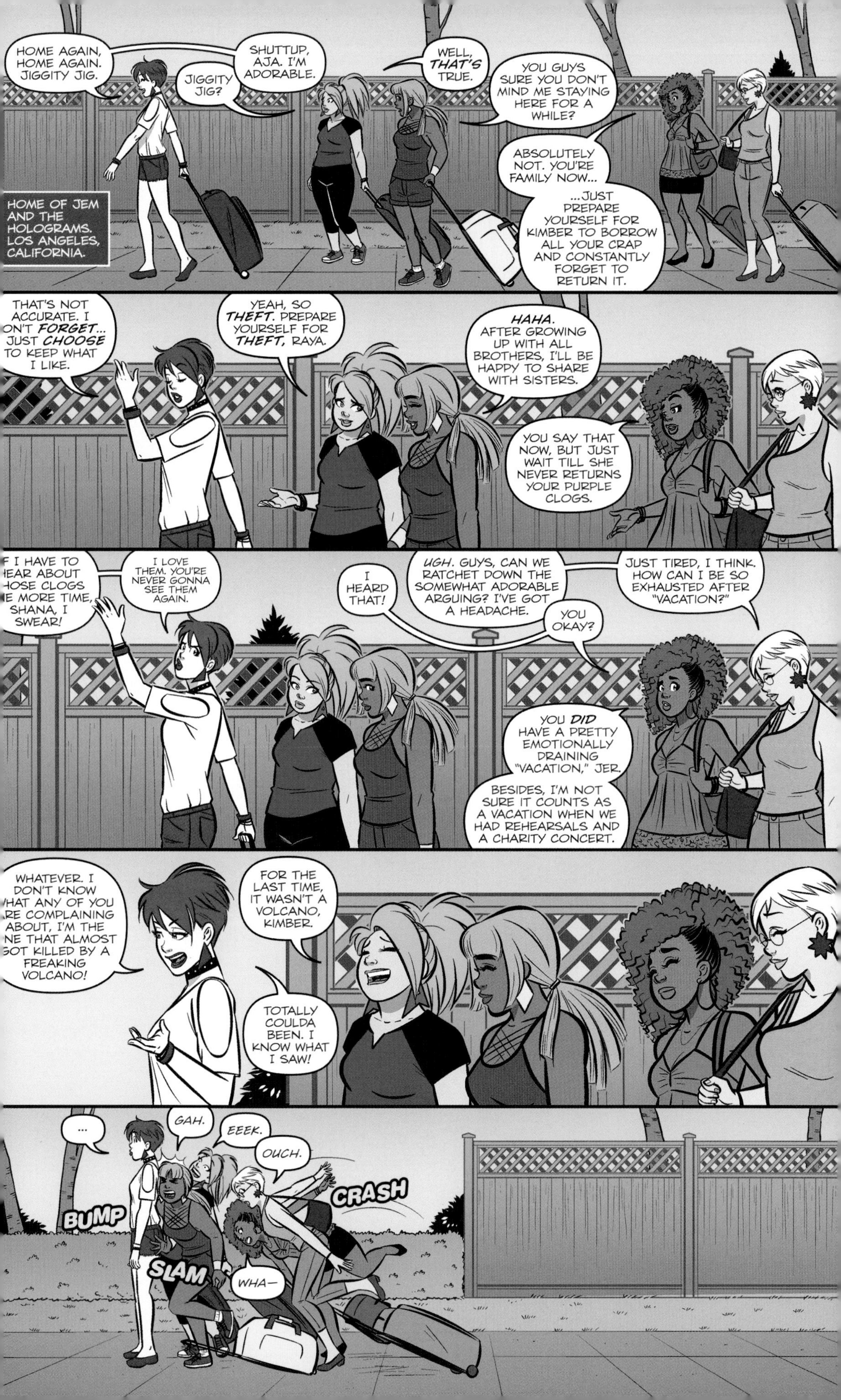

HOME AGAIN, HOME AGAIN. JIGGITY JIG.
JIGGITY JIG?
SHUTTUP, AJA. I'M ADORABLE.
WELL, THAT'S TRUE.
YOU GUYS SURE YOU DON'T MIND ME STAYING HERE FOR A WHILE?
ABSOLUTELY NOT. YOU'RE FAMILY NOW...
...JUST PREPARE YOURSELF FOR KIMBER TO BORROW ALL YOUR CRAP AND CONSTANTLY FORGET TO RETURN IT.
HOME OF JEM AND THE HOLOGRAMS. LOS ANGELES, CALIFORNIA.
THAT'S NOT ACCURATE. I ON'T FORGET... JUST CHOOSE TO KEEP WHAT I LIKE.
YEAH, SO THEFT. PREPARE YOURSELF FOR THEFT, RAYA.
HAHA. AFTER GROWING UP WITH ALL BROTHERS, I'LL BE HAPPY TO SHARE WITH SISTERS.
YOU SAY THAT NOW, BUT JUST WAIT TILL SHE NEVER RETURNS YOUR PURPLE CLOGS.
F I HAVE TO HEAR ABOUT HOSE CLOGS E MORE TIME, SHANA, I SWEAR!
I LOVE THEM. YOU'RE NEVER GONNA SEE THEM AGAIN.
I HEARD THAT!
UGH. GUYS, CAN WE RATCHET DOWN THE SOMEWHAT ADORABLE ARGUING? I'VE GOT A HEADACHE.
YOU OKAY?
JUST TIRED, I THINK. HOW CAN I BE SO EXHAUSTED AFTER "VACATION?"
YOU DID HAVE A PRETTY EMOTIONALLY DRAINING "VACATION," JER.
BESIDES, I'M NOT SURE IT COUNTS AS A VACATION WHEN WE HAD REHEARSALS AND A CHARITY CONCERT.
WHATEVER. I DON'T KNOW HAT ANY OF YOU RE COMPLAINING ABOUT, I'M THE NE THAT ALMOST GOT KILLED BY A FREAKING VOLCANO!
FOR THE LAST TIME, IT WASN'T A VOLCANO, KIMBER.
TOTALLY COULDA BEEN. I KNOW WHAT I SAW!
...
GAH.
EEEK.
OUCH.
CRASH
BUMP
SLAM
WHA—

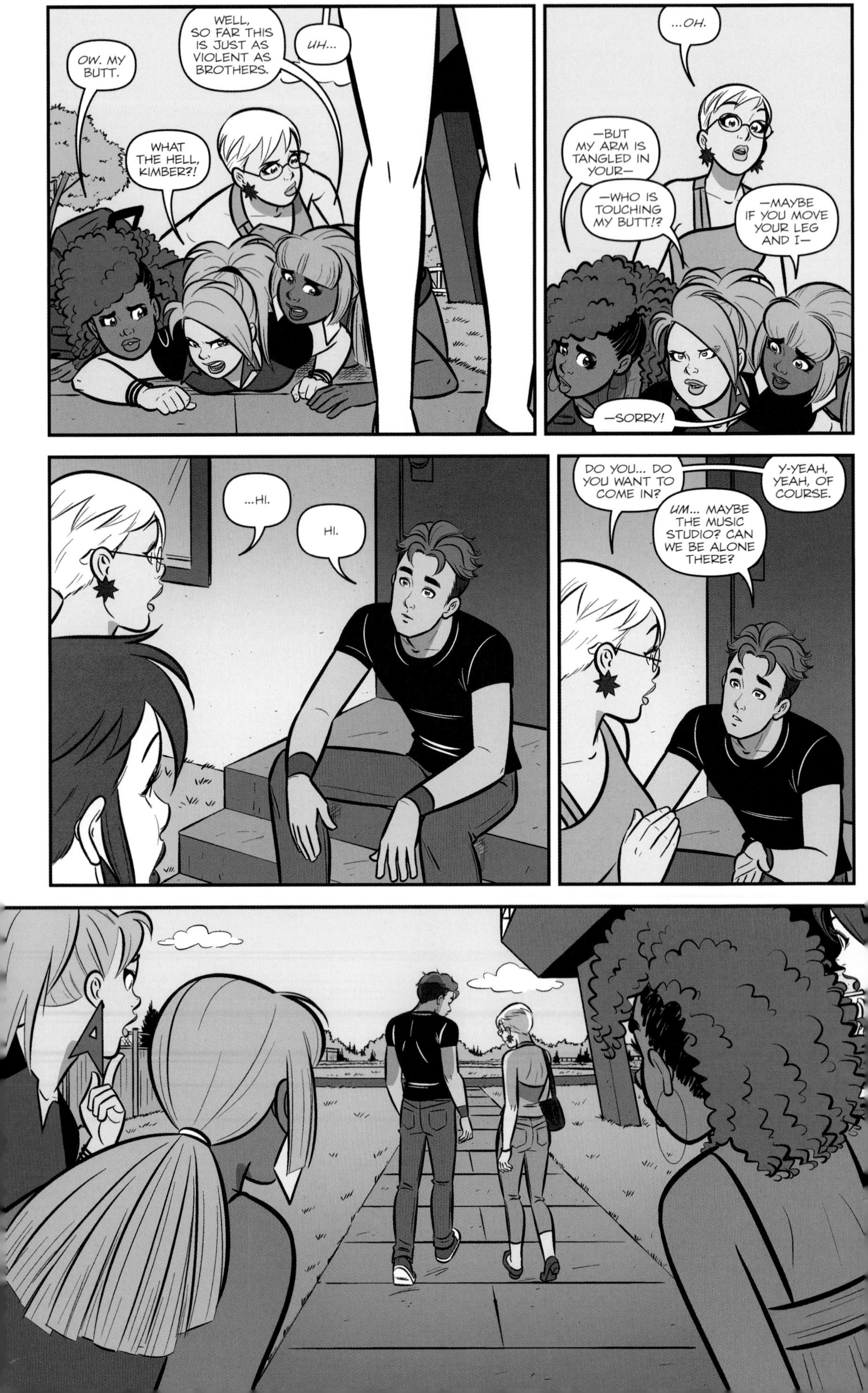
OW. MY BUTT.
WELL, SO FAR THIS IS JUST AS VIOLENT AS BROTHERS.
UH...
WHAT THE HELL, KIMBER?!
...OH.
—BUT MY ARM IS TANGLED IN YOUR—
—WHO IS TOUCHING MY BUTT!?
—MAYBE IF YOU MOVE YOUR LEG AND I—
—SORRY!
...HI.
HI.
DO YOU... DO YOU WANT TO COME IN?
Y-YEAH, YEAH, OF COURSE.
UM... MAYBE THE MUSIC STUDIO? CAN WE BE ALONE THERE?

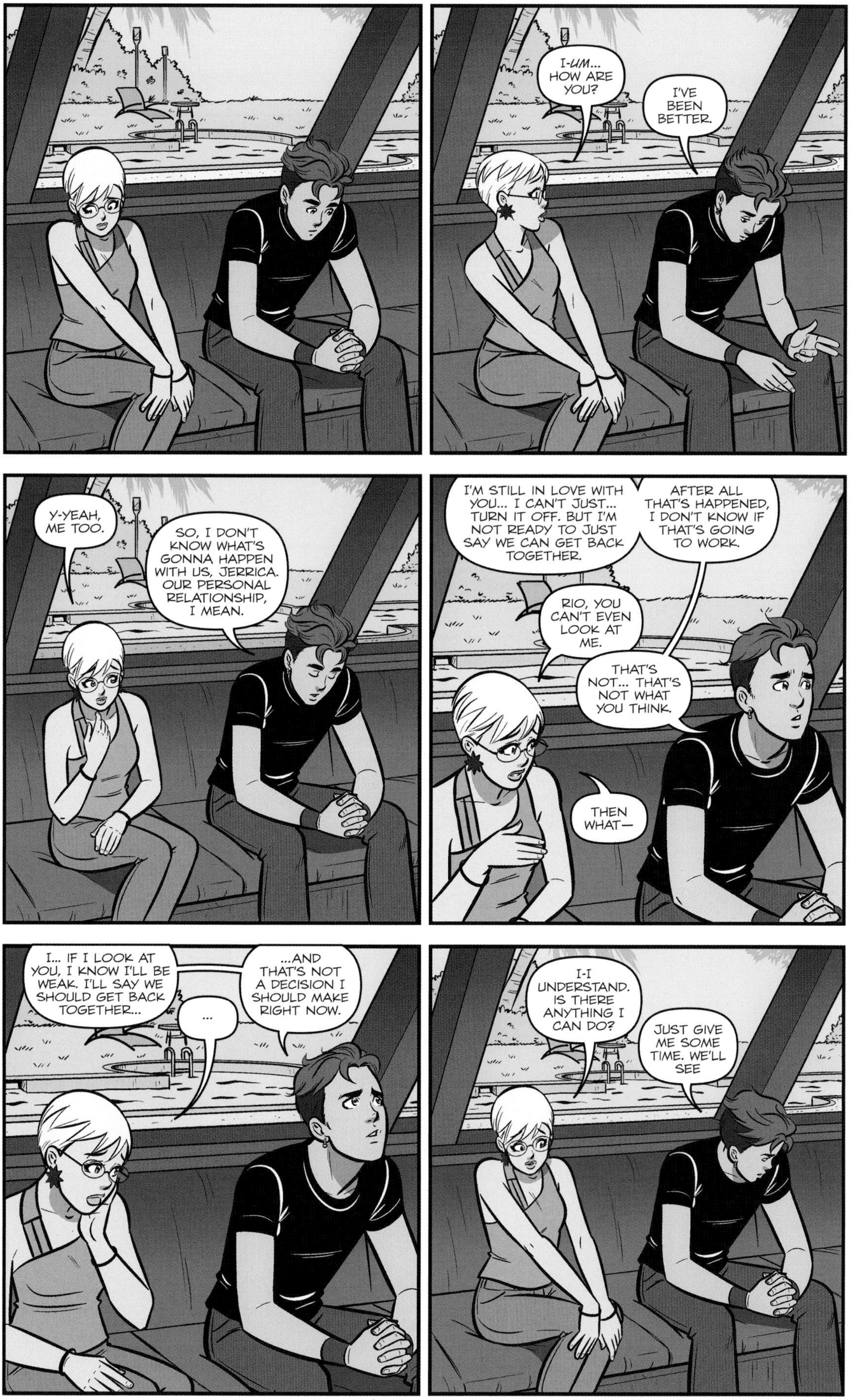
I-UM... HOW ARE YOU?
I'VE BEEN BETTER.
Y-YEAH, ME TOO.
SO, I DON'T KNOW WHAT'S GONNA HAPPEN WITH US, JERRICA. OUR PERSONAL RELATIONSHIP, I MEAN.
I'M STILL IN LOVE WITH YOU... I CAN'T JUST... TURN IT OFF. BUT I'M NOT READY TO JUST SAY WE CAN GET BACK TOGETHER.
AFTER ALL THAT'S HAPPENED, I DON'T KNOW IF THAT'S GOING TO WORK.
RIO, YOU CAN'T EVEN LOOK AT ME.
THAT'S NOT... THAT'S NOT WHAT YOU THINK.
THEN WHAT—
I... IF I LOOK AT YOU, I KNOW I'LL BE WEAK. I'LL SAY WE SHOULD GET BACK TOGETHER...
...AND THAT'S NOT A DECISION I SHOULD MAKE RIGHT NOW.
...
I-I UNDERSTAND. IS THERE ANYTHING I CAN DO?
JUST GIVE ME SOME TIME. WE'LL SEE

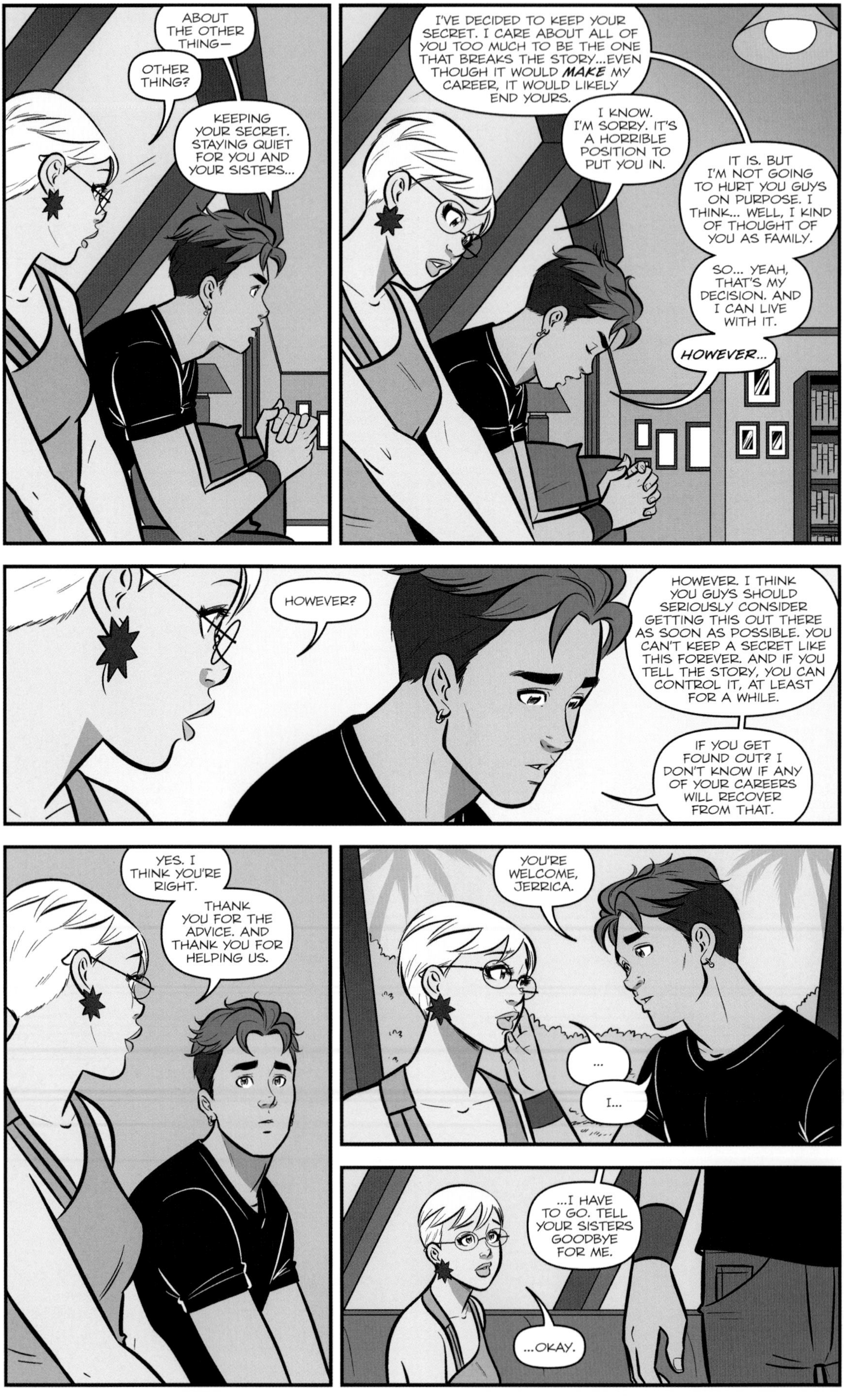

ABOUT THE OTHER THING—
OTHER THING?
KEEPING YOUR SECRET. STAYING QUIET FOR YOU AND YOUR SISTERS...
I'VE DECIDED TO KEEP YOUR SECRET. I CARE ABOUT ALL OF YOU TOO MUCH TO BE THE ONE THAT BREAKS THE STORY...EVEN THOUGH IT WOULD MAKE MY CAREER, IT WOULD LIKELY END YOURS.
I KNOW. I'M SORRY. IT'S A HORRIBLE POSITION TO PUT YOU IN.
IT IS. BUT I'M NOT GOING TO HURT YOU GUYS ON PURPOSE. I THINK... WELL, I KIND OF THOUGHT OF YOU AS FAMILY.
SO... YEAH, THAT'S MY DECISION. AND I CAN LIVE WITH IT.
HOWEVER...
HOWEVER?
HOWEVER. I THINK YOU GUYS SHOULD SERIOUSLY CONSIDER GETTING THIS OUT THERE AS SOON AS POSSIBLE. YOU CAN'T KEEP A SECRET LIKE THIS FOREVER. AND IF YOU TELL THE STORY, YOU CAN CONTROL IT, AT LEAST FOR A WHILE.
IF YOU GET FOUND OUT? I DON'T KNOW IF ANY OF YOUR CAREERS WILL RECOVER FROM THAT.
YES. I THINK YOU'RE RIGHT.
THANK YOU FOR THE ADVICE. AND THANK YOU FOR HELPING US.
YOU'RE WELCOME, JERRICA.
...
I...
...I HAVE TO GO. TELL YOUR SISTERS GOODBYE FOR ME.
...OKAY.

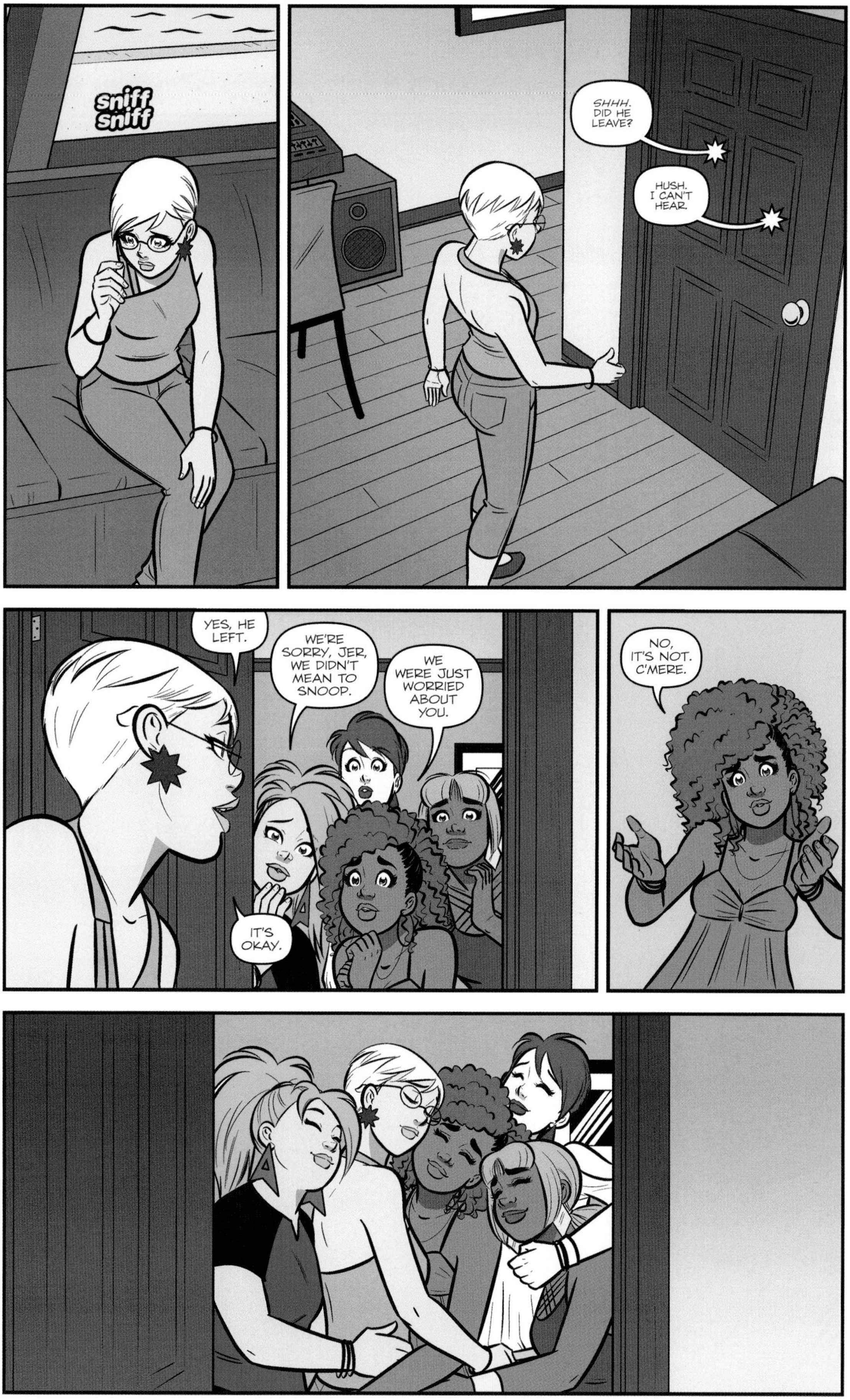
sniff sniff
SHHH. DID HE LEAVE?
HUSH. I CAN'T HEAR.
YES, HE LEFT.
IT'S OKAY.
WE'RE SORRY, JER, WE DIDN'T MEAN TO SNOOP.
WE WERE JUST WORRIED ABOUT YOU.
NO, IT'S NOT. C'MERE.

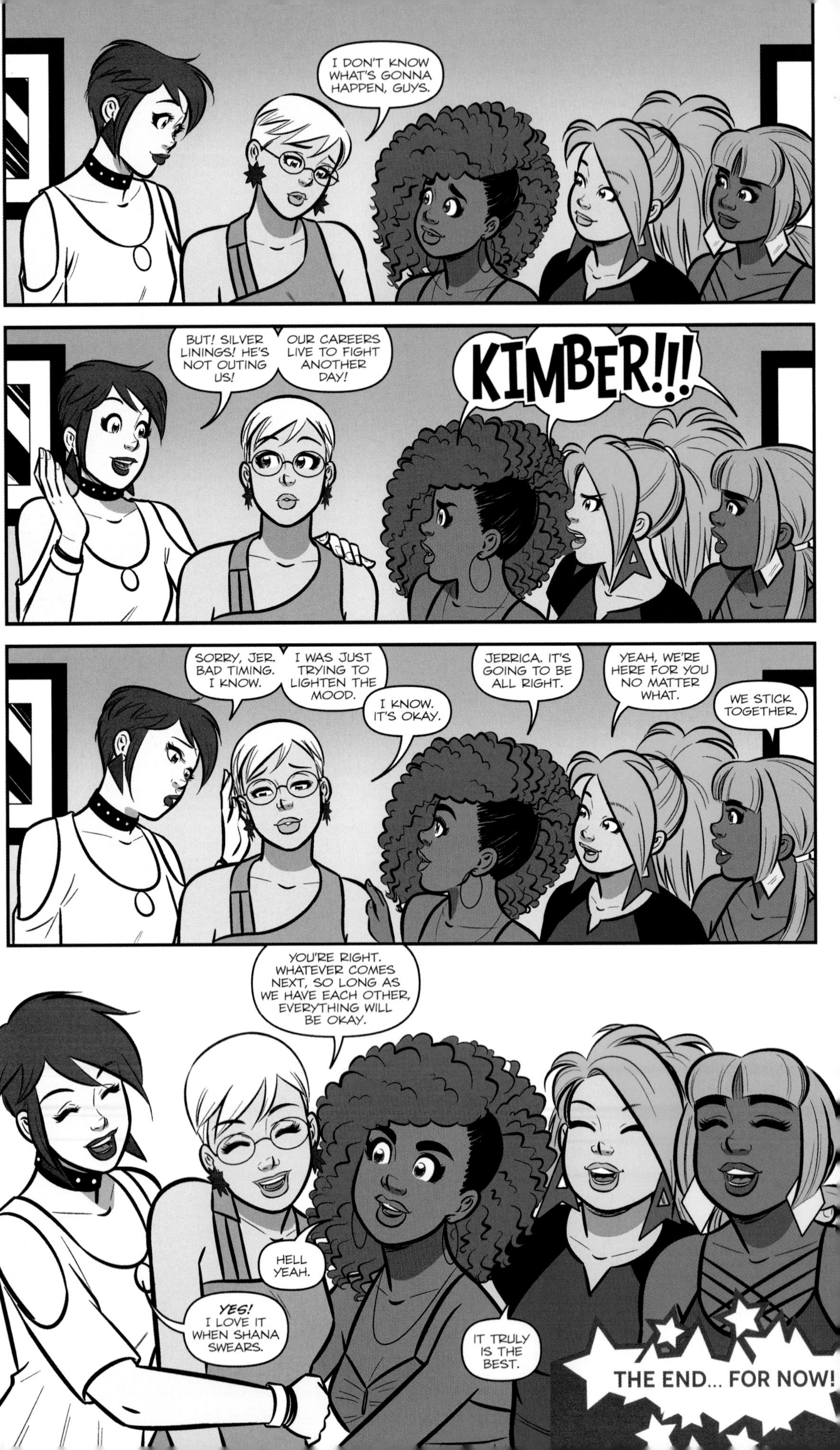
I DON'T KNOW WHAT'S GONNA HAPPEN, GUYS.
BUT! SILVER LININGS! HE'S NOT OUTING US!
OUR CAREERS LIVE TO FIGHT ANOTHER DAY!
KIMBER!!!
SORRY, JER. BAD TIMING. I KNOW.
I WAS JUST TRYING TO LIGHTEN THE MOOD.
I KNOW. IT'S OKAY.
JERRICA. IT'S GOING TO BE ALL RIGHT.
YEAH, WE'RE HERE FOR YOU NO MATTER WHAT.
WE STICK TOGETHER.
YOU'RE RIGHT. WHATEVER COMES NEXT, SO LONG AS WE HAVE EACH OTHER, EVERYTHING WILL BE OKAY.
HELL YEAH.
YES! I LOVE IT WHEN SHANA SWEARS.
IT TRULY IS THE BEST.
THE END... FOR NOW!

4 ANNUAL 2017
ART BY **W. SCOTT FORBES**

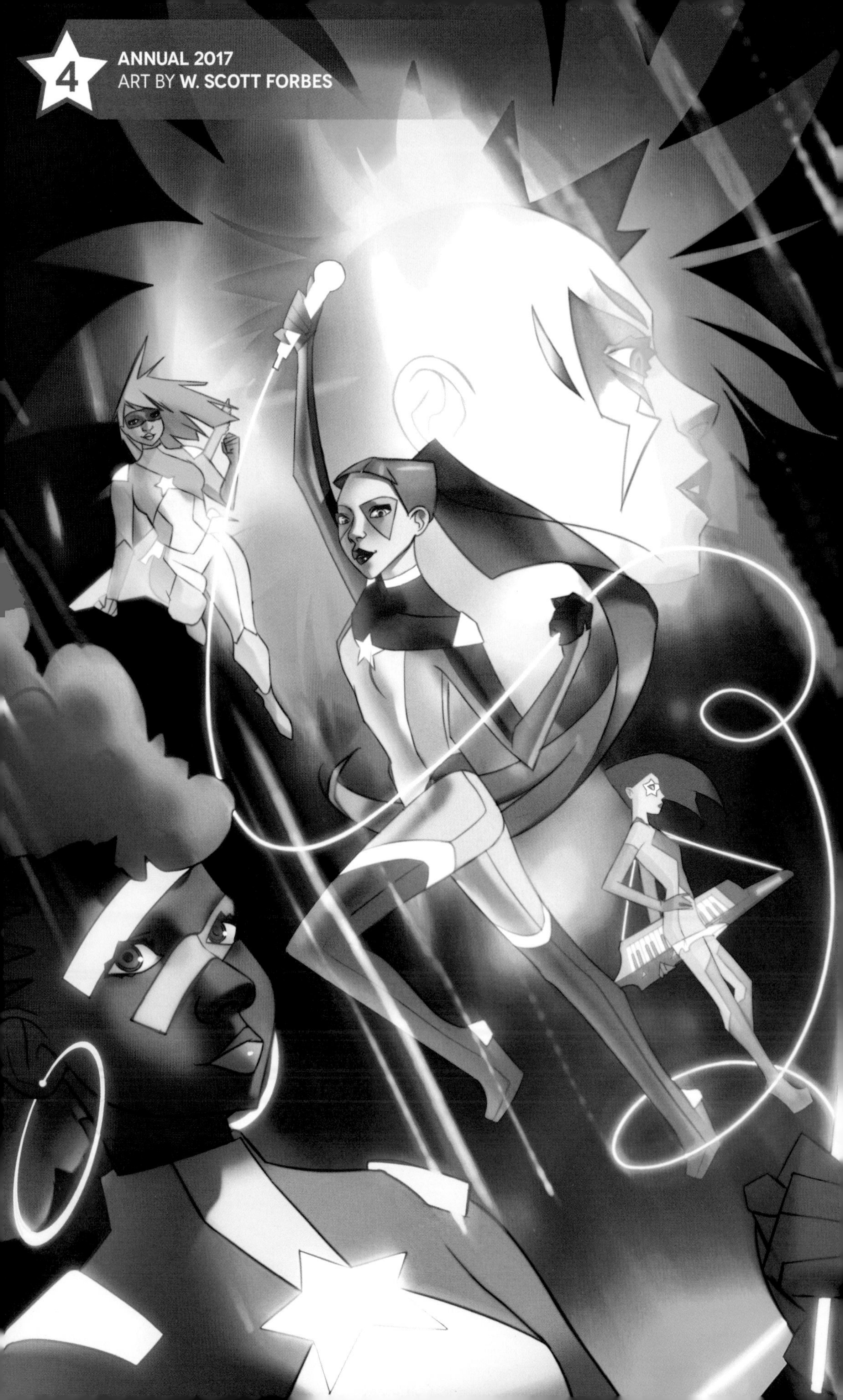

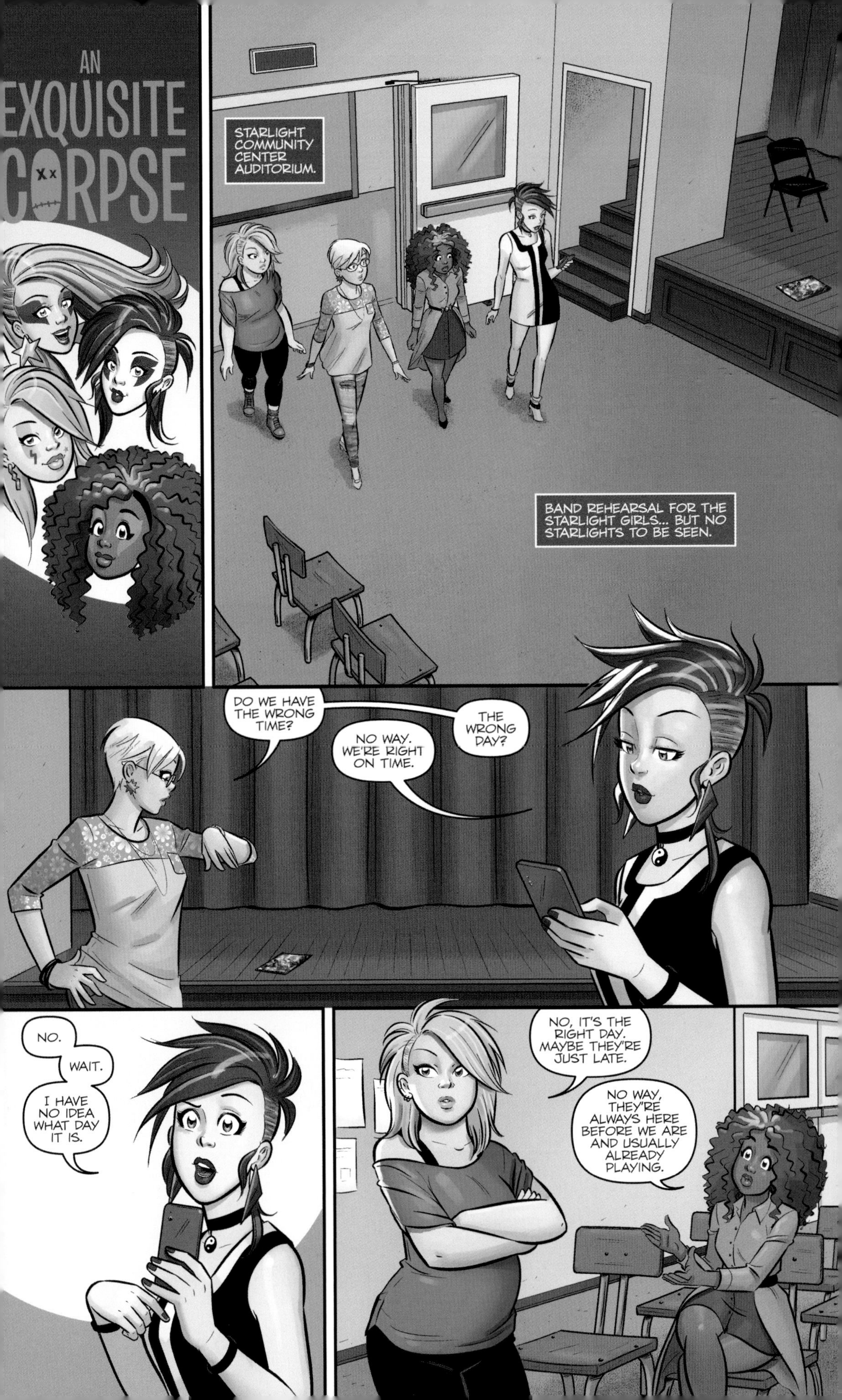

AN EXQUISITE CORPSE
STARLIGHT COMMUNITY CENTER AUDITORIUM.
BAND REHEARSAL FOR THE STARLIGHT GIRLS... BUT NO STARLIGHTS TO BE SEEN.
DO WE HAVE THE WRONG TIME?
THE WRONG DAY?
NO WAY. WE'RE RIGHT ON TIME.
NO.
WAIT.
I HAVE NO IDEA WHAT DAY IT IS.
NO, IT'S THE RIGHT DAY. MAYBE THEY'RE JUST LATE.
NO WAY, THEY'RE ALWAYS HERE BEFORE WE ARE AND USUALLY ALREADY PLAYING.

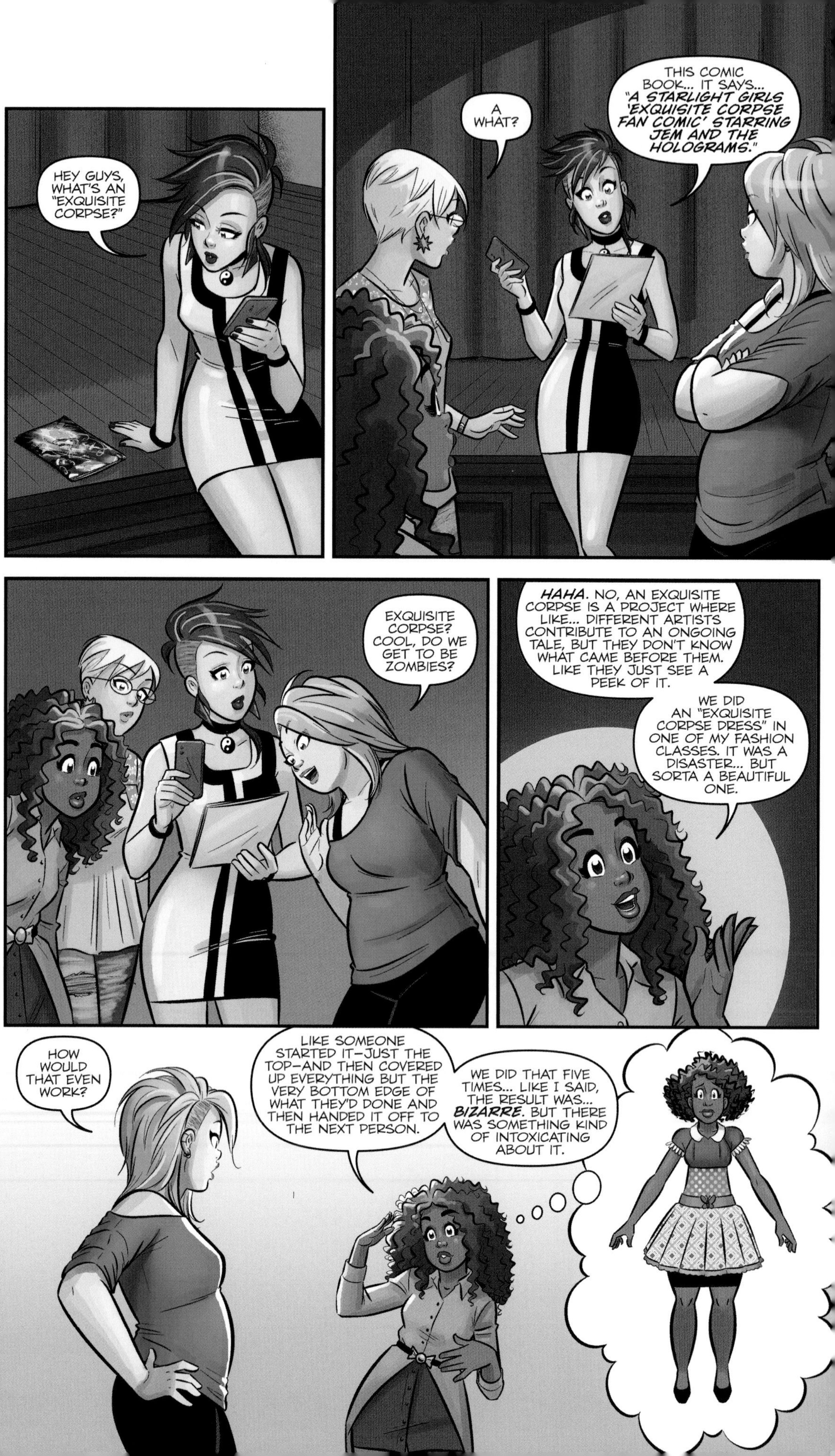

HEY GUYS, WHAT'S AN "EXQUISITE CORPSE?"
A WHAT?
THIS COMIC BOOK... IT SAYS... "A STARLIGHT GIRLS 'EXQUISITE CORPSE FAN COMIC' STARRING JEM AND THE HOLOGRAMS."
EXQUISITE CORPSE? COOL, DO WE GET TO BE ZOMBIES?
HAHA. NO, AN EXQUISITE CORPSE IS A PROJECT WHERE LIKE... DIFFERENT ARTISTS CONTRIBUTE TO AN ONGOING TALE, BUT THEY DON'T KNOW WHAT CAME BEFORE THEM. LIKE THEY JUST SEE A PEEK OF IT.
WE DID AN "EXQUISITE CORPSE DRESS" IN ONE OF MY FASHION CLASSES. IT WAS A DISASTER... BUT SORTA A BEAUTIFUL ONE.
HOW WOULD THAT EVEN WORK?
LIKE SOMEONE STARTED IT—JUST THE TOP—AND THEN COVERED UP EVERYTHING BUT THE VERY BOTTOM EDGE OF WHAT THEY'D DONE AND THEN HANDED IT OFF TO THE NEXT PERSON.
WE DID THAT FIVE TIMES... LIKE I SAID, THE RESULT WAS... BIZARRE. BUT THERE WAS SOMETHING KIND OF INTOXICATING ABOUT IT.

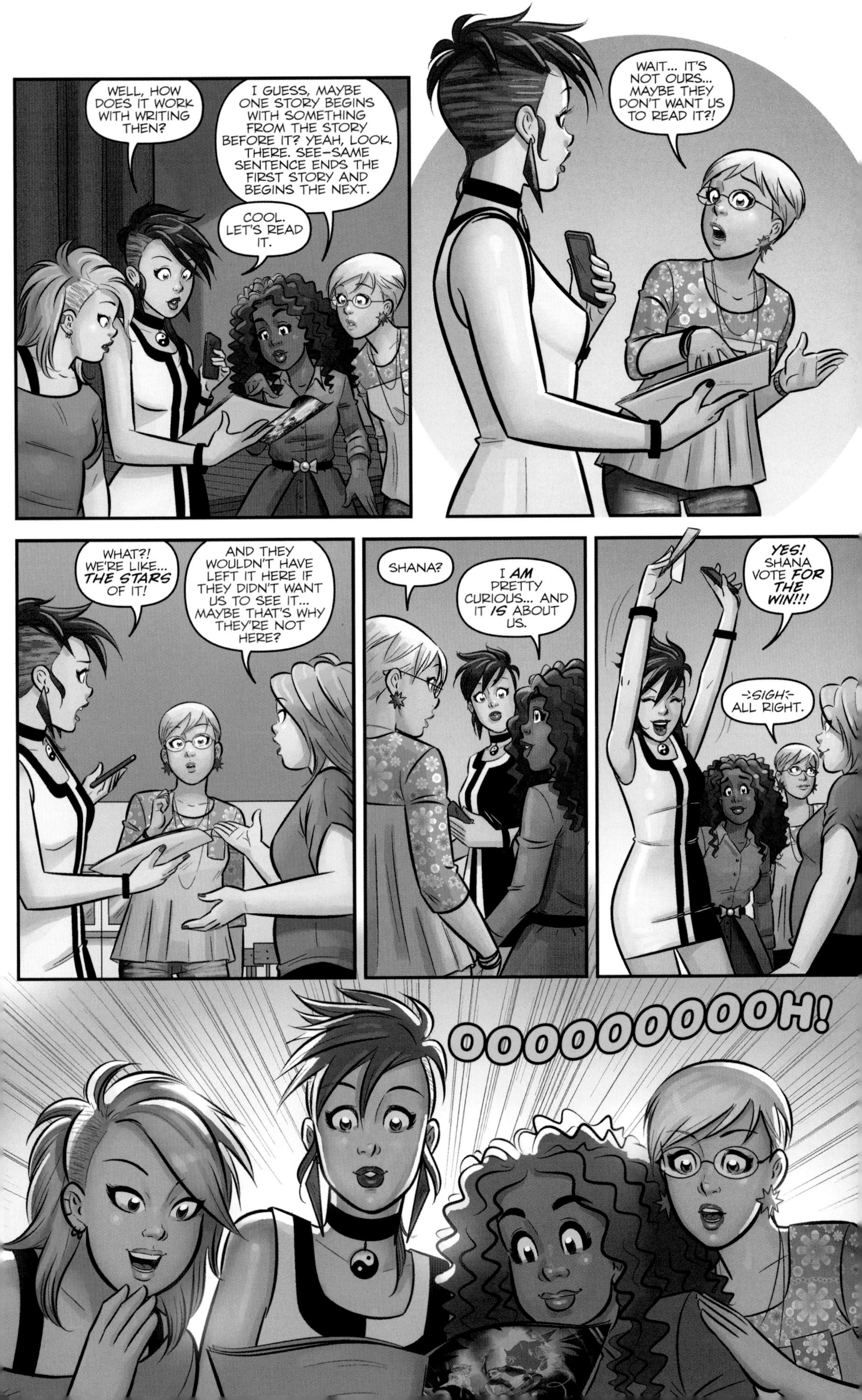
WELL, HOW DOES IT WORK WITH WRITING THEN?
I GUESS, MAYBE ONE STORY BEGINS WITH SOMETHING FROM THE STORY BEFORE IT? YEAH, LOOK. THERE. SEE–SAME SENTENCE ENDS THE FIRST STORY AND BEGINS THE NEXT.
COOL. LET'S READ IT.
WAIT... IT'S NOT OURS... MAYBE THEY DON'T WANT US TO READ IT?!
WHAT?! WE'RE LIKE... THE STARS OF IT!
AND THEY WOULDN'T HAVE LEFT IT HERE IF THEY DIDN'T WANT US TO SEE IT... MAYBE THAT'S WHY THEY'RE NOT HERE?
SHANA?
I AM PRETTY CURIOUS... AND IT IS ABOUT US.
YES! SHANA VOTE FOR THE WIN!!!
-SIGH- ALL RIGHT.
OOOOOOOOOOH!

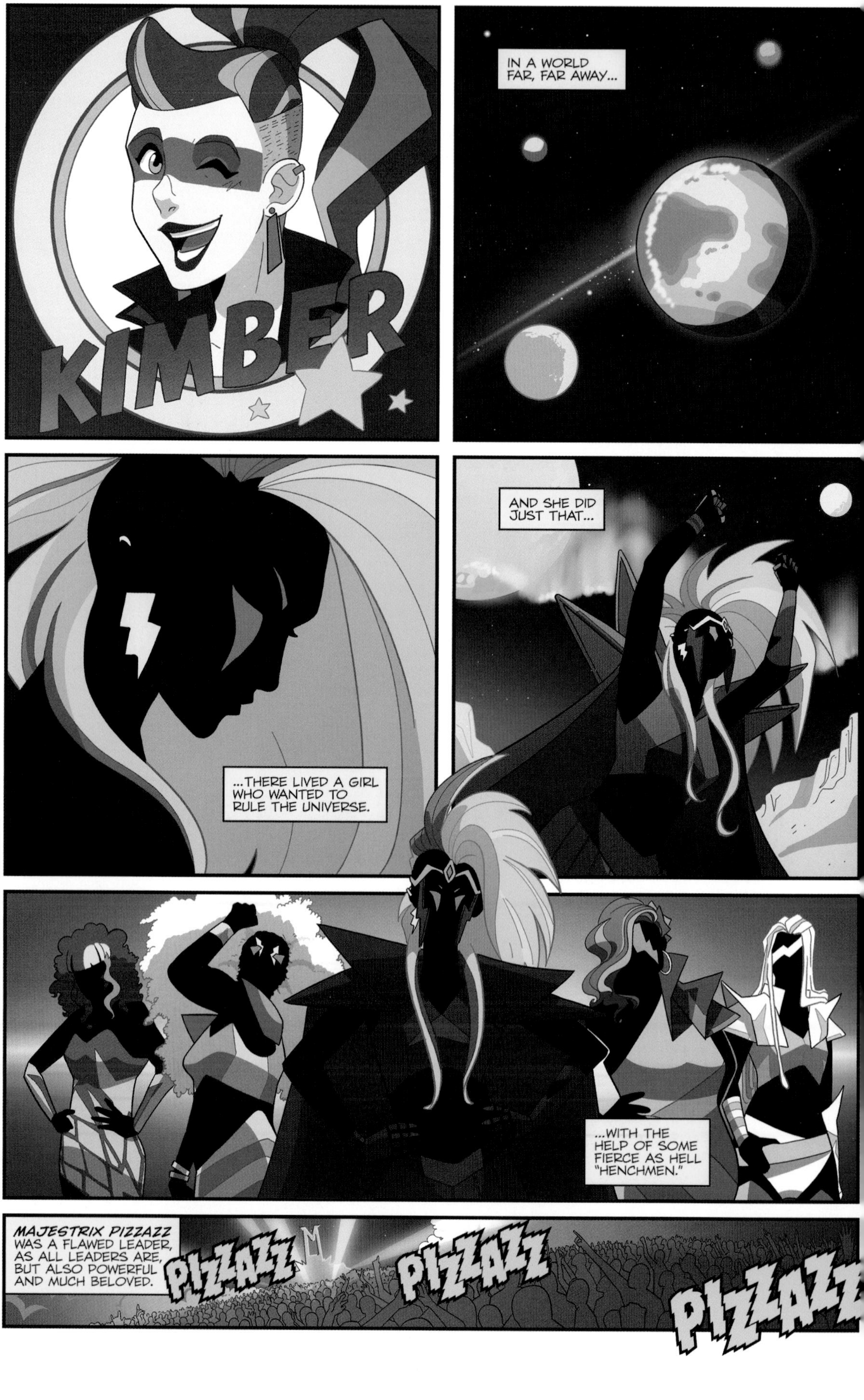
KIMBER
IN A WORLD FAR, FAR AWAY...
...THERE LIVED A GIRL WHO WANTED TO RULE THE UNIVERSE.
AND SHE DID JUST THAT...
...WITH THE HELP OF SOME FIERCE AS HELL "HENCHMEN."
MAJESTRIX PIZZAZZ WAS A FLAWED LEADER, AS ALL LEADERS ARE, BUT ALSO POWERFUL AND MUCH BELOVED.
PIZZAZZ
PIZZAZZ
PIZZAZZ

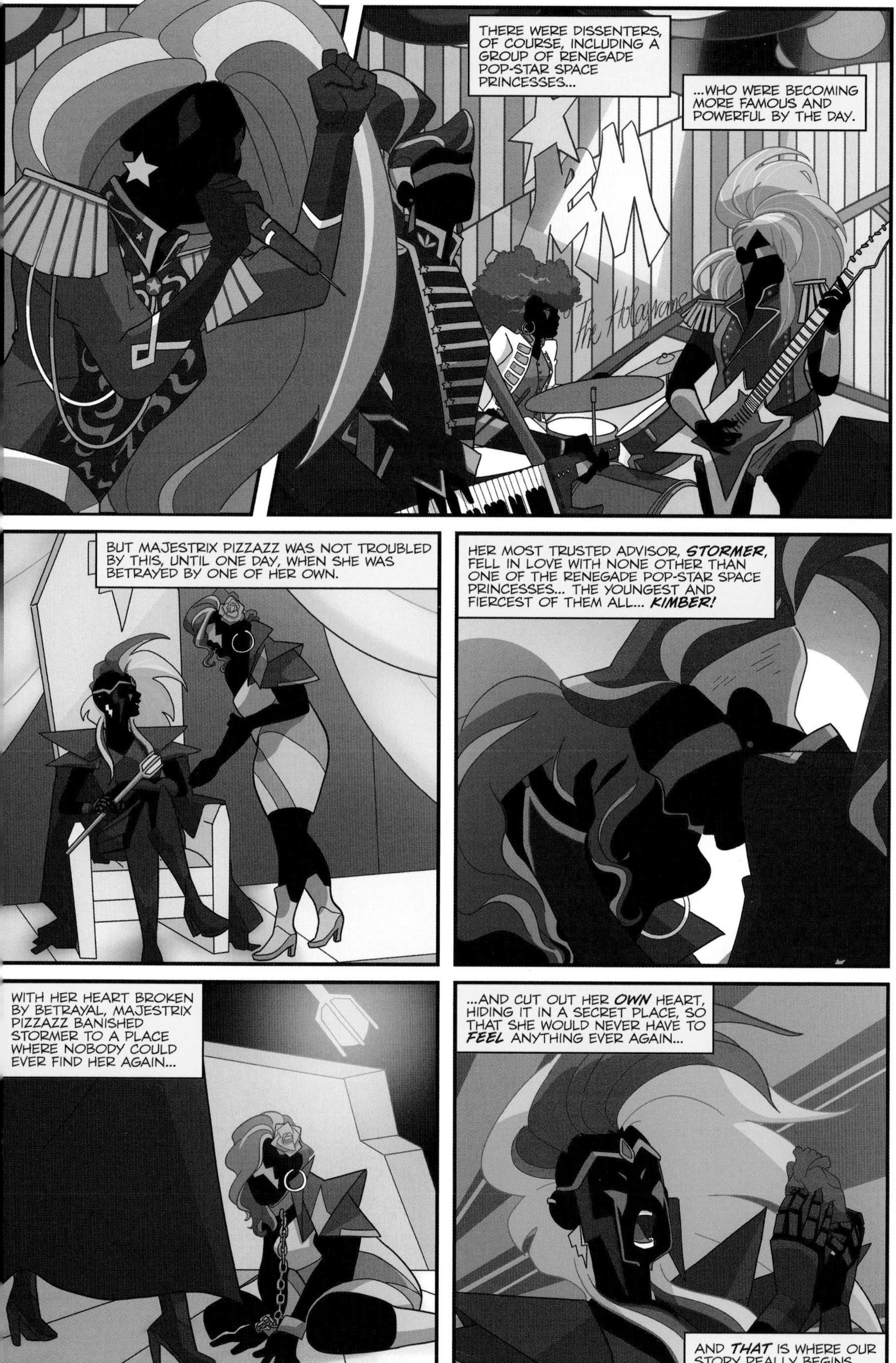
THERE WERE DISSENTERS, OF COURSE, INCLUDING A GROUP OF RENEGADE POP-STAR SPACE PRINCESSES...
...WHO WERE BECOMING MORE FAMOUS AND POWERFUL BY THE DAY.
BUT MAJESTRIX PIZZAZZ WAS NOT TROUBLED BY THIS, UNTIL ONE DAY, WHEN SHE WAS BETRAYED BY ONE OF HER OWN.
HER MOST TRUSTED ADVISOR, STORMER, FELL IN LOVE WITH NONE OTHER THAN ONE OF THE RENEGADE POP-STAR SPACE PRINCESSES... THE YOUNGEST AND FIERCEST OF THEM ALL... KIMBER!
WITH HER HEART BROKEN BY BETRAYAL, MAJESTRIX PIZZAZZ BANISHED STORMER TO A PLACE WHERE NOBODY COULD EVER FIND HER AGAIN...
...AND CUT OUT HER OWN HEART, HIDING IT IN A SECRET PLACE, SO THAT SHE WOULD NEVER HAVE TO FEEL ANYTHING EVER AGAIN...
AND THAT IS WHERE OUR STORY REALLY BEGINS...

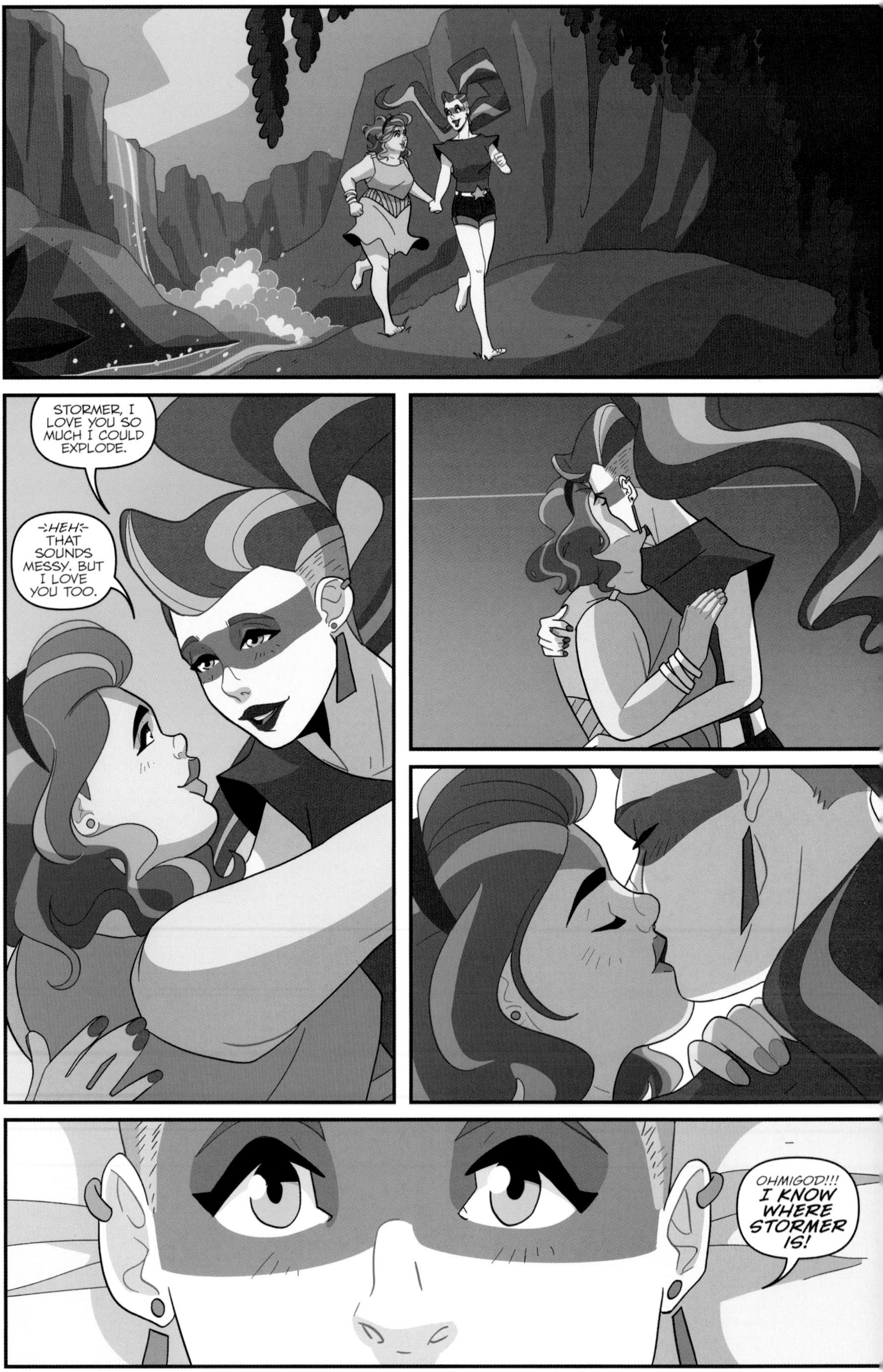

STORMER, I LOVE YOU SO MUCH I COULD EXPLODE.
-HEH- THAT SOUNDS MESSY. BUT I LOVE YOU TOO.
OHMIGOD!!! I KNOW WHERE STORMER IS!

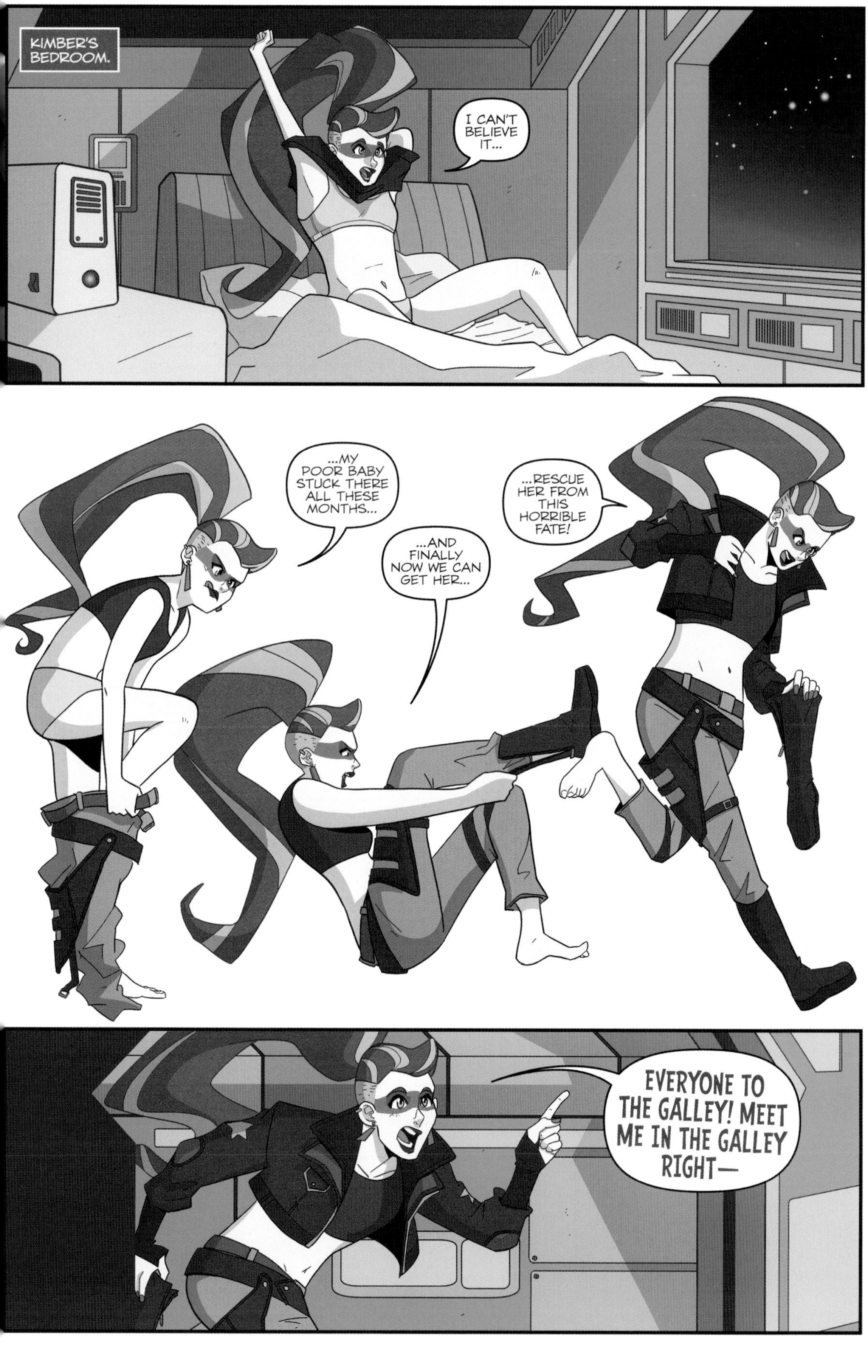
KIMBER'S BEDROOM.
I CAN'T BELIEVE IT...
...MY POOR BABY STUCK THERE ALL THESE MONTHS...
...AND FINALLY NOW WE CAN GET HER...
...RESCUE HER FROM THIS HORRIBLE FATE!
EVERYONE TO THE GALLEY! MEET ME IN THE GALLEY RIGHT—

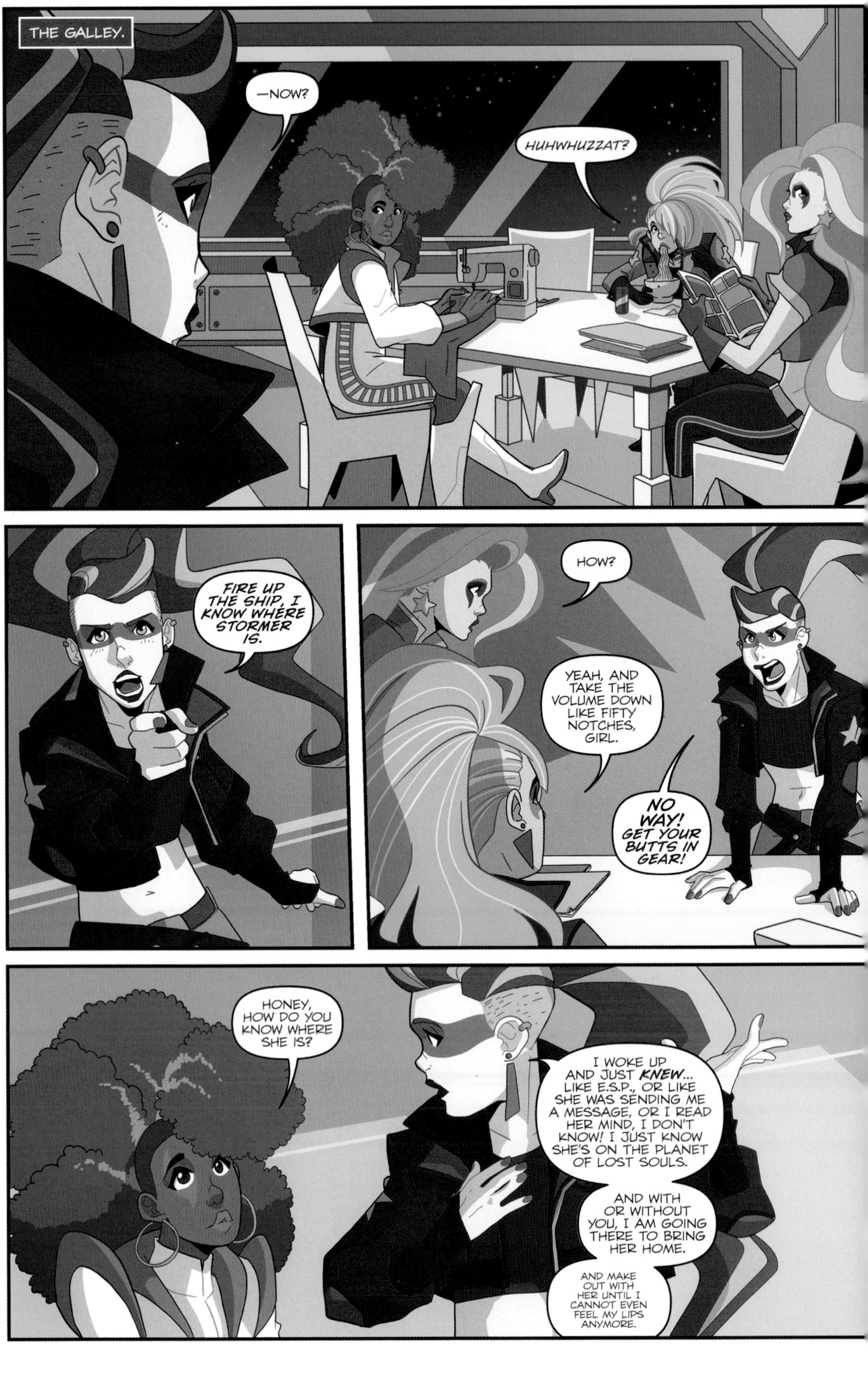
THE GALLEY.
—NOW?
HUHWHUZZAT?
FIRE UP THE SHIP, I KNOW WHERE STORMER IS.
HOW?
YEAH, AND TAKE THE VOLUME DOWN LIKE FIFTY NOTCHES, GIRL.
NO WAY! GET YOUR BUTTS IN GEAR!
HONEY, HOW DO YOU KNOW WHERE SHE IS?
I WOKE UP AND JUST KNEW... LIKE E.S.P., OR LIKE SHE WAS SENDING ME A MESSAGE, OR I READ HER MIND, I DON'T KNOW! I JUST KNOW SHE'S ON THE PLANET OF LOST SOULS.
AND WITH OR WITHOUT YOU, I AM GOING THERE TO BRING HER HOME.
AND MAKE OUT WITH HER UNTIL I CANNOT EVEN FEEL MY LIPS ANYMORE.

WOW. THE PLANET OF LOST SOULS.

YEAH, THAT PLACE IS NO JOKE.

MAKES SENSE THOUGH.

YES, IT DOES. TOTALLY SEEMS LIKE SOMETHING PIZZAZZ WOULD DO.

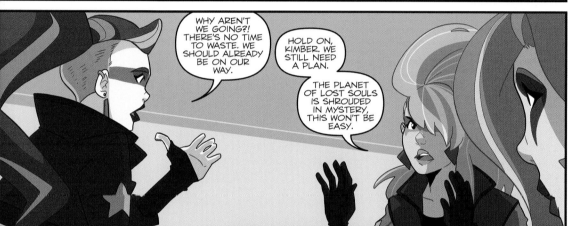

WHY AREN'T WE GOING?! THERE'S NO TIME TO WASTE. WE SHOULD ALREADY BE ON OUR WAY.

HOLD ON, KIMBER. WE STILL NEED A PLAN.

THE PLANET OF LOST SOULS IS SHROUDED IN MYSTERY, THIS WON'T BE EASY.

WE CAN STILL USE THE EXISTING PLAN WE WERE ALREADY WORKING ON TO FIND STORMER, JUST MODIFY IT TO SOLVING THE MYSTERIES OF THE PLANET OF LOST SOULS.

WAIT. THERE'S A PLAN?!

CAN SOMEONE PLEASE AT LEAST TELL ME THE PLAN?!

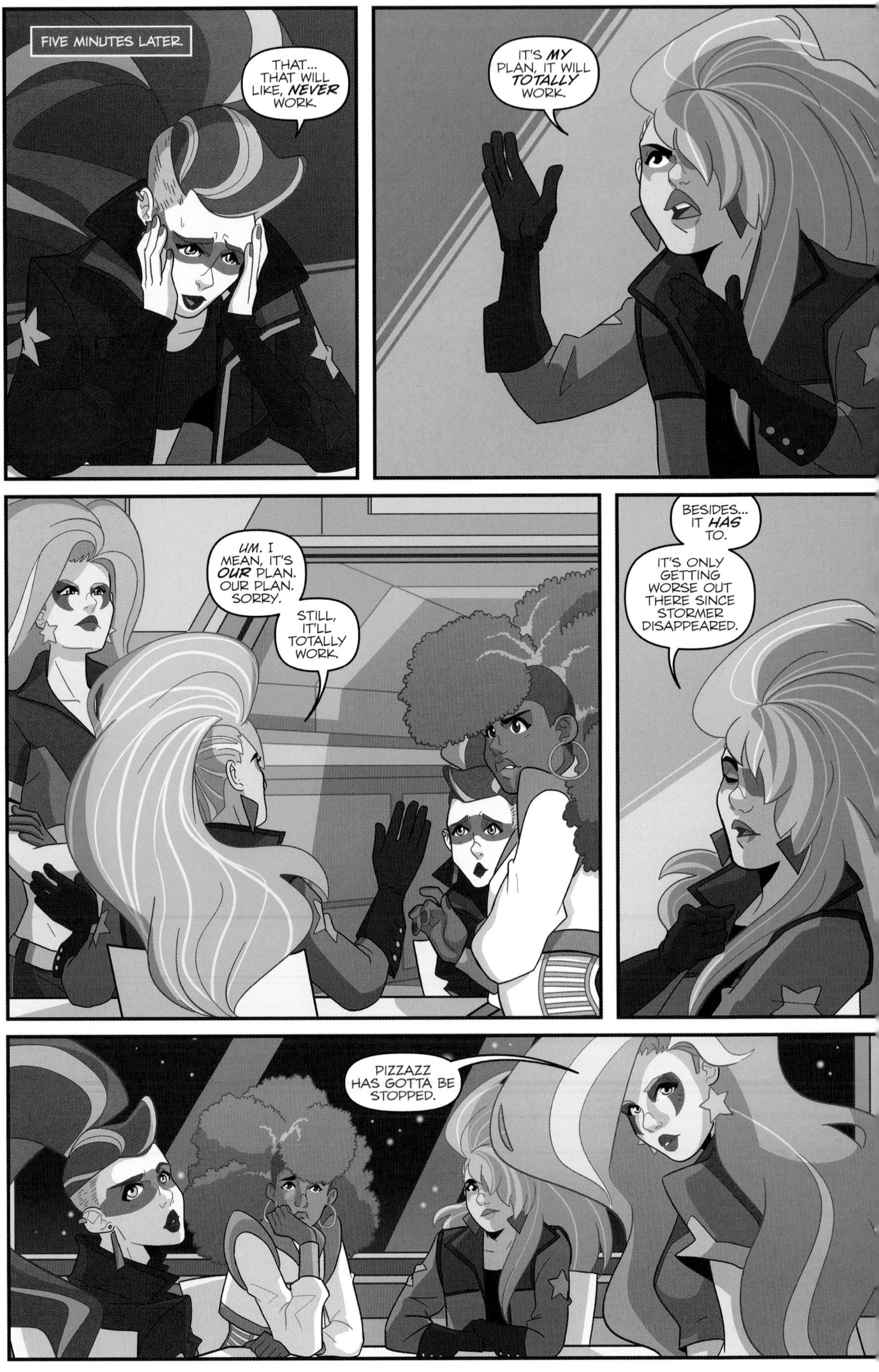
FIVE MINUTES LATER.
THAT... THAT WILL LIKE, NEVER WORK.
IT'S MY PLAN, IT WILL TOTALLY WORK.
UM. I MEAN, IT'S OUR PLAN. OUR PLAN. SORRY.
STILL, IT'LL TOTALLY WORK.
BESIDES... IT HAS TO.
IT'S ONLY GETTING WORSE OUT THERE SINCE STORMER DISAPPEARED.
PIZZAZZ HAS GOTTA BE STOPPED.

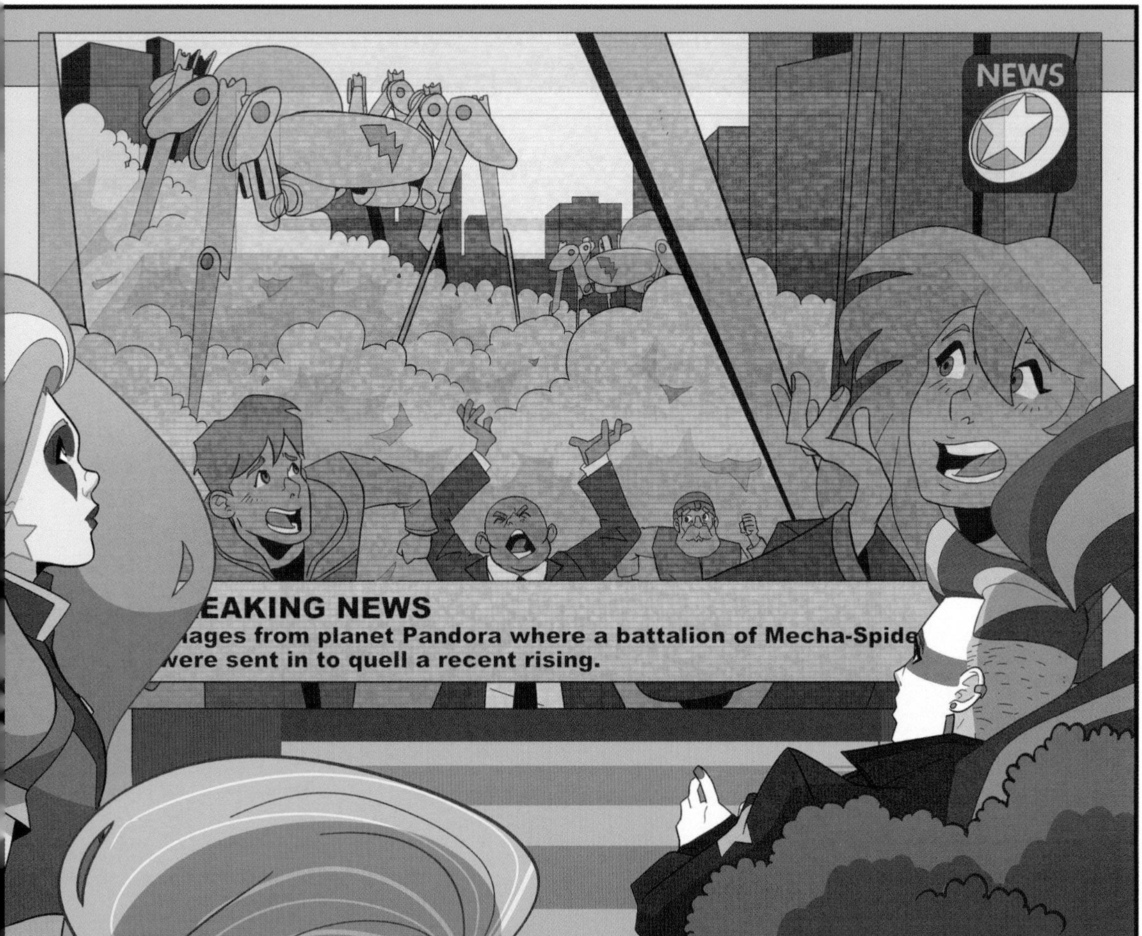
NEWS
EAKING NEWS
nages from planet Pandora where a battalion of Mecha-Spide
were sent in to quell a recent rising.

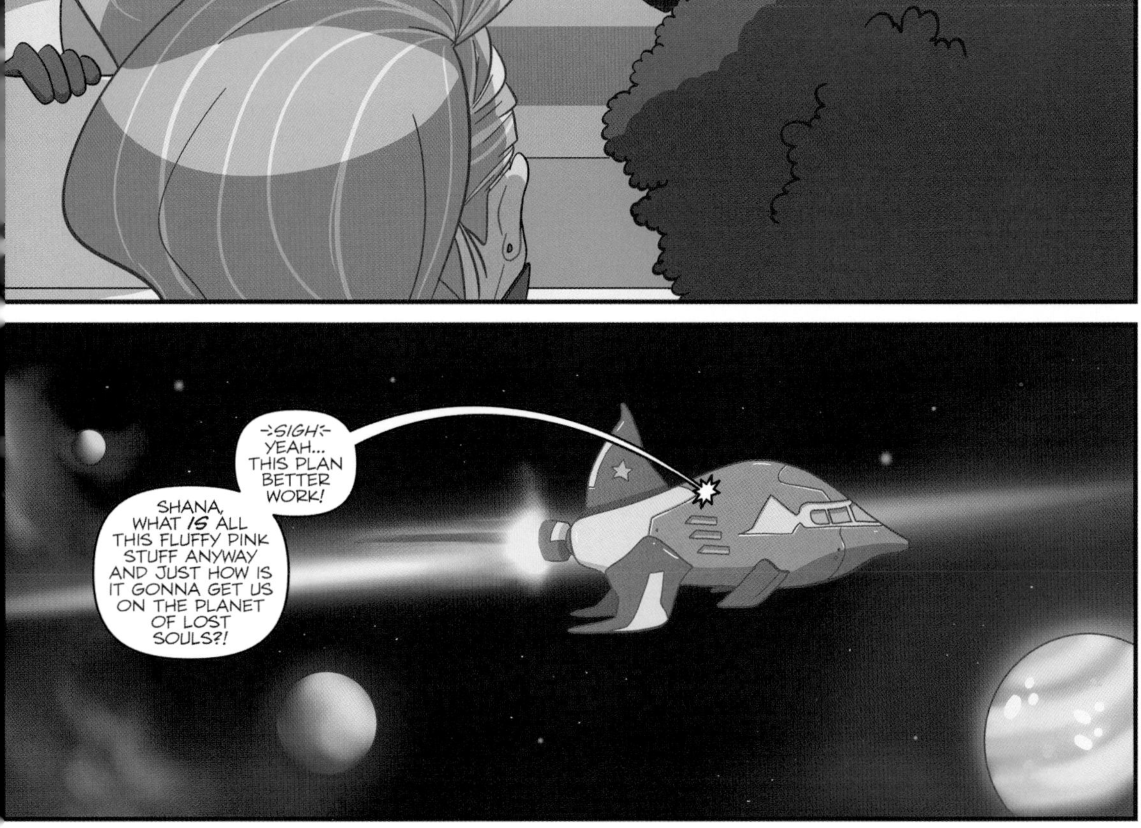
SHANA, WHAT *IS* ALL THIS FLUFFY PINK STUFF ANYWAY AND JUST HOW IS IT GONNA GET US ON THE PLANET OF LOST SOULS?!
-SIGH- YEAH... THIS PLAN BETTER WORK!

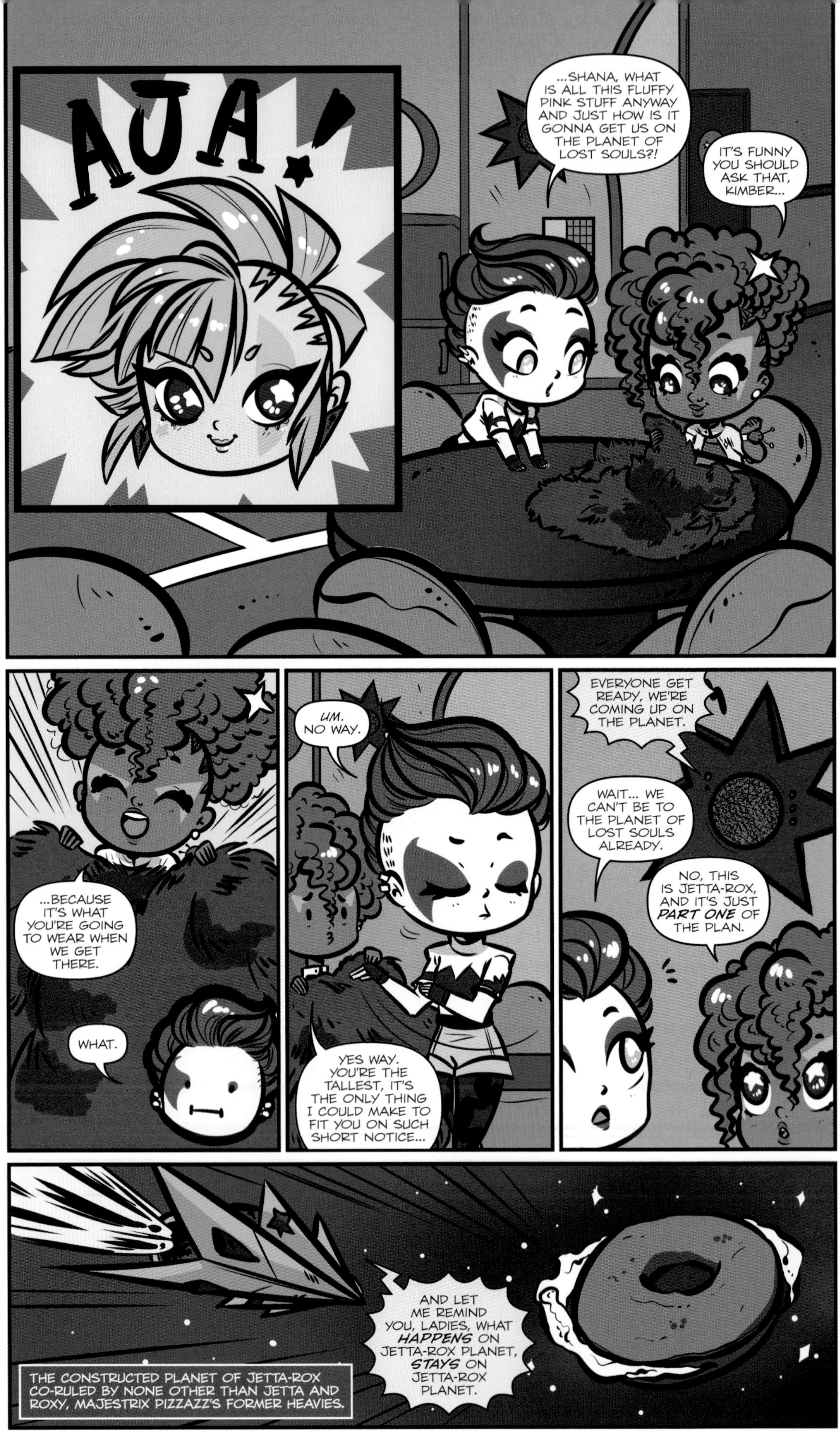
AJA!
...SHANA, WHAT IS ALL THIS FLUFFY PINK STUFF ANYWAY AND JUST HOW IS IT GONNA GET US ON THE PLANET OF LOST SOULS?!
IT'S FUNNY YOU SHOULD ASK THAT, KIMBER...
...BECAUSE IT'S WHAT YOU'RE GOING TO WEAR WHEN WE GET THERE.
WHAT.
UM. NO WAY.
YES WAY. YOU'RE THE TALLEST, IT'S THE ONLY THING I COULD MAKE TO FIT YOU ON SUCH SHORT NOTICE...
EVERYONE GET READY, WE'RE COMING UP ON THE PLANET.
WAIT... WE CAN'T BE TO THE PLANET OF LOST SOULS ALREADY.
NO, THIS IS JETTA-ROX, AND IT'S JUST PART ONE OF THE PLAN.
THE CONSTRUCTED PLANET OF JETTA-ROX CO-RULED BY NONE OTHER THAN JETTA AND ROXY, MAJESTRIX PIZZAZZ'S FORMER HEAVIES.
AND LET ME REMIND YOU, LADIES, WHAT HAPPENS ON JETTA-ROX PLANET, STAYS ON JETTA-ROX PLANET.

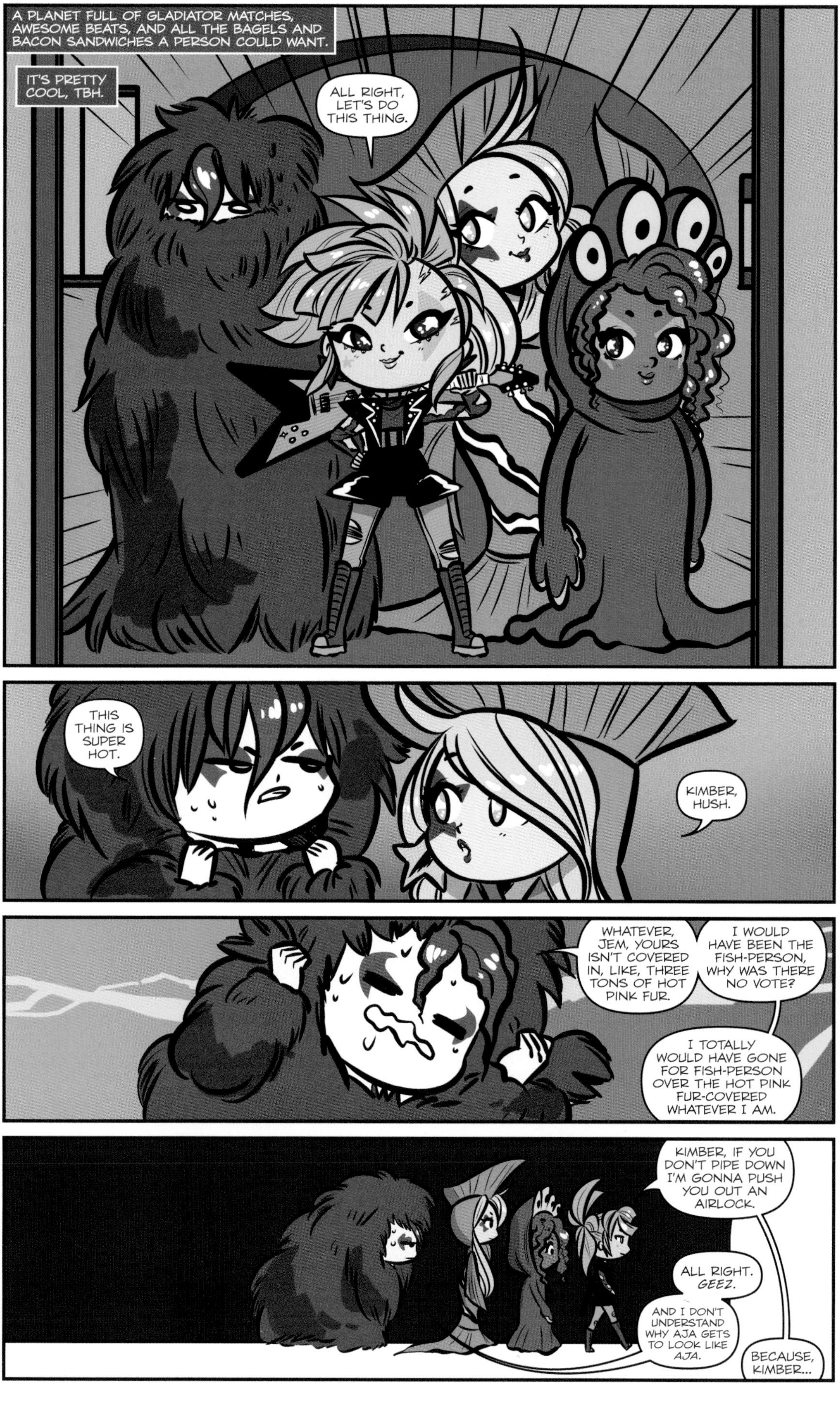
A PLANET FULL OF GLADIATOR MATCHES, AWESOME BEATS, AND ALL THE BAGELS AND BACON SANDWICHES A PERSON COULD WANT.
IT'S PRETTY COOL, TBH.
ALL RIGHT, LET'S DO THIS THING.
THIS THING IS SUPER HOT.
KIMBER, HUSH.
WHATEVER, JEM, YOURS ISN'T COVERED IN, LIKE, THREE TONS OF HOT PINK FUR.
I WOULD HAVE BEEN THE FISH-PERSON, WHY WAS THERE NO VOTE?
I TOTALLY WOULD HAVE GONE FOR FISH-PERSON OVER THE HOT PINK FUR-COVERED WHATEVER I AM.
KIMBER, IF YOU DON'T PIPE DOWN I'M GONNA PUSH YOU OUT AN AIRLOCK.
ALL RIGHT. *GEEZ.*
AND I DON'T UNDERSTAND WHY AJA GETS TO LOOK LIKE AJA.
BECAUSE, KIMBER...

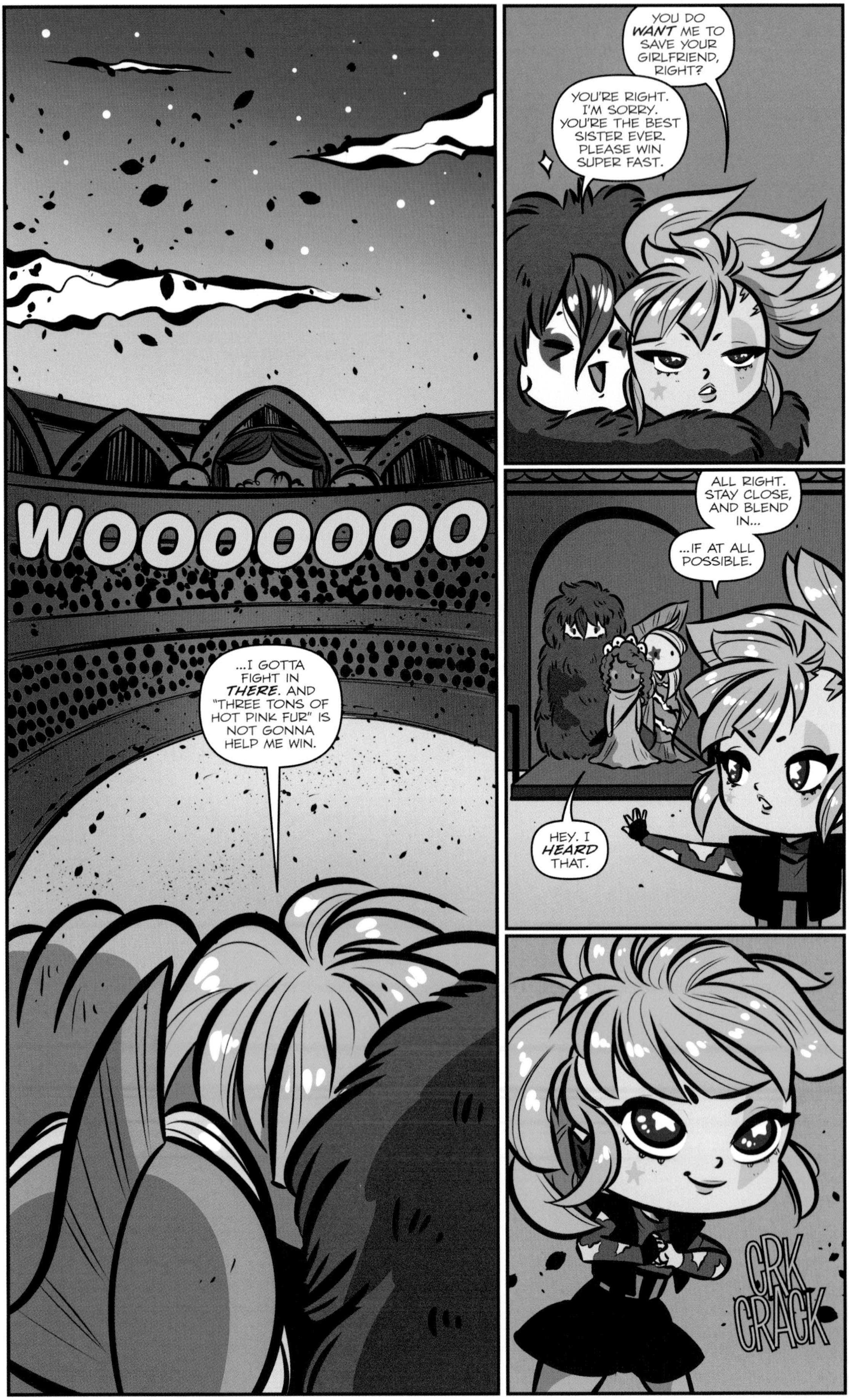
WOOOOOOO
...I GOTTA FIGHT IN **THERE**. AND "THREE TONS OF HOT PINK FUR" IS NOT GONNA HELP ME WIN.
YOU DO **WANT** ME TO SAVE YOUR GIRLFRIEND, RIGHT?
YOU'RE RIGHT. I'M SORRY. YOU'RE THE BEST SISTER EVER. PLEASE WIN SUPER FAST.
ALL RIGHT. STAY CLOSE, AND BLEND IN...
...IF AT ALL POSSIBLE.
HEY. I **HEARD** THAT.
GRK CRACK

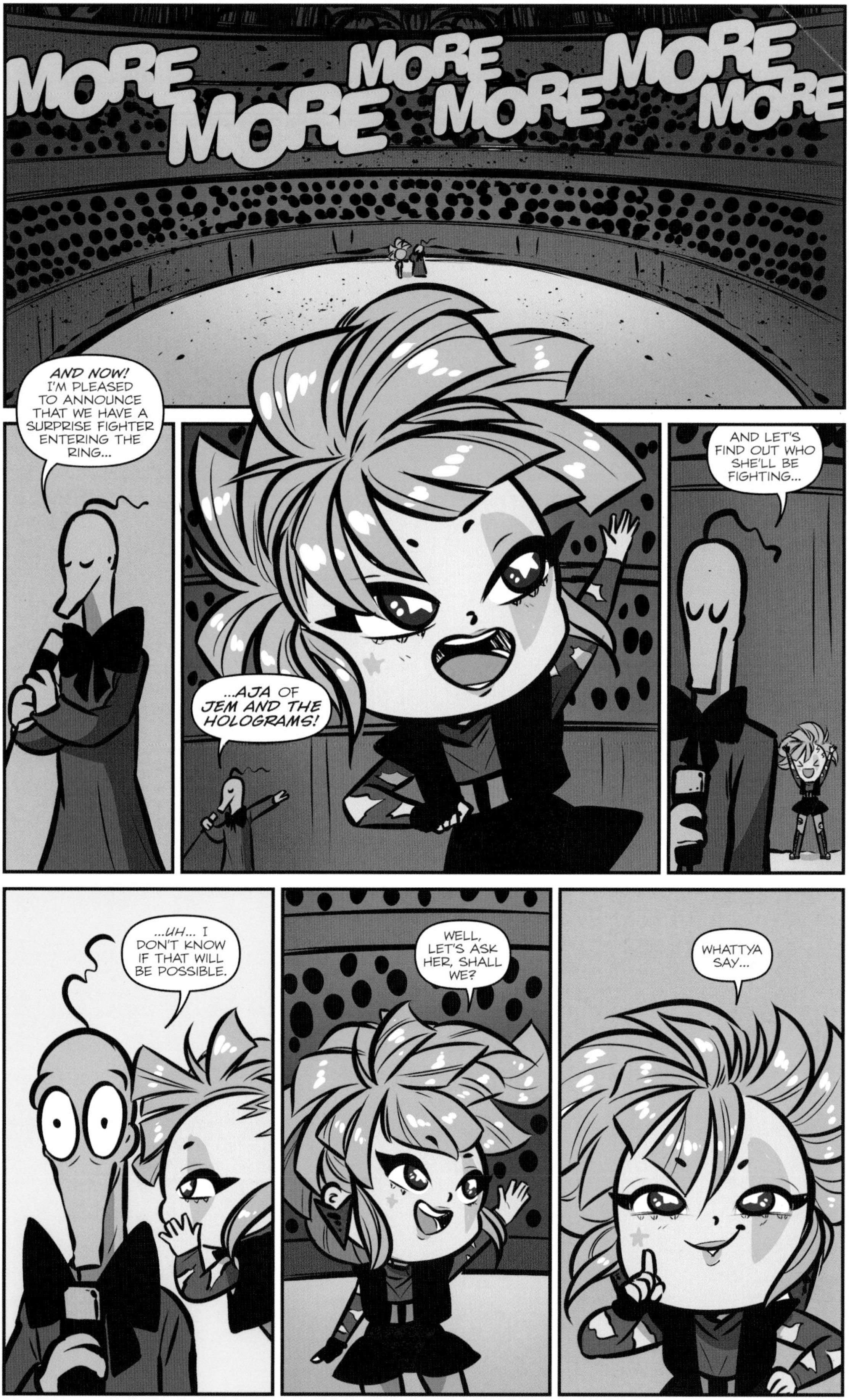
MORE MORE MORE MORE MORE MORE MORE
AND NOW! I'M PLEASED TO ANNOUNCE THAT WE HAVE A SURPRISE FIGHTER ENTERING THE RING...
...AJA OF JEM AND THE HOLOGRAMS!
AND LET'S FIND OUT WHO SHE'LL BE FIGHTING...
...UH... I DON'T KNOW IF THAT WILL BE POSSIBLE.
WELL, LET'S ASK HER, SHALL WE?
WHATTYA SAY...

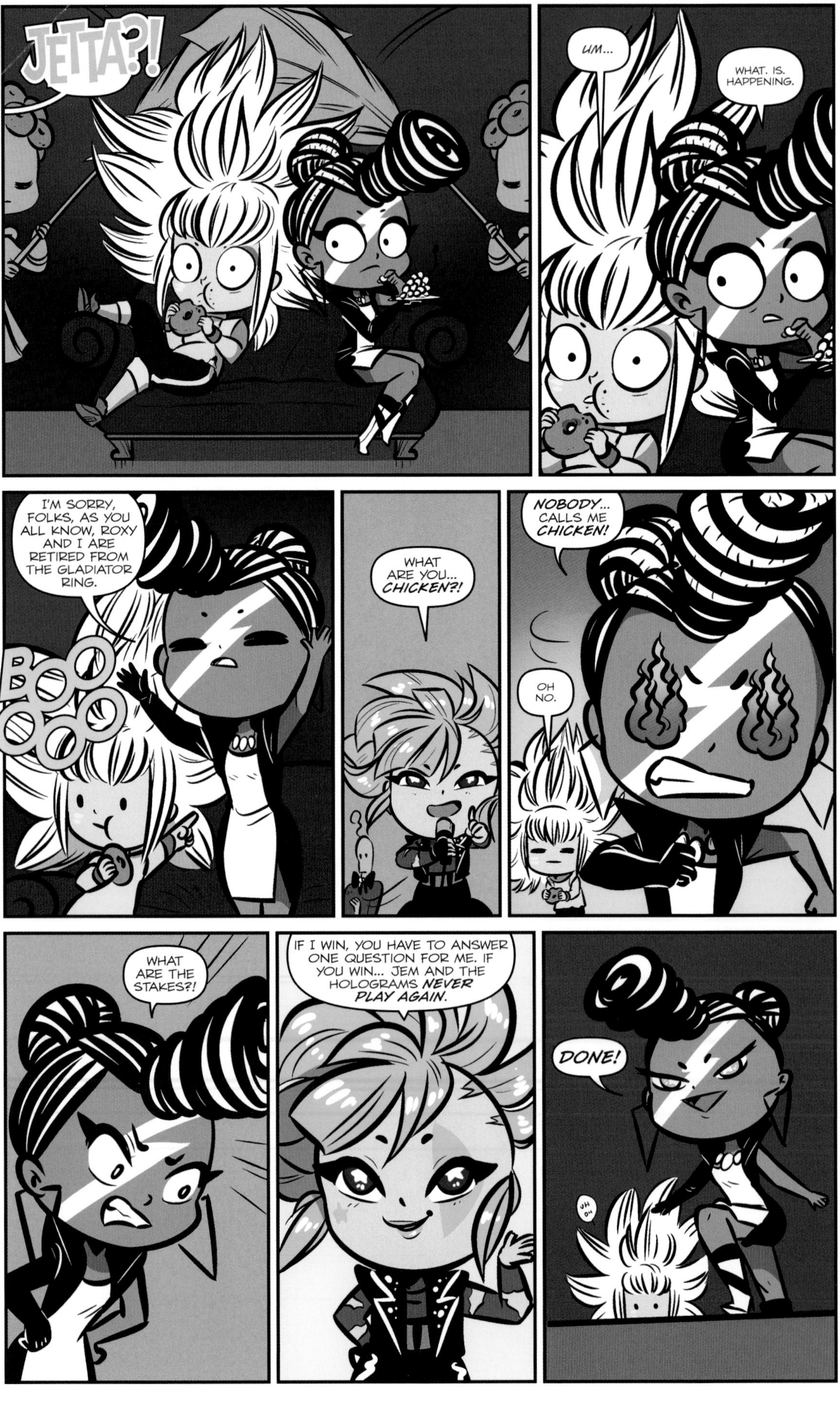

JETTA?!
UM...
WHAT. IS. HAPPENING.
I'M SORRY, FOLKS, AS YOU ALL KNOW, ROXY AND I ARE RETIRED FROM THE GLADIATOR RING.
BOOOOOO
WHAT ARE YOU... CHICKEN?!
NOBODY... CALLS ME CHICKEN!
OH NO.
WHAT ARE THE STAKES?!
IF I WIN, YOU HAVE TO ANSWER ONE QUESTION FOR ME. IF YOU WIN... JEM AND THE HOLOGRAMS NEVER PLAY AGAIN.
DONE!
UH OH

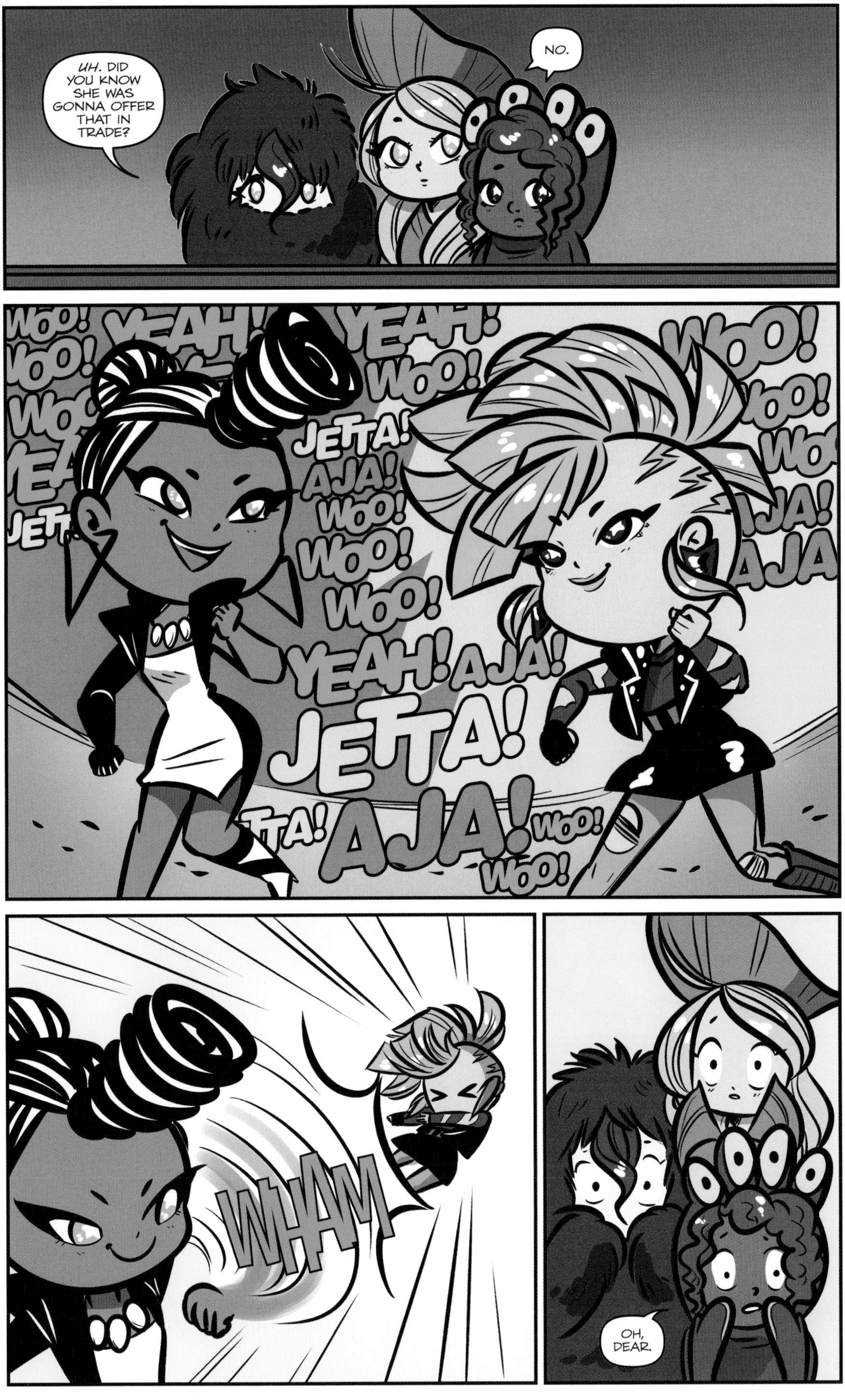
UH. DID YOU KNOW SHE WAS GONNA OFFER THAT IN TRADE?
NO.
WOO! YEAH! YEAH! WOO! WOO! WOO!
JETTA! AJA! WOO! WOO! WOO!
YEAH! AJA! JETTA!
AJA! WOO! WOO!
WHAM
OH, DEAR.

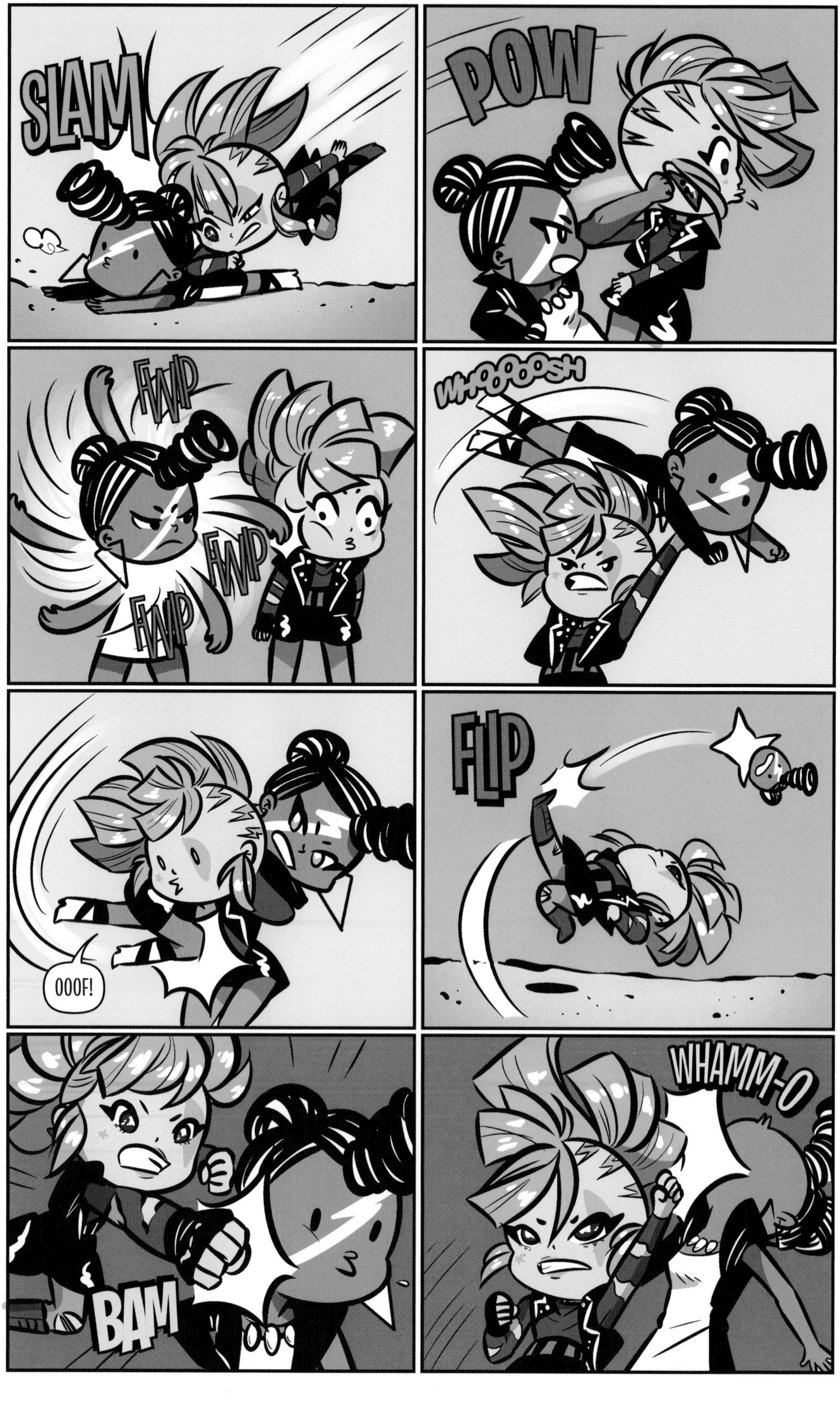
SLAM
POW
FWIP
FWIP
FWIP
WHOOOOOSH
OOOF!
FLIP
BAM
WHAMM-O

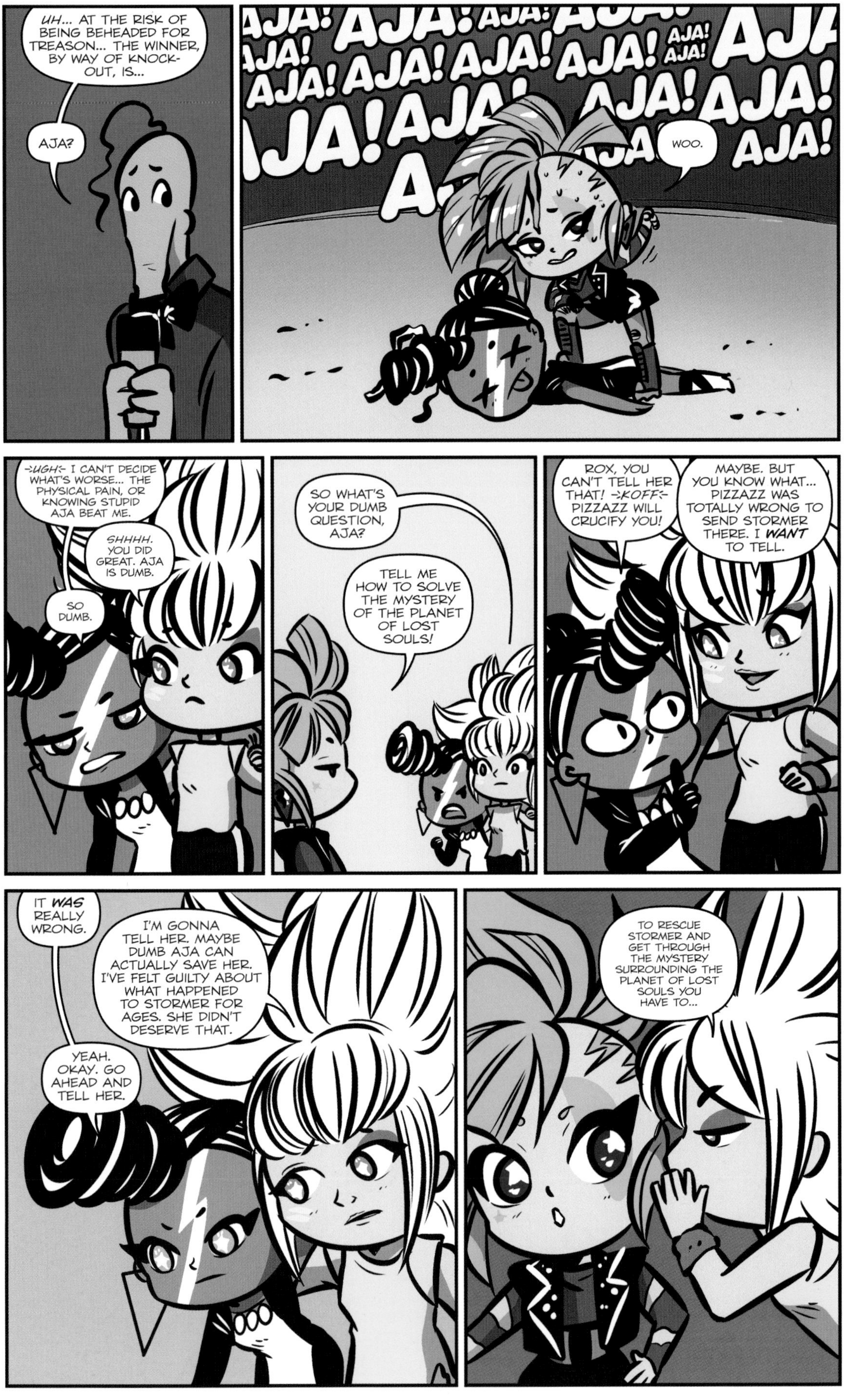
UH... AT THE RISK OF BEING BEHEADED FOR TREASON... THE WINNER, BY WAY OF KNOCK-OUT, IS...
AJA?
AJA! AJA! AJA! AJA! AJA! AJA! AJA! AJA! AJA! AJA! AJA! AJA! AJA! AJA! AJA!
WOO.
~UGH~ I CAN'T DECIDE WHAT'S WORSE... THE PHYSICAL PAIN, OR KNOWING STUPID AJA BEAT ME.
SHHHH. YOU DID GREAT. AJA IS DUMB.
SO DUMB.
SO WHAT'S YOUR DUMB QUESTION, AJA?
TELL ME HOW TO SOLVE THE MYSTERY OF THE PLANET OF LOST SOULS!
ROX, YOU CAN'T TELL HER THAT! ~KOFF~ PIZZAZZ WILL CRUCIFY YOU!
MAYBE. BUT YOU KNOW WHAT... PIZZAZZ WAS TOTALLY WRONG TO SEND STORMER THERE. I WANT TO TELL.
IT WAS REALLY WRONG.
I'M GONNA TELL HER. MAYBE DUMB AJA CAN ACTUALLY SAVE HER. I'VE FELT GUILTY ABOUT WHAT HAPPENED TO STORMER FOR AGES. SHE DIDN'T DESERVE THAT.
YEAH. OKAY. GO AHEAD AND TELL HER.
TO RESCUE STORMER AND GET THROUGH THE MYSTERY SURROUNDING THE PLANET OF LOST SOULS YOU HAVE TO...

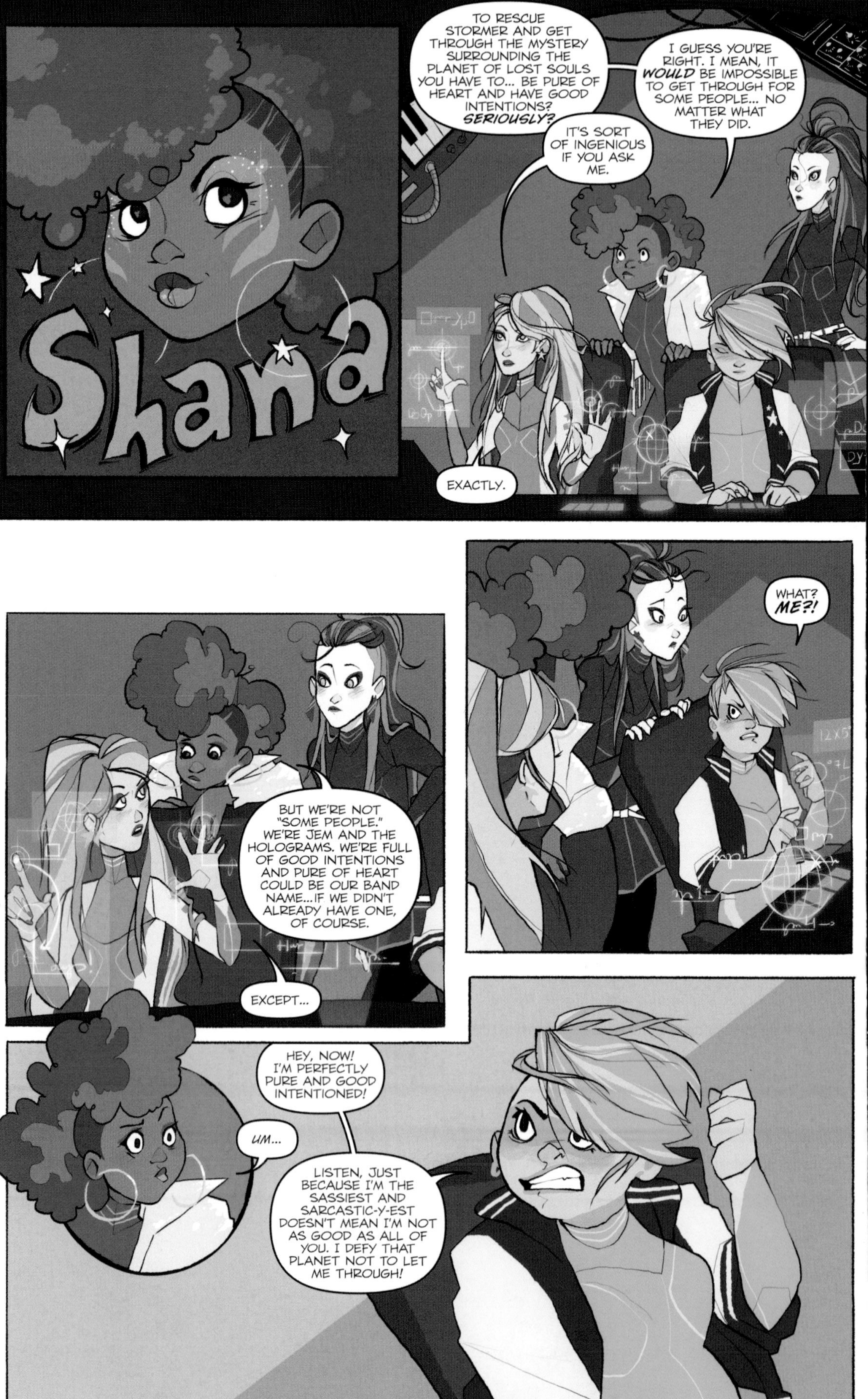
Shana
TO RESCUE STORMER AND GET THROUGH THE MYSTERY SURROUNDING THE PLANET OF LOST SOULS YOU HAVE TO... BE PURE OF HEART AND HAVE GOOD INTENTIONS? SERIOUSLY?
IT'S SORT OF INGENIOUS IF YOU ASK ME.
I GUESS YOU'RE RIGHT. I MEAN, IT WOULD BE IMPOSSIBLE TO GET THROUGH FOR SOME PEOPLE... NO MATTER WHAT THEY DID.
EXACTLY.
BUT WE'RE NOT "SOME PEOPLE." WE'RE JEM AND THE HOLOGRAMS. WE'RE FULL OF GOOD INTENTIONS AND PURE OF HEART COULD BE OUR BAND NAME...IF WE DIDN'T ALREADY HAVE ONE, OF COURSE.
EXCEPT...
WHAT? ME?!
HEY, NOW! I'M PERFECTLY PURE AND GOOD INTENTIONED!
UM...
LISTEN, JUST BECAUSE I'M THE SASSIEST AND SARCASTIC-Y-EST DOESN'T MEAN I'M NOT AS GOOD AS ALL OF YOU. I DEFY THAT PLANET NOT TO LET ME THROUGH!

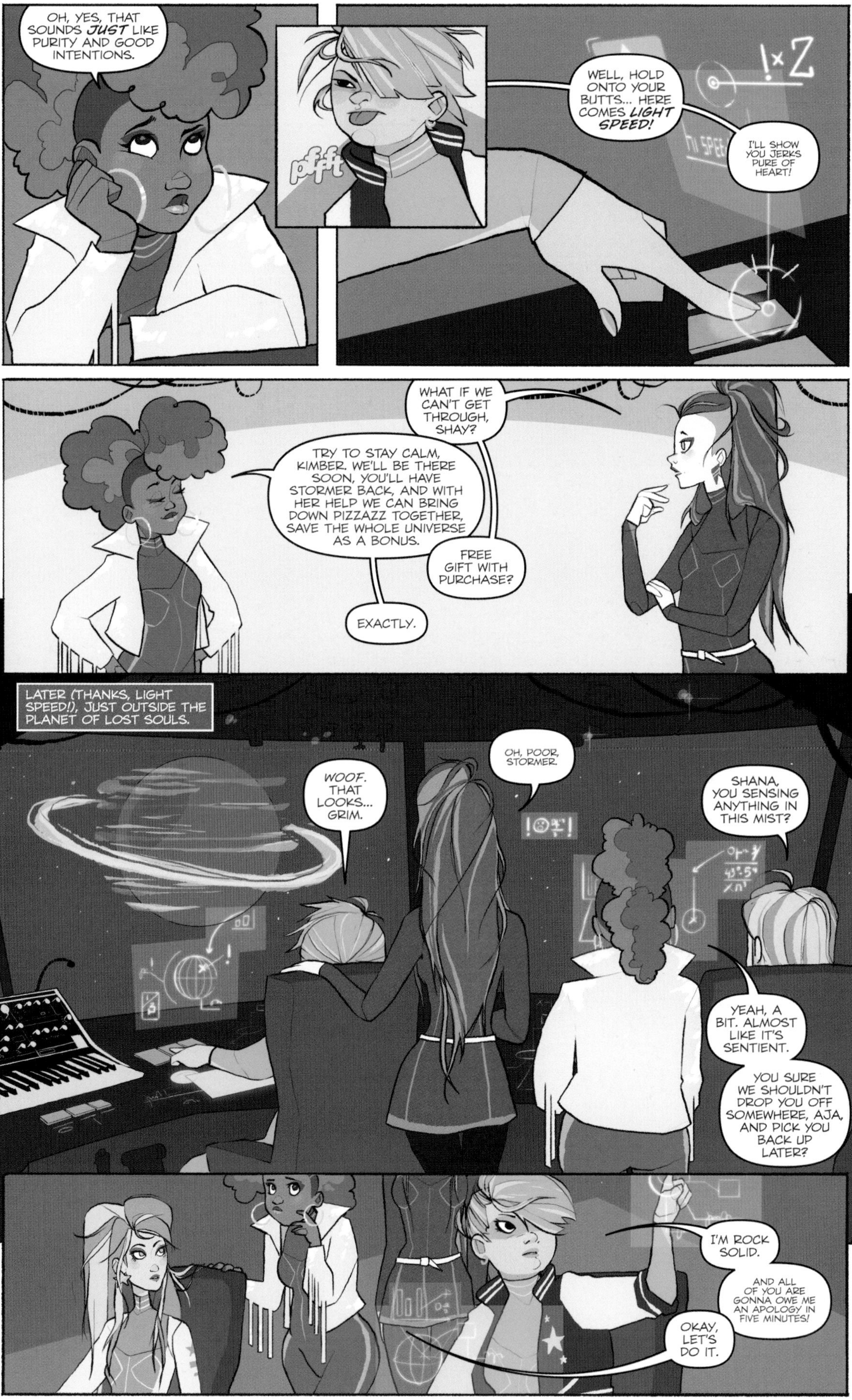
OH, YES, THAT SOUNDS JUST LIKE PURITY AND GOOD INTENTIONS.
pfft
WELL, HOLD ONTO YOUR BUTTS... HERE COMES LIGHT SPEED!
I'LL SHOW YOU JERKS PURE OF HEART!
WHAT IF WE CAN'T GET THROUGH, SHAY?
TRY TO STAY CALM, KIMBER. WE'LL BE THERE SOON, YOU'LL HAVE STORMER BACK, AND WITH HER HELP WE CAN BRING DOWN PIZZAZZ TOGETHER, SAVE THE WHOLE UNIVERSE AS A BONUS.
FREE GIFT WITH PURCHASE?
EXACTLY.
LATER (THANKS, LIGHT SPEED!), JUST OUTSIDE THE PLANET OF LOST SOULS.
WOOF. THAT LOOKS... GRIM.
OH, POOR, STORMER.
SHANA, YOU SENSING ANYTHING IN THIS MIST?
YEAH, A BIT. ALMOST LIKE IT'S SENTIENT.
YOU SURE WE SHOULDN'T DROP YOU OFF SOMEWHERE, AJA, AND PICK YOU BACK UP LATER?
I'M ROCK SOLID.
AND ALL OF YOU ARE GONNA OWE ME AN APOLOGY IN FIVE MINUTES!
OKAY, LET'S DO IT.

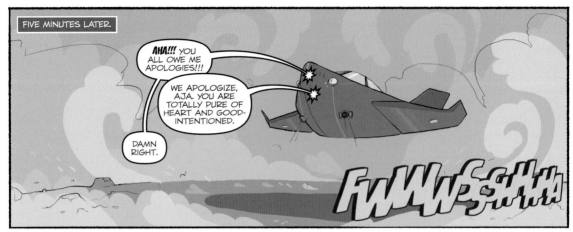

AHA!!! YOU ALL OWE ME APOLOGIES!!!

WE APOLOGIZE, AJA. YOU ARE TOTALLY PURE OF HEART AND GOOD-INTENTIONED.

DAMN RIGHT.

FWWWSSHHH

I WONDER HOW LONG IT WILL TAKE TO FIND HER?

I DON'T KNOW, SWEETIE, BUT WE'LL STAY HERE AS LONG AS IT...

KIMBER!

...TAKES?

STORMER!

KIMBER!

WELL THAT WAS FAST.

IT'D BE GREAT IF TAKING DOWN PIZZAZZ IS THIS EASY.

NO KIDDING.

STORMER, I KNOW YOU'VE BEEN THROUGH A LOT. WE DON'T WANT TO RUSH YOU...

...BUT?

—BUT WE REALLY NEED YOUR HELP TO TAKE DOWN PIZZAZZ.

YEAH, EVER SINCE SHE BANISHED YOU, SHE'S BEEN OUT OF CONTROL. THINGS ARE GETTING REALLY BAD OUT THERE. IT'S LIKE SHE...

DOESN'T HAVE A HEART.

UH... YEAH. KINDA *EXACTLY* LIKE THAT.

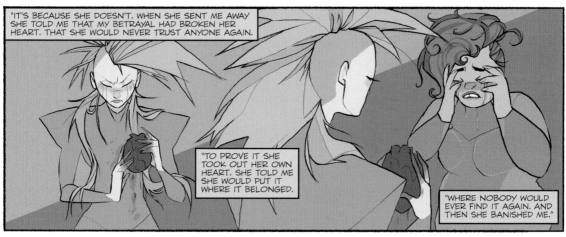

"IT'S BECAUSE SHE DOESN'T. WHEN SHE SENT ME AWAY SHE TOLD ME THAT MY BETRAYAL HAD BROKEN HER HEART. THAT SHE WOULD NEVER TRUST ANYONE AGAIN.

"TO PROVE IT SHE TOOK OUT HER OWN HEART. SHE TOLD ME SHE WOULD PUT IT WHERE IT BELONGED.

"WHERE NOBODY WOULD EVER FIND IT AGAIN. AND THEN SHE BANISHED ME."

DO YOU KNOW WHERE SHE SENT IT?

IF WE COULD PUT IT BACK INSIDE HER MAYBE IT WOULD HELP HER UNDERSTAND WHAT SHE'S DOING TO THE WORLD.

I'M SORRY, I DON'T KNOW WHERE IT IS.

SHE EXILED ME THAT SAME DAY.

I HAVEN'T SEEN HER... *ANYONE*, SINCE.

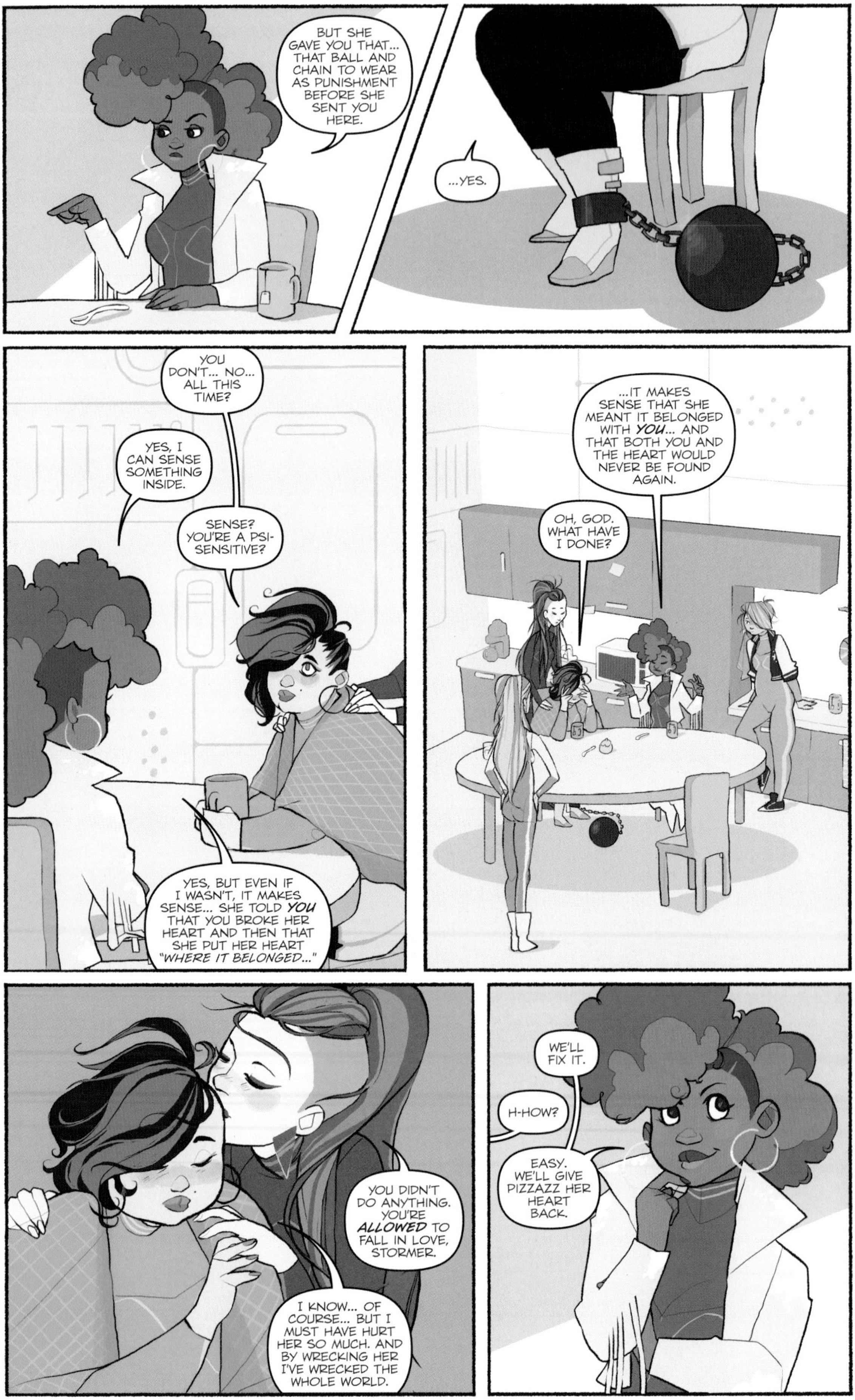
BUT SHE GAVE YOU THAT... THAT BALL AND CHAIN TO WEAR AS PUNISHMENT BEFORE SHE SENT YOU HERE.
...YES.
YOU DON'T... NO... ALL THIS TIME?
YES, I CAN SENSE SOMETHING INSIDE.
SENSE? YOU'RE A PSI-SENSITIVE?
YES, BUT EVEN IF I WASN'T, IT MAKES SENSE... SHE TOLD *YOU* THAT YOU BROKE HER HEART AND THEN THAT SHE PUT HER HEART "*WHERE IT BELONGED...*"
...IT MAKES SENSE THAT SHE MEANT IT BELONGED WITH *YOU*... AND THAT BOTH YOU AND THE HEART WOULD NEVER BE FOUND AGAIN.
OH, GOD. WHAT HAVE I DONE?
YOU DIDN'T DO ANYTHING. YOU'RE *ALLOWED* TO FALL IN LOVE, STORMER.
I KNOW... OF COURSE... BUT I MUST HAVE HURT HER SO MUCH. AND BY WRECKING HER I'VE WRECKED THE WHOLE WORLD.
WE'LL FIX IT.
H-HOW?
EASY. WE'LL GIVE PIZZAZZ HER HEART BACK.

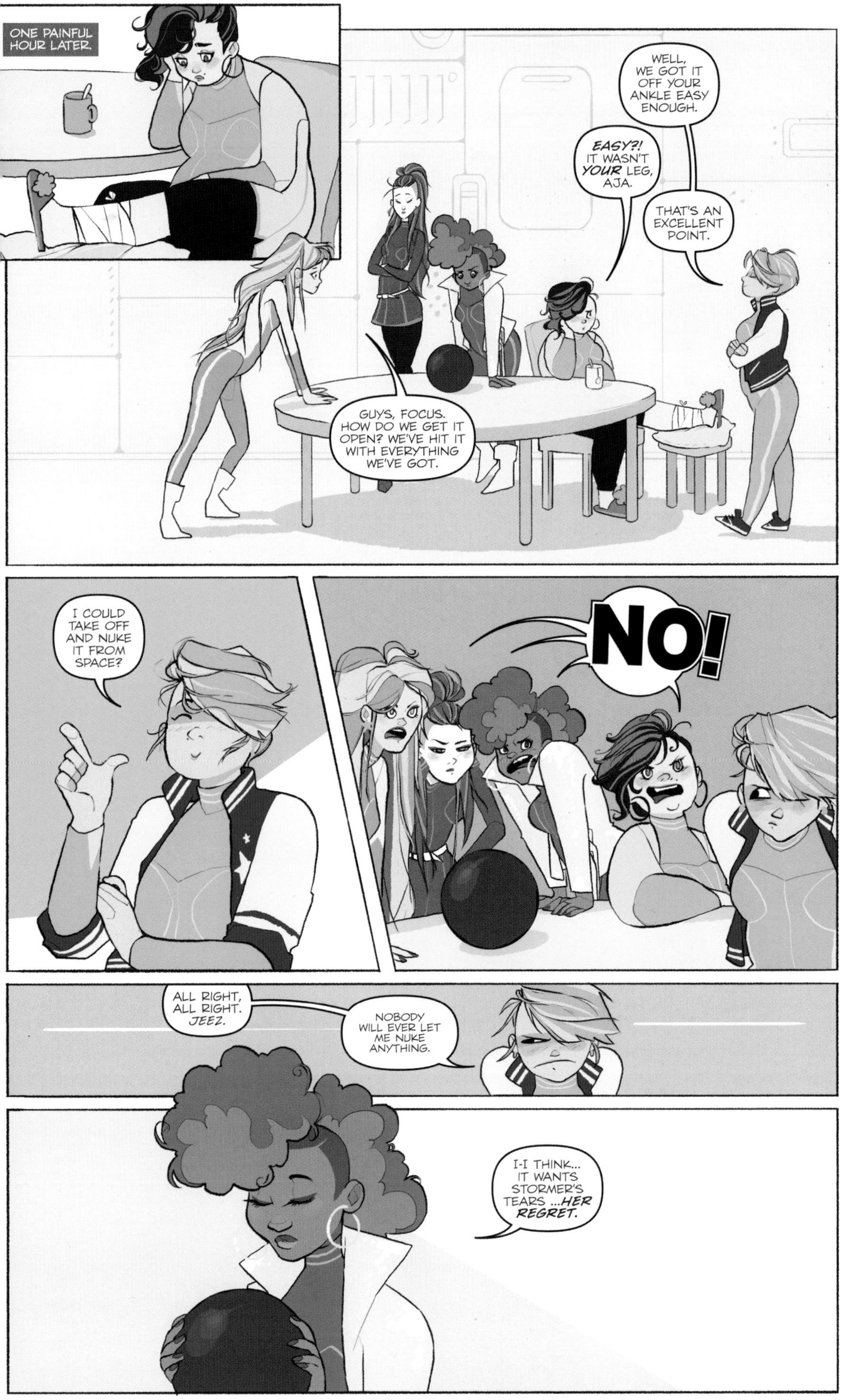
ONE PAINFUL HOUR LATER.
WELL, WE GOT IT OFF YOUR ANKLE EASY ENOUGH.
EASY?! IT WASN'T YOUR LEG, AJA.
THAT'S AN EXCELLENT POINT.
GUYS, FOCUS. HOW DO WE GET IT OPEN? WE'VE HIT IT WITH EVERYTHING WE'VE GOT.
I COULD TAKE OFF AND NUKE IT FROM SPACE?
NO!
ALL RIGHT, ALL RIGHT. JEEZ.
NOBODY WILL EVER LET ME NUKE ANYTHING.
I-I THINK... IT WANTS STORMER'S TEARS ...HER REGRET.

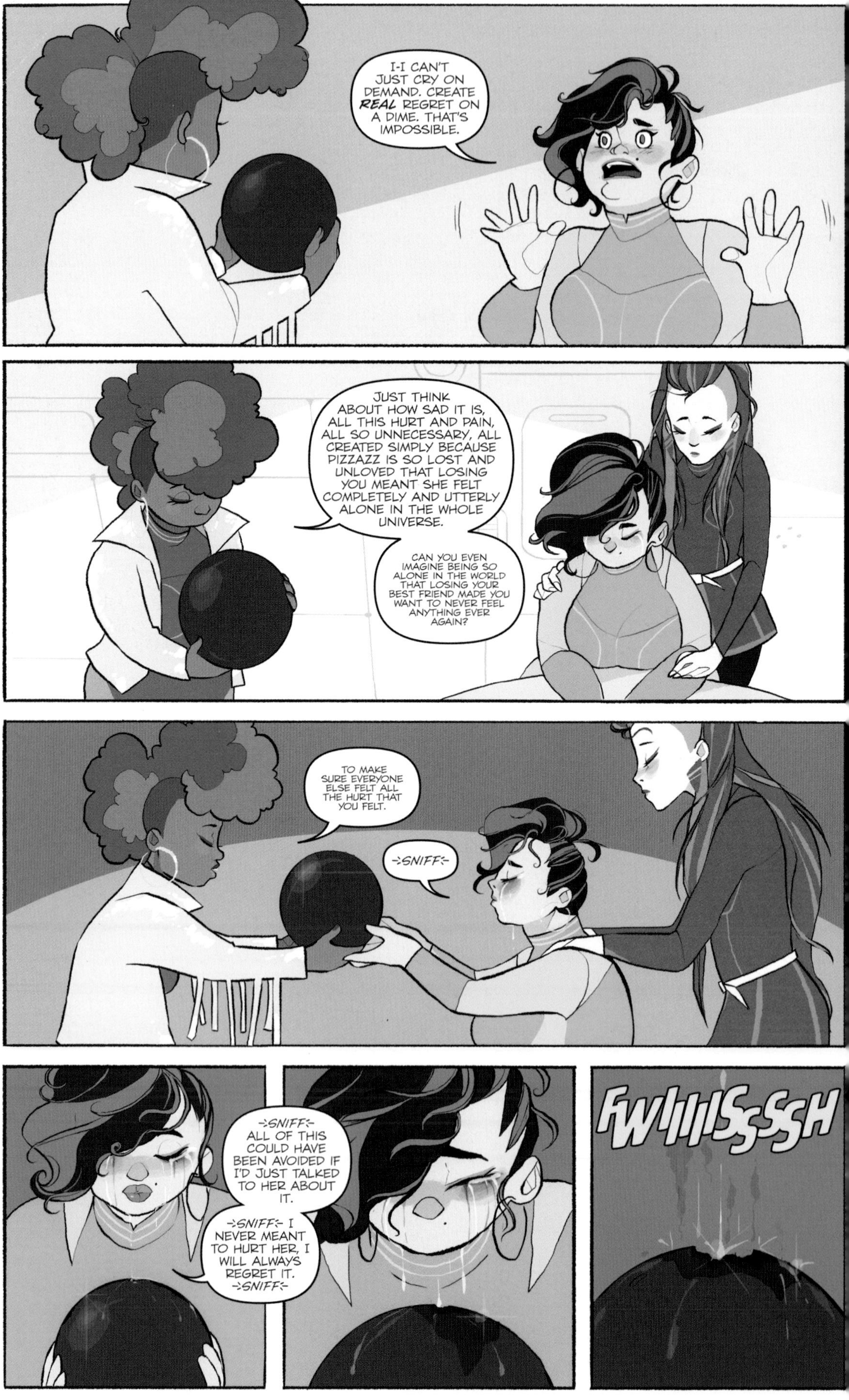
I-I CAN'T JUST CRY ON DEMAND. CREATE *REAL* REGRET ON A DIME. THAT'S IMPOSSIBLE.
JUST THINK ABOUT HOW SAD IT IS, ALL THIS HURT AND PAIN, ALL SO UNNECESSARY, ALL CREATED SIMPLY BECAUSE PIZZAZZ IS SO LOST AND UNLOVED THAT LOSING YOU MEANT SHE FELT COMPLETELY AND UTTERLY ALONE IN THE WHOLE UNIVERSE.
CAN YOU EVEN IMAGINE BEING SO ALONE IN THE WORLD THAT LOSING YOUR BEST FRIEND MADE YOU WANT TO NEVER FEEL ANYTHING EVER AGAIN?
TO MAKE SURE EVERYONE ELSE FELT ALL THE HURT THAT YOU FELT.
-SNIFF-
-SNIFF- ALL OF THIS COULD HAVE BEEN AVOIDED IF I'D JUST TALKED TO HER ABOUT IT.
-SNIFF- I NEVER MEANT TO HURT HER, I WILL ALWAYS REGRET IT. -SNIFF-
FWIIIIISSSSH

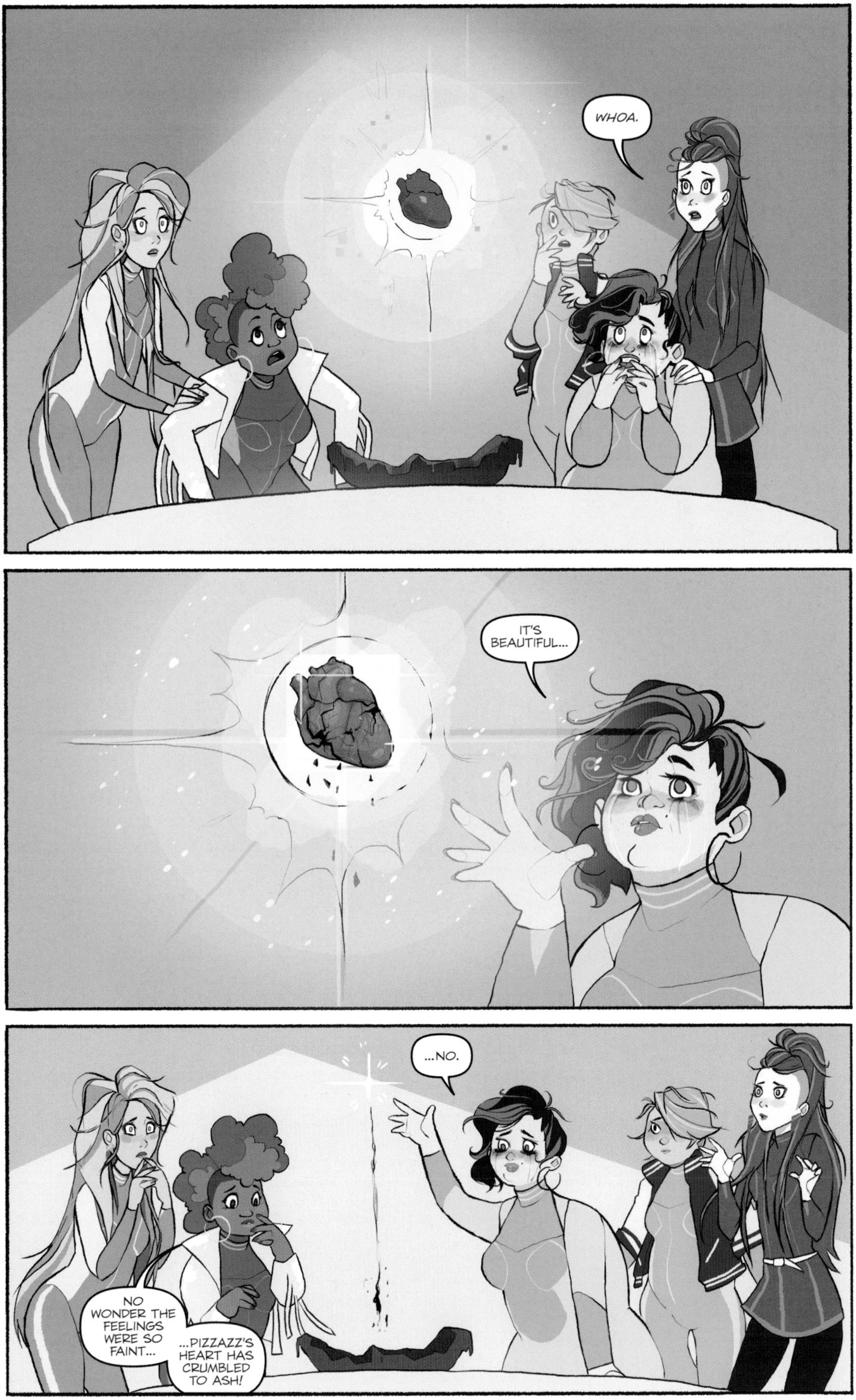
WHOA.
IT'S BEAUTIFUL...
...NO.
NO WONDER THE FEELINGS WERE SO FAINT...
...PIZZAZZ'S HEART HAS CRUMBLED TO ASH!

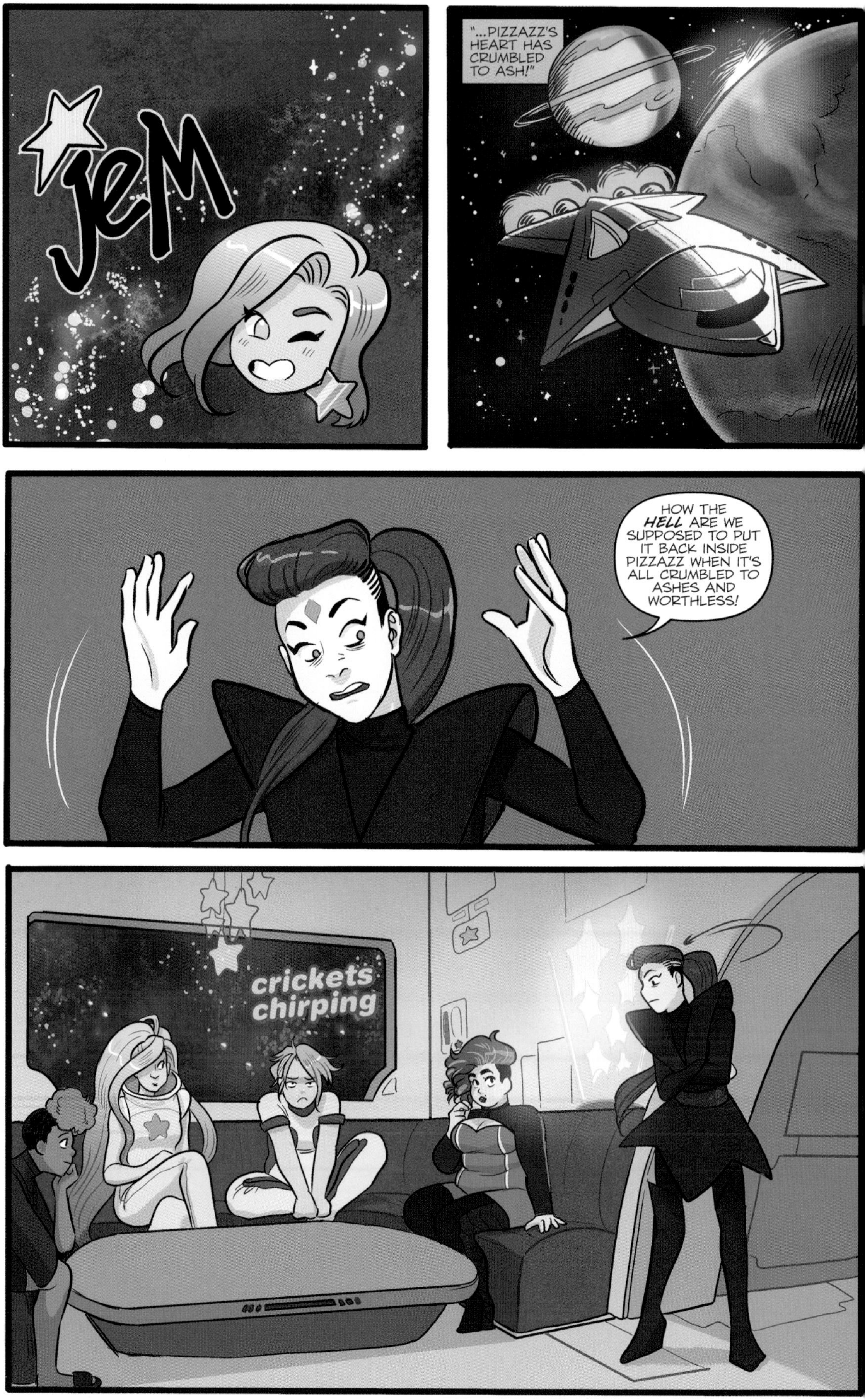
JEM
"...PIZZAZZ'S HEART HAS CRUMBLED TO ASH!"
HOW THE *HELL* ARE WE SUPPOSED TO PUT IT BACK INSIDE PIZZAZZ WHEN IT'S ALL CRUMBLED TO ASHES AND WORTHLESS!
crickets chirping

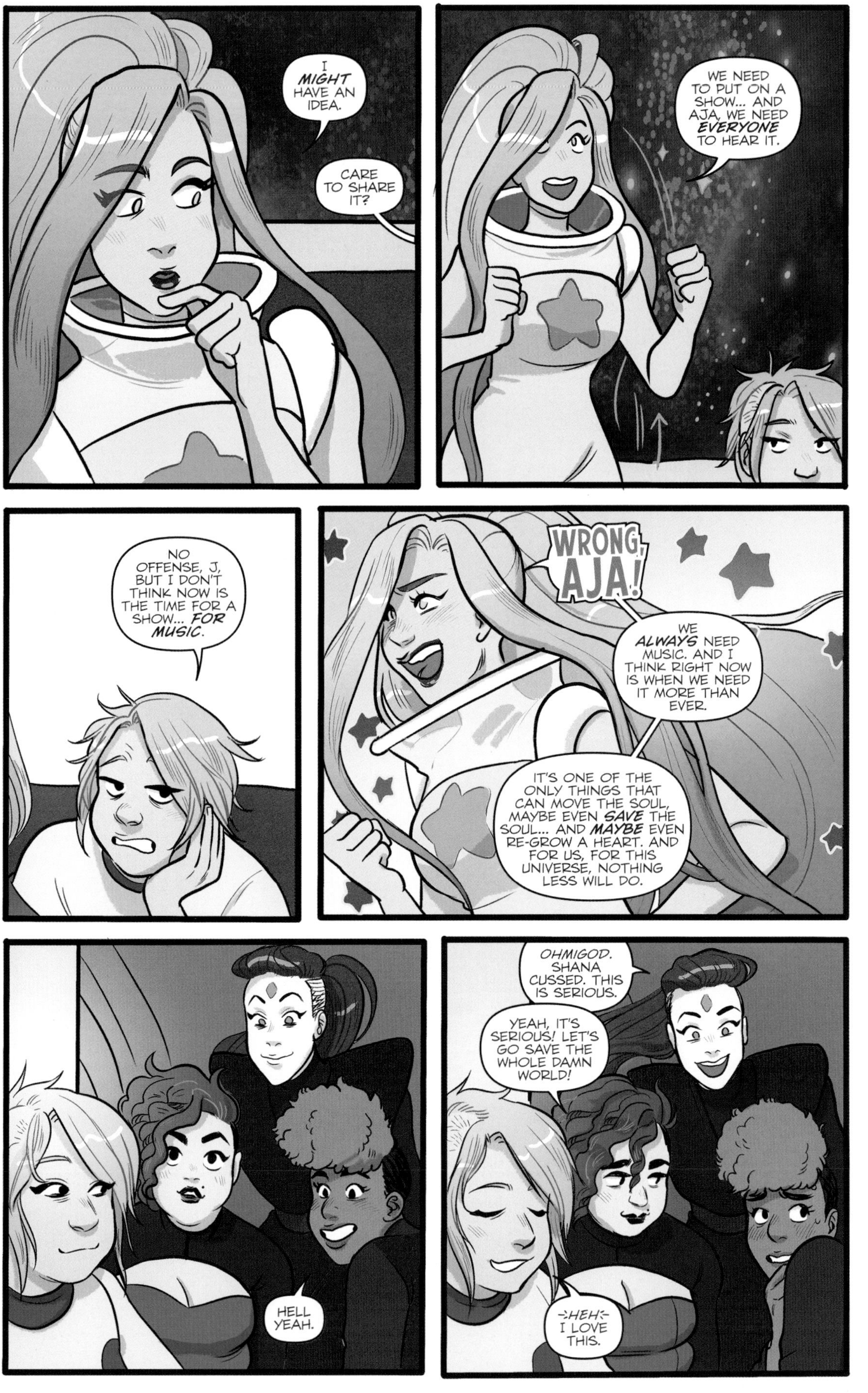
I *MIGHT* HAVE AN IDEA.
CARE TO SHARE IT?
WE NEED TO PUT ON A SHOW... AND AJA, WE NEED *EVERYONE* TO HEAR IT.
NO OFFENSE, J, BUT I DON'T THINK NOW IS THE TIME FOR A SHOW... *FOR MUSIC*.
WRONG, AJA!
WE *ALWAYS* NEED MUSIC. AND I THINK RIGHT NOW IS WHEN WE NEED IT MORE THAN EVER.
IT'S ONE OF THE ONLY THINGS THAT CAN MOVE THE SOUL, MAYBE EVEN *SAVE* THE SOUL... AND *MAYBE* EVEN RE-GROW A HEART. AND FOR US, FOR THIS UNIVERSE, NOTHING LESS WILL DO.
HELL YEAH.
OHMIGOD. SHANA CUSSED. THIS IS SERIOUS.
YEAH, IT'S SERIOUS! LET'S GO SAVE THE WHOLE DAMN WORLD!
HEH I LOVE THIS.

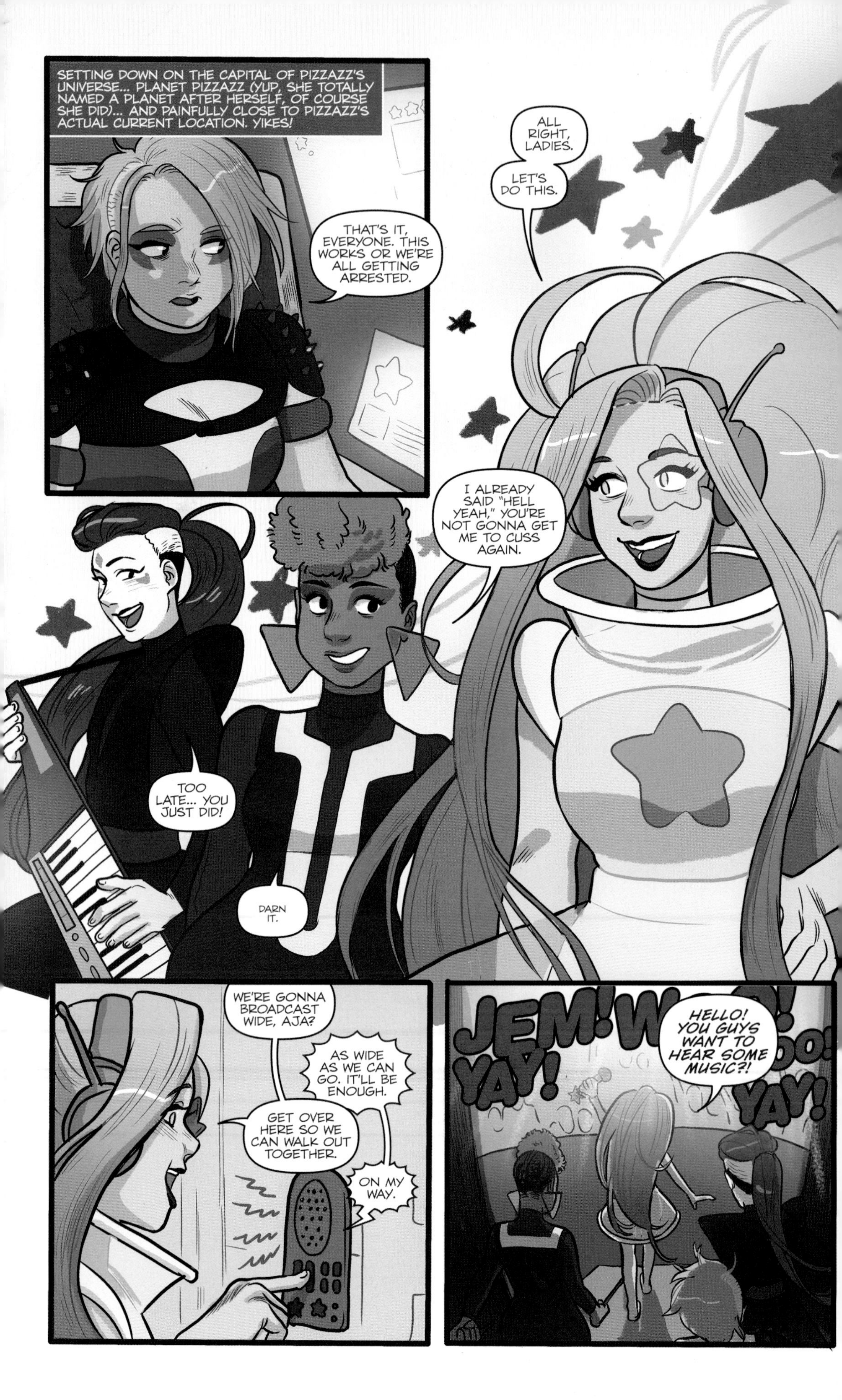
SETTING DOWN ON THE CAPITAL OF PIZZAZZ'S UNIVERSE... PLANET PIZZAZZ (YUP, SHE TOTALLY NAMED A PLANET AFTER HERSELF, OF COURSE SHE DID)... AND PAINFULLY CLOSE TO PIZZAZZ'S ACTUAL CURRENT LOCATION. YIKES!
THAT'S IT, EVERYONE. THIS WORKS OR WE'RE ALL GETTING ARRESTED.
ALL RIGHT, LADIES.
LET'S DO THIS.
I ALREADY SAID "HELL YEAH," YOU'RE NOT GONNA GET ME TO CUSS AGAIN.
TOO LATE... YOU JUST DID!
DARN IT.
WE'RE GONNA BROADCAST WIDE, AJA?
AS WIDE AS WE CAN GO. IT'LL BE ENOUGH.
GET OVER HERE SO WE CAN WALK OUT TOGETHER.
ON MY WAY.
JEM!
YAY!
HELLO! YOU GUYS WANT TO HEAR SOME MUSIC?!
YAY!

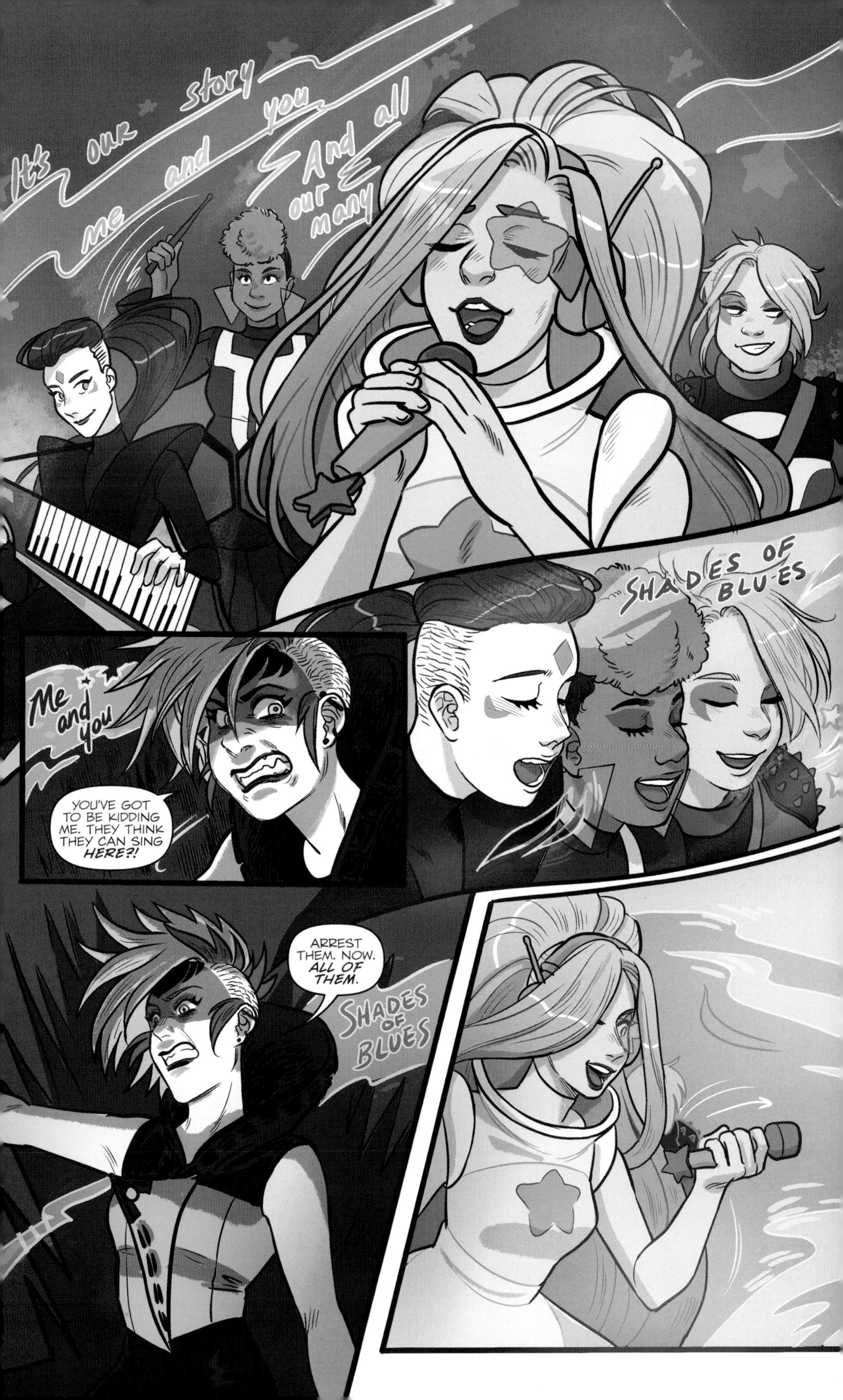
It's our story
me and you
And all our many
SHADES OF BLUES
Me and you
YOU'VE GOT TO BE KIDDING ME. THEY THINK THEY CAN SING HERE?!
ARREST THEM. NOW. ALL OF THEM.
SHADES OF BLUES

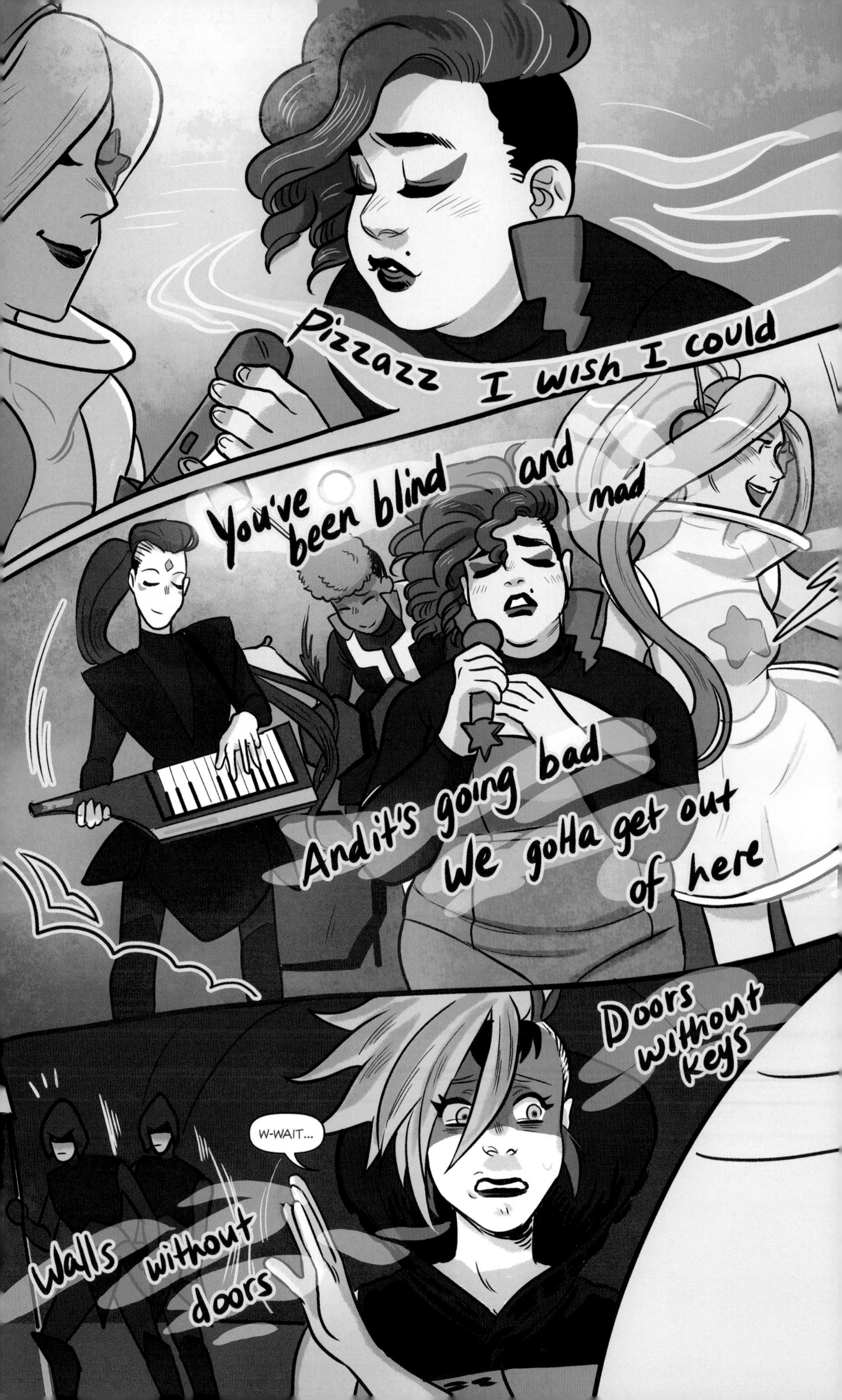

Pizzazz I wish I could
You've been blind and mad
And it's going bad
We gotta get out of here
Doors without keys
W-WAIT...
Walls without doors

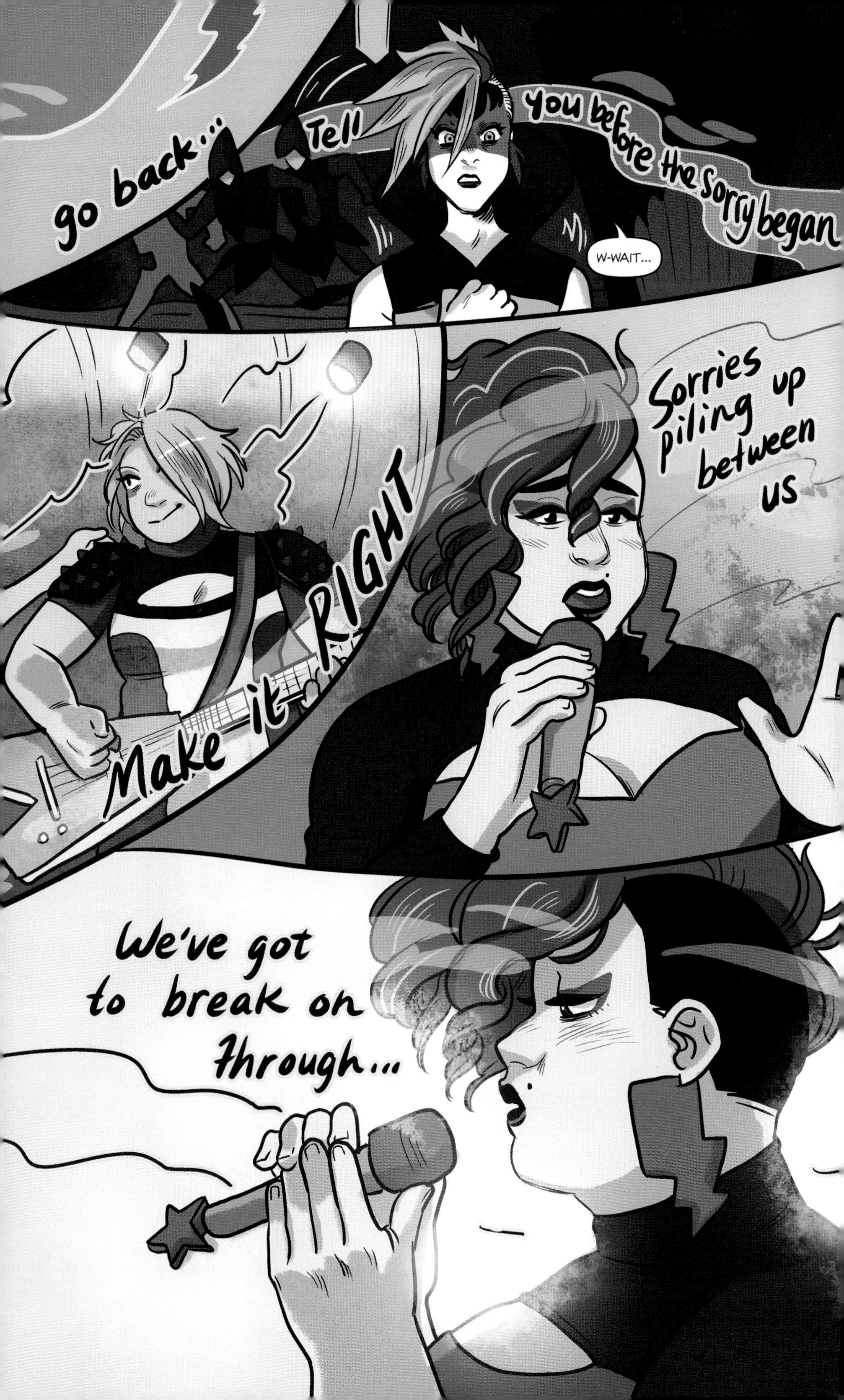
go back...
Tell
you before the sorry began
W-WAIT...
Make it RIGHT
Sorries piling up between us
We've got to break on through...

It's up to you
All I want is your face to see
There's truth inside of me
And I need you to forgive
Only you can make it Right
Only you can bring the light

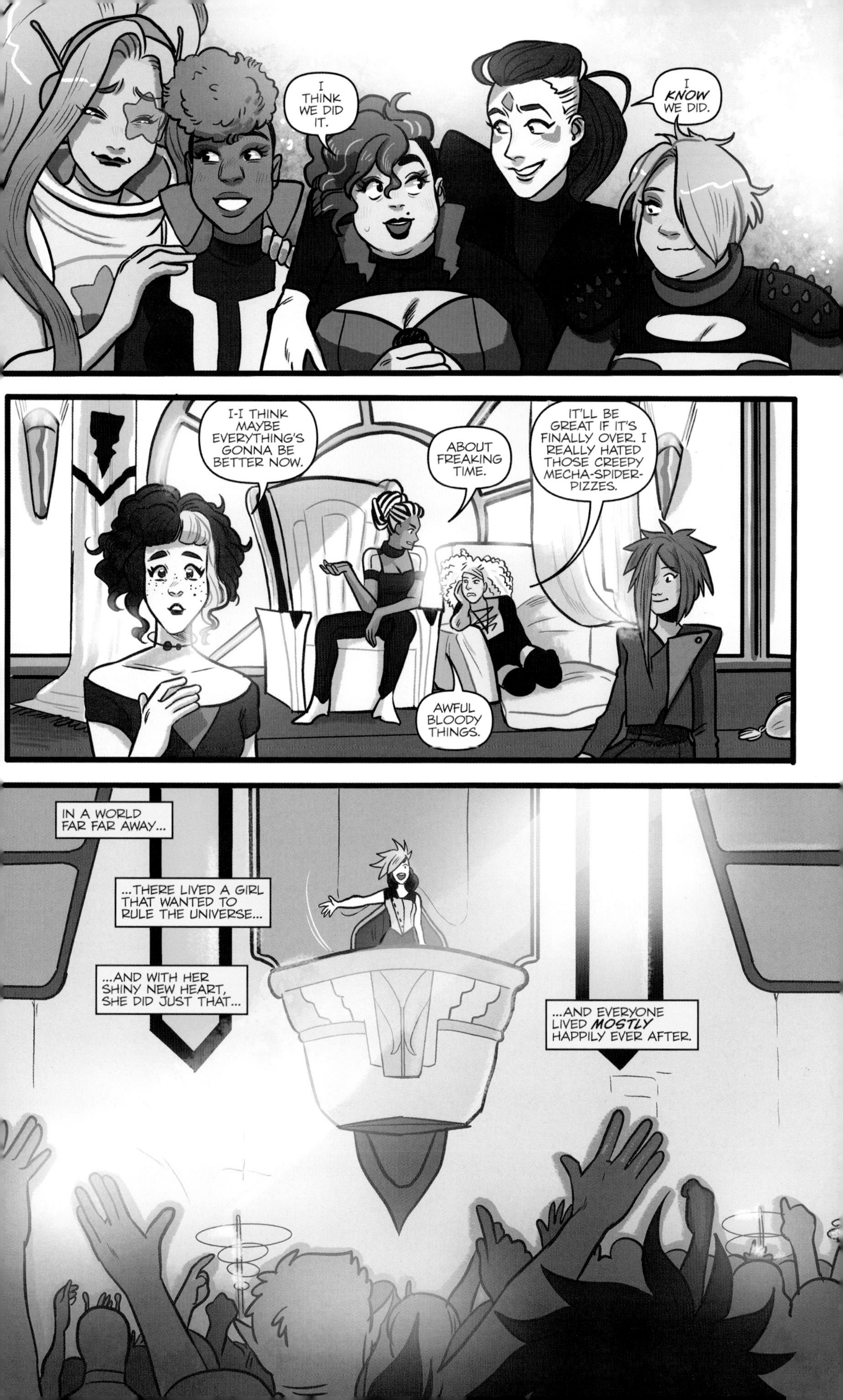
I THINK WE DID IT.
I KNOW WE DID.
I-I THINK MAYBE EVERYTHING'S GONNA BE BETTER NOW.
ABOUT FREAKING TIME.
IT'LL BE GREAT IF IT'S FINALLY OVER. I REALLY HATED THOSE CREEPY MECHA-SPIDER-PIZZES.
AWFUL BLOODY THINGS.
IN A WORLD FAR FAR AWAY...
...THERE LIVED A GIRL THAT WANTED TO RULE THE UNIVERSE...
...AND WITH HER SHINY NEW HEART, SHE DID JUST THAT...
...AND EVERYONE LIVED MOSTLY HAPPILY EVER AFTER.

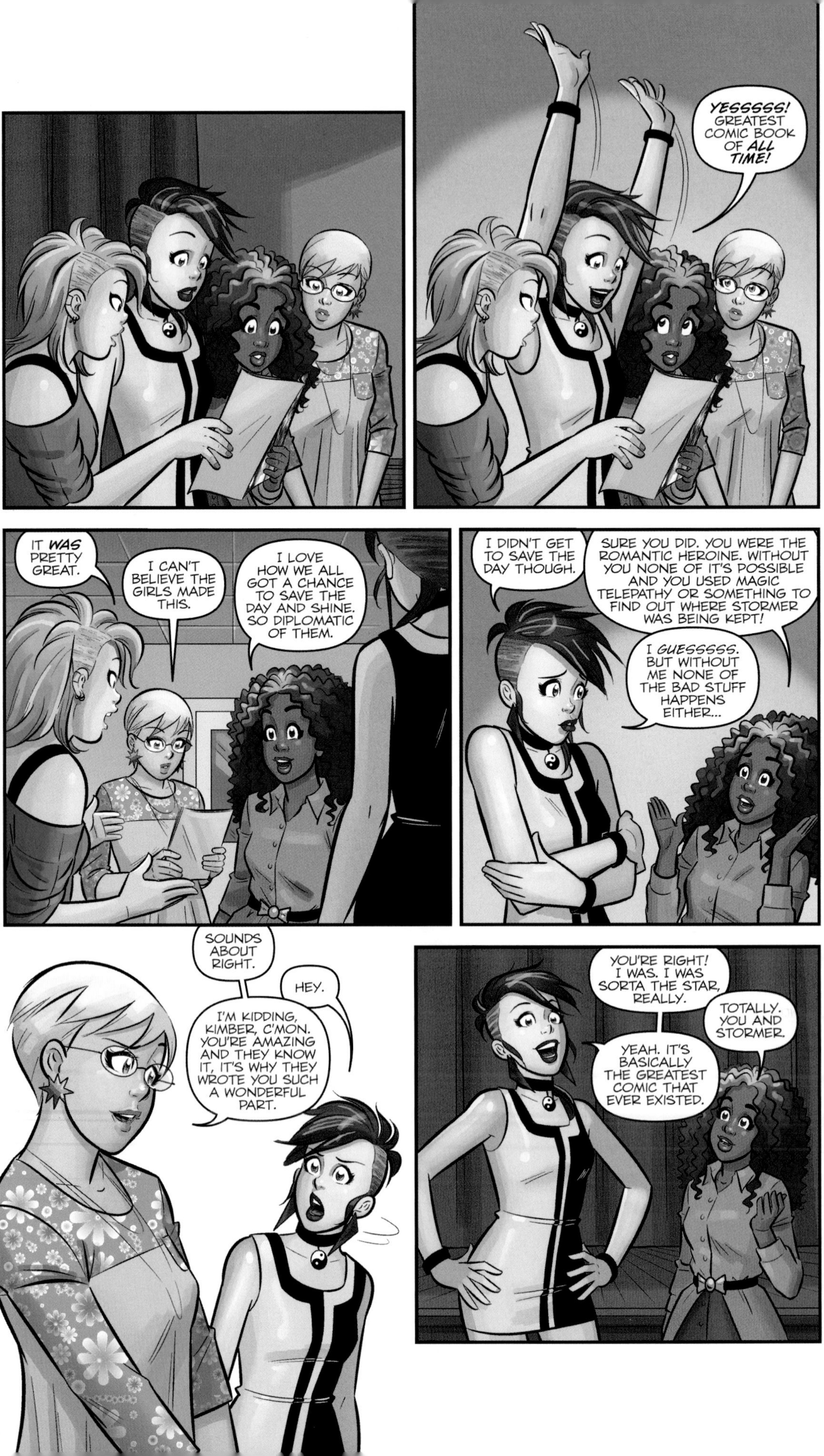

YESSSSS! GREATEST COMIC BOOK OF ALL TIME!
IT WAS PRETTY GREAT.
I CAN'T BELIEVE THE GIRLS MADE THIS.
I LOVE HOW WE ALL GOT A CHANCE TO SAVE THE DAY AND SHINE. SO DIPLOMATIC OF THEM.
I DIDN'T GET TO SAVE THE DAY THOUGH.
SURE YOU DID. YOU WERE THE ROMANTIC HEROINE. WITHOUT YOU NONE OF IT'S POSSIBLE AND YOU USED MAGIC TELEPATHY OR SOMETHING TO FIND OUT WHERE STORMER WAS BEING KEPT!
I GUESSSSS. BUT WITHOUT ME NONE OF THE BAD STUFF HAPPENS EITHER...
SOUNDS ABOUT RIGHT.
HEY.
I'M KIDDING, KIMBER, C'MON. YOU'RE AMAZING AND THEY KNOW IT, IT'S WHY THEY WROTE YOU SUCH A WONDERFUL PART.
YOU'RE RIGHT! I WAS. I WAS SORTA THE STAR, REALLY.
YEAH. IT'S BASICALLY THE GREATEST COMIC THAT EVER EXISTED.
TOTALLY. YOU AND STORMER.

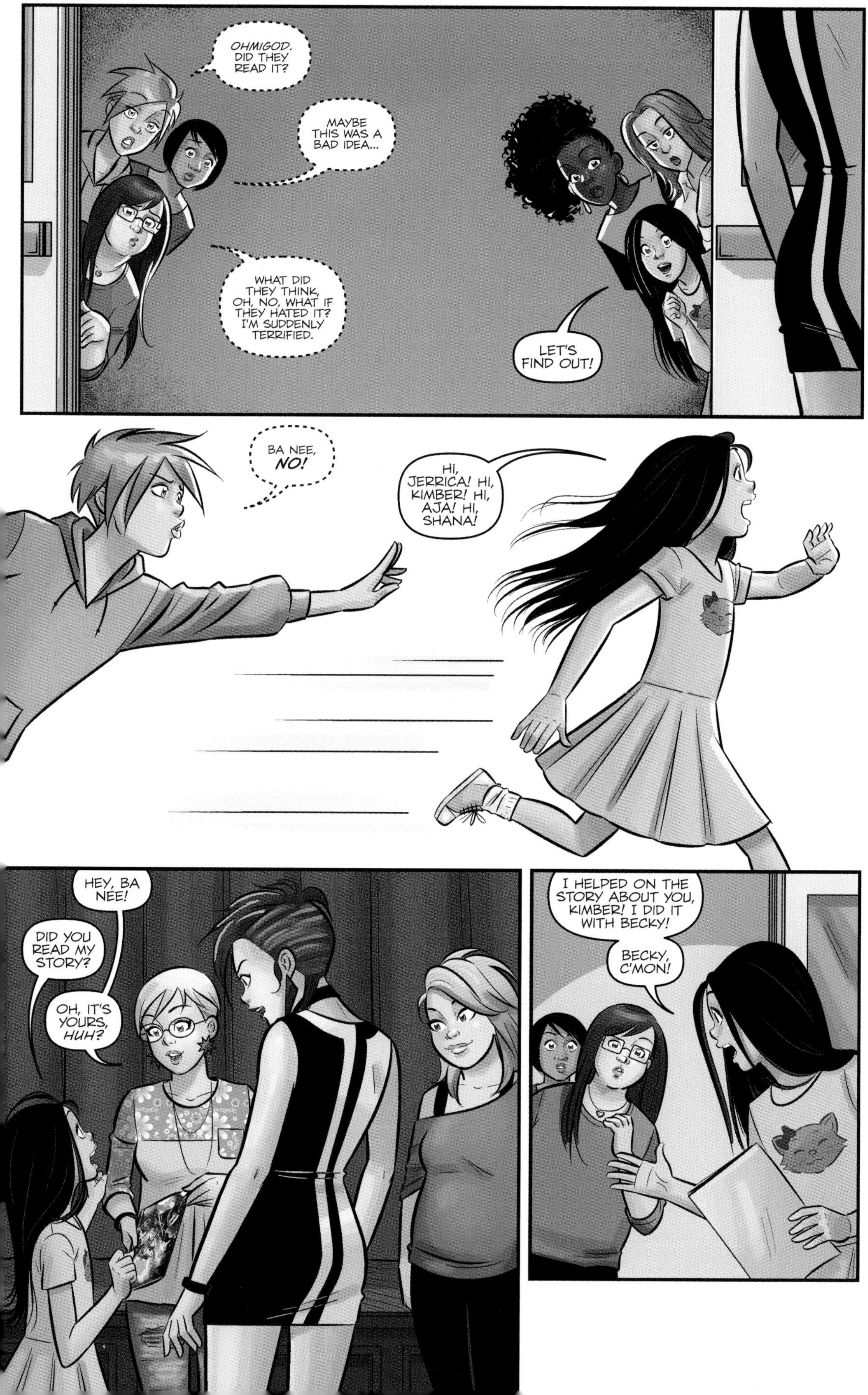
OHMIGOD. DID THEY READ IT?
MAYBE THIS WAS A BAD IDEA...
WHAT DID THEY THINK, OH, NO, WHAT IF THEY HATED IT? I'M SUDDENLY TERRIFIED.
LET'S FIND OUT!
BA NEE, *NO!*
HI, JERRICA! HI, KIMBER! HI, AJA! HI, SHANA!
HEY, BA NEE!
DID YOU READ MY STORY?
OH, IT'S YOURS, *HUH?*
I HELPED ON THE STORY ABOUT YOU, KIMBER! I DID IT WITH BECKY!
BECKY, C'MON!

EXIT

YOU GUYS, COME TALK TO US ABOUT THIS AMAZING COMIC.

YOU *LIKED* IT?

WE *LOVED* IT.

WHAT WAS YOUR FAVORITE PART?

OBVIOUSLY THE SHANA STORY IS THE BEST.

NO WAY!

WE DID THE SHANA ONE.

IT'S SO GOOD YOU GUYS. SO CREATIVE.

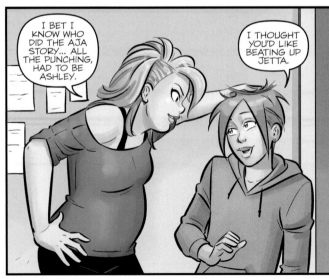

I BET I KNOW WHO DID THE AJA STORY... ALL THE PUNCHING, HAD TO BE ASHLEY.

I THOUGHT YOU'D LIKE BEATING UP JETTA.

I DO, I REALLY REALLY DO.

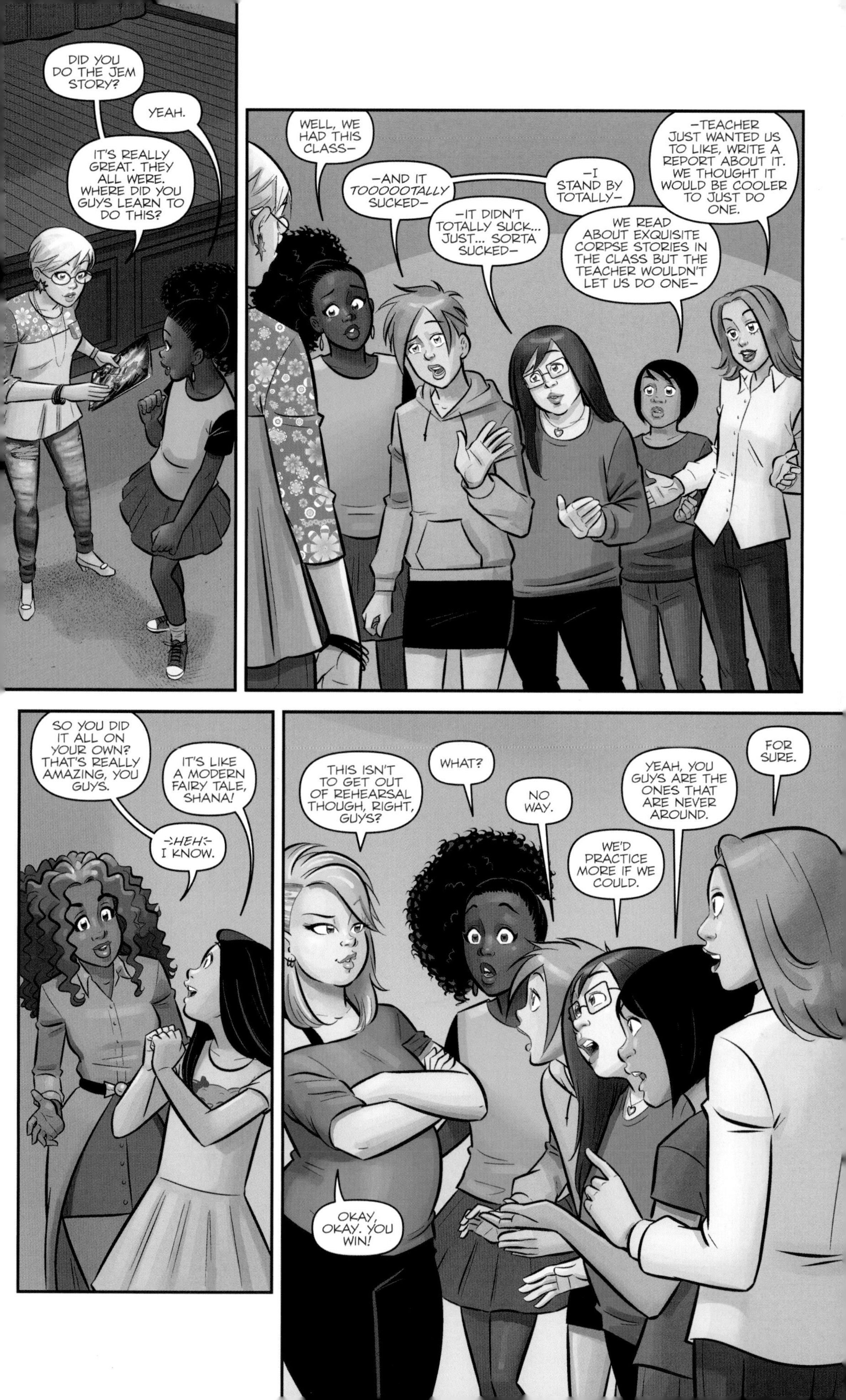
DID YOU DO THE JEM STORY?
YEAH.
IT'S REALLY GREAT. THEY ALL WERE. WHERE DID YOU GUYS LEARN TO DO THIS?
WELL, WE HAD THIS CLASS—
—AND IT TOOOOOTALLY SUCKED—
—I STAND BY TOTALLY—
—IT DIDN'T TOTALLY SUCK... JUST... SORTA SUCKED—
WE READ ABOUT EXQUISITE CORPSE STORIES IN THE CLASS BUT THE TEACHER WOULDN'T LET US DO ONE—
—TEACHER JUST WANTED US TO LIKE, WRITE A REPORT ABOUT IT. WE THOUGHT IT WOULD BE COOLER TO JUST DO ONE.
SO YOU DID IT ALL ON YOUR OWN? THAT'S REALLY AMAZING, YOU GUYS.
IT'S LIKE A MODERN FAIRY TALE, SHANA!
HEH I KNOW.
THIS ISN'T TO GET OUT OF REHEARSAL THOUGH, RIGHT, GUYS?
WHAT?
NO WAY.
WE'D PRACTICE MORE IF WE COULD.
YEAH, YOU GUYS ARE THE ONES THAT ARE NEVER AROUND.
FOR SURE.
OKAY, OKAY. YOU WIN!

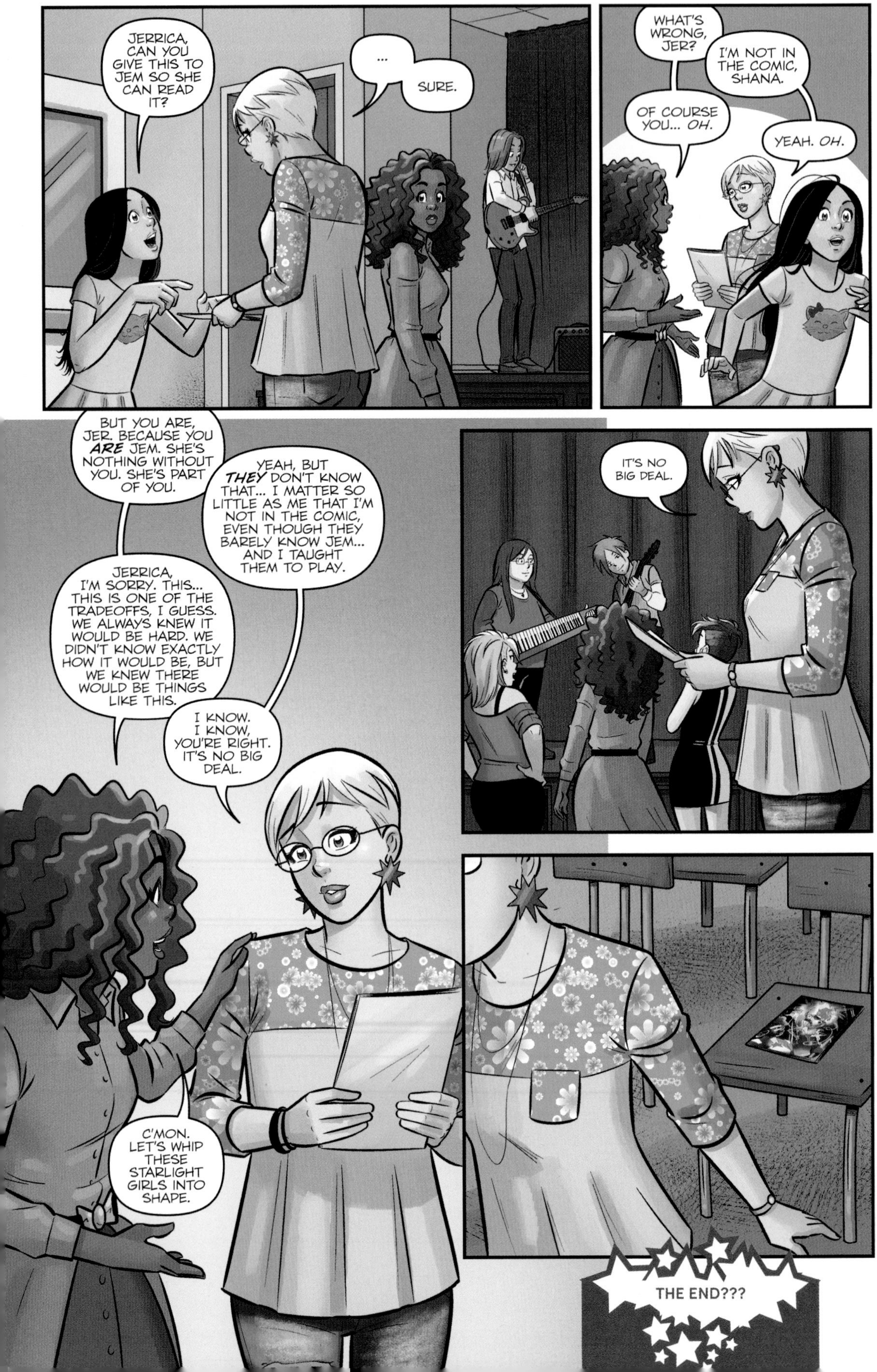
JERRICA, CAN YOU GIVE THIS TO JEM SO SHE CAN READ IT?
...
SURE.
WHAT'S WRONG, JER?
I'M NOT IN THE COMIC, SHANA.
OF COURSE YOU... OH.
YEAH. OH.
BUT YOU ARE, JER. BECAUSE YOU ARE JEM. SHE'S NOTHING WITHOUT YOU. SHE'S PART OF YOU.
YEAH, BUT THEY DON'T KNOW THAT... I MATTER SO LITTLE AS ME THAT I'M NOT IN THE COMIC, EVEN THOUGH THEY BARELY KNOW JEM... AND I TAUGHT THEM TO PLAY.
JERRICA, I'M SORRY. THIS... THIS IS ONE OF THE TRADEOFFS, I GUESS. WE ALWAYS KNEW IT WOULD BE HARD. WE DIDN'T KNOW EXACTLY HOW IT WOULD BE, BUT WE KNEW THERE WOULD BE THINGS LIKE THIS.
I KNOW. I KNOW, YOU'RE RIGHT. IT'S NO BIG DEAL.
IT'S NO BIG DEAL.
C'MON. LET'S WHIP THESE STARLIGHT GIRLS INTO SHAPE.
THE END???

Riot

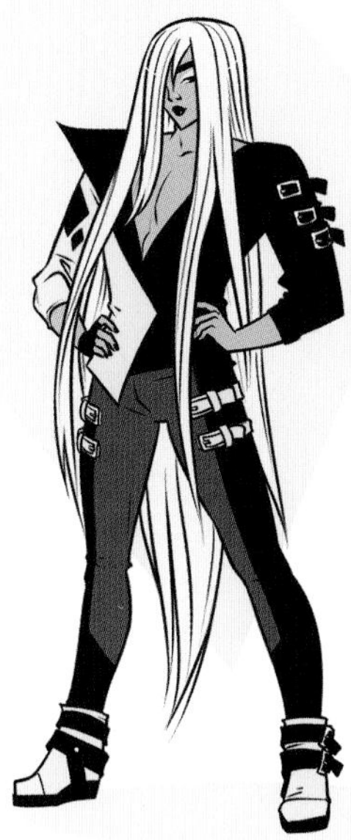

NAME: Rory Llewelyn

AGE: 25

HEIGHT: 5'9"

INSTRUMENT(S): Vocals, Piano

LOVES: Fame & fortune, comics (especially rare European ones), Germany, independent films, bratwurst & sauerkraut, poetry readings, being in control, private islands, and Jem.

HATES: Being controlled, the military, imperfections, big budget action movies, and sell-outs.

PRIZED POSSESSION: Signed Moebius print.

VOTED MOST LIKELY TO: Charm you.

Minx

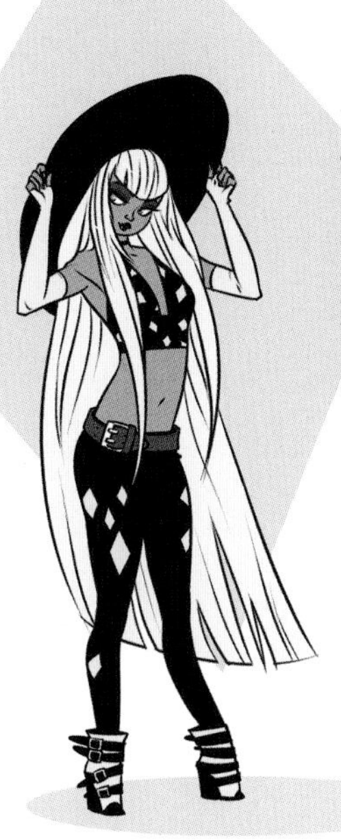

NAME: Ingrid Kruger

AGE: 25

HEIGHT: 5'4"

INSTRUMENT: Keyboard

LOVES: Tech, fashion (especially fabulous hats and shoes), flirting, travel, sparkling water, football (aka "American soccer"), underground parties, Löwensenf, knacker (knackwurst), and Haribo Happy Cola.

HATES: Commitment, rejection, American chocolate, and Americans (with a few exceptions!).

PRIZED POSSESSION: Karl Lagerfeld vintage couture gown.

VOTED MOST LIKELY TO: Create drama.

Rapture

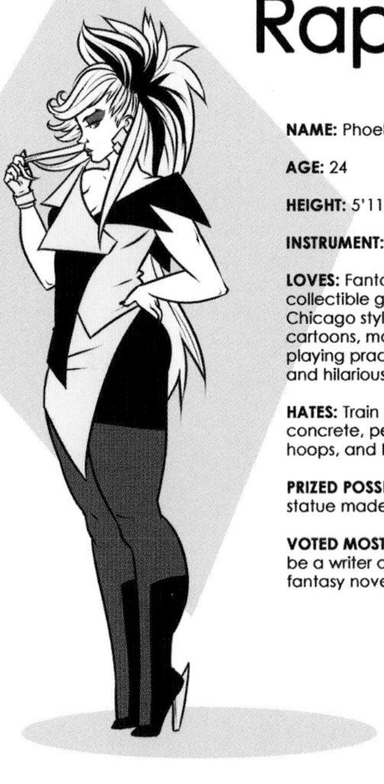

NAME: Phoebe Ashe

AGE: 24

HEIGHT: 5'11"

INSTRUMENT: Guitar

LOVES: Fantasy novels and films, collectible griffins, horses, Ramen, Chicago style deep dish pizza, cartoons, manipulating people, playing practical jokes, gossip, and hilarious GIFs.

HATES: Train travel, bare feet on concrete, peanut butter, hula hoops, and New York style pizza.

PRIZED POSSESSION: Antique griffin statue made of carved jade.

VOTED MOST LIKELY TO: Secretly be a writer of self-published fantasy novels.

Raya

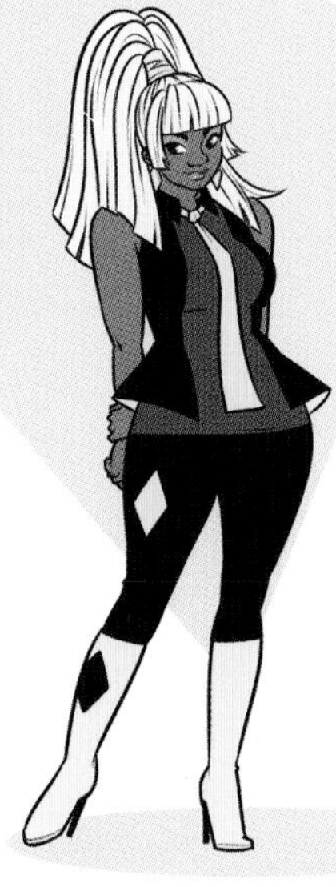

NAME: Carmen Alonso

AGE: 24

HEIGHT: 5'5"

INSTRUMENT: Drums

LOVES: Her brothers, Greece, archery, milkshakes, authentic Mexican food, coffee, young adult novels, horror movies, carnivals, dogs, the ocean, loyalty, and flying.

HATES: Her brothers, drama, fake people, and long car trips.

PRIZED POSSESSION: Custom hand-made bow & arrows.

VOTED MOST LIKELY TO: Keep a secret.

ART BY **GISELE LAGACE**
COLORS BY **JASON MILLET**

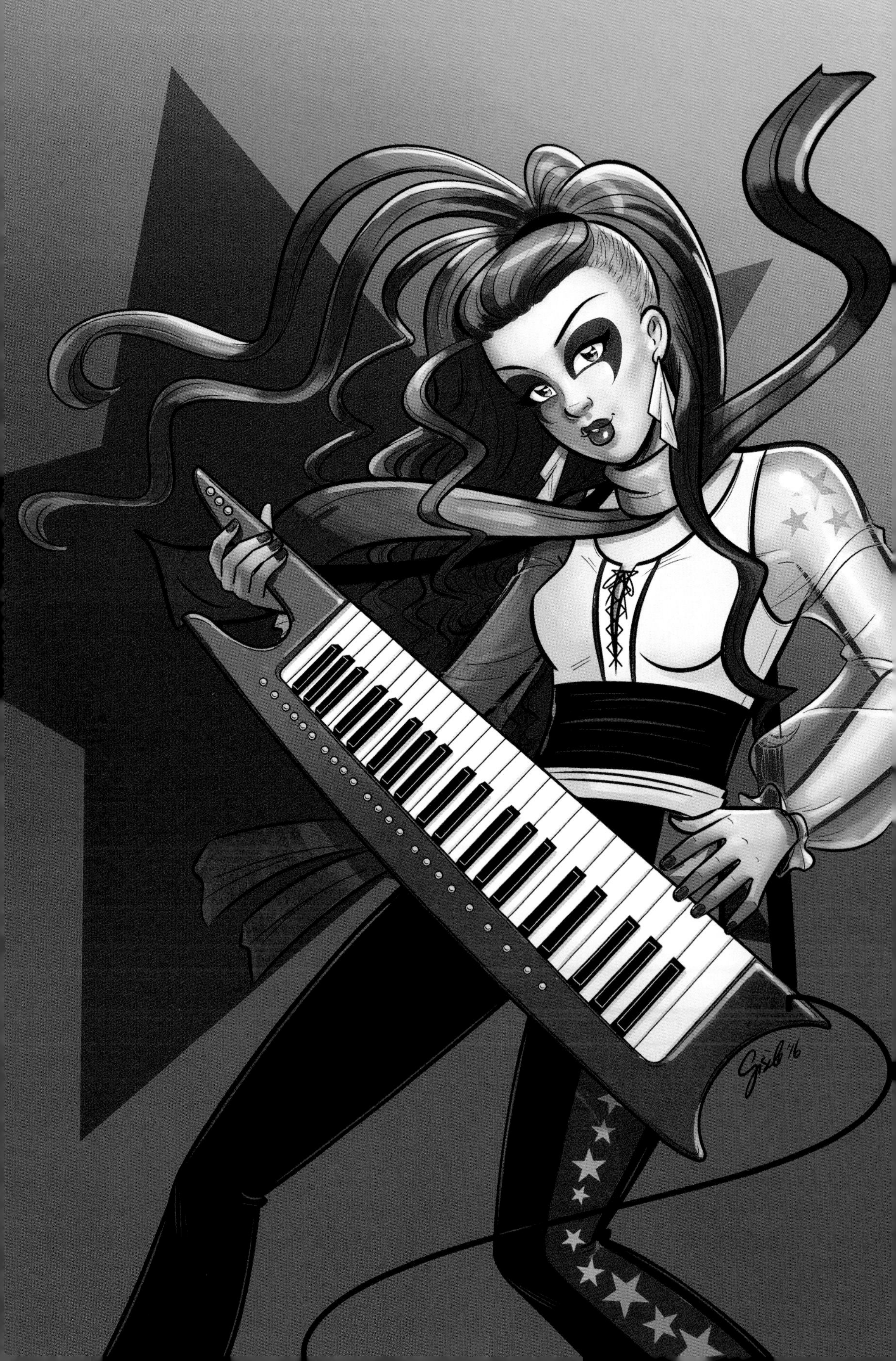

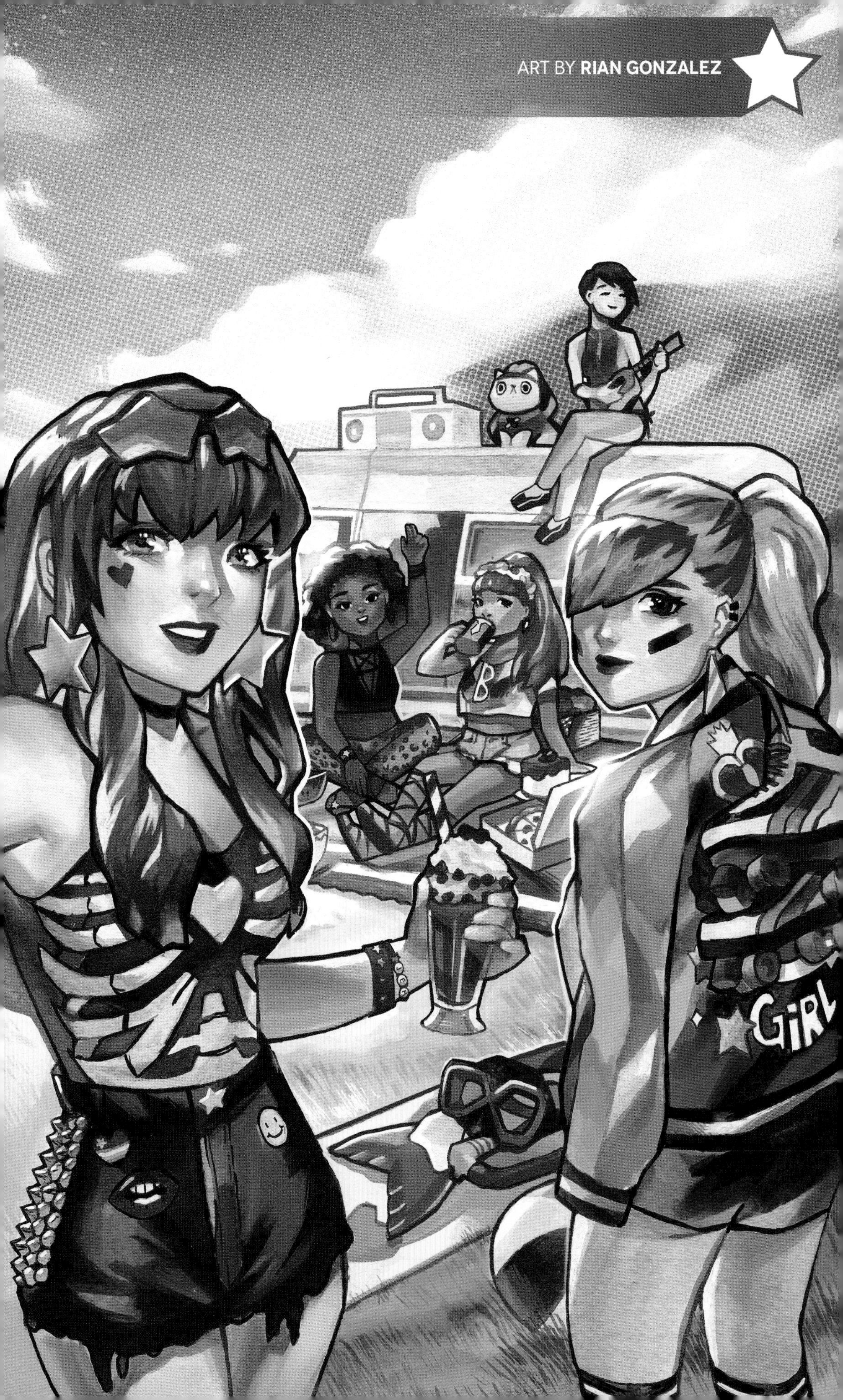
GIRL

ART BY **RIAN GONZALEZ**

ART BY **YOSHI YOSHITANI**

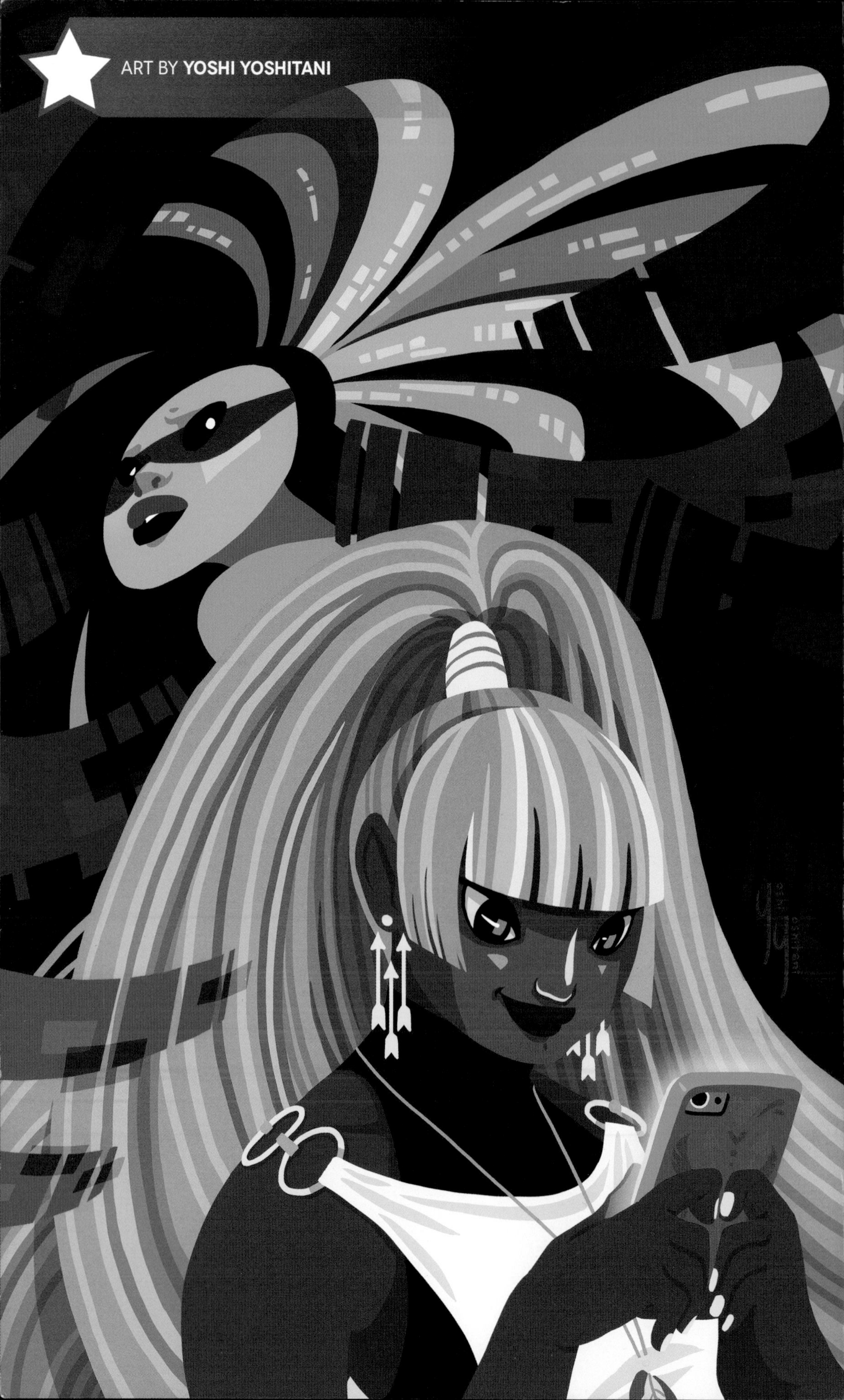

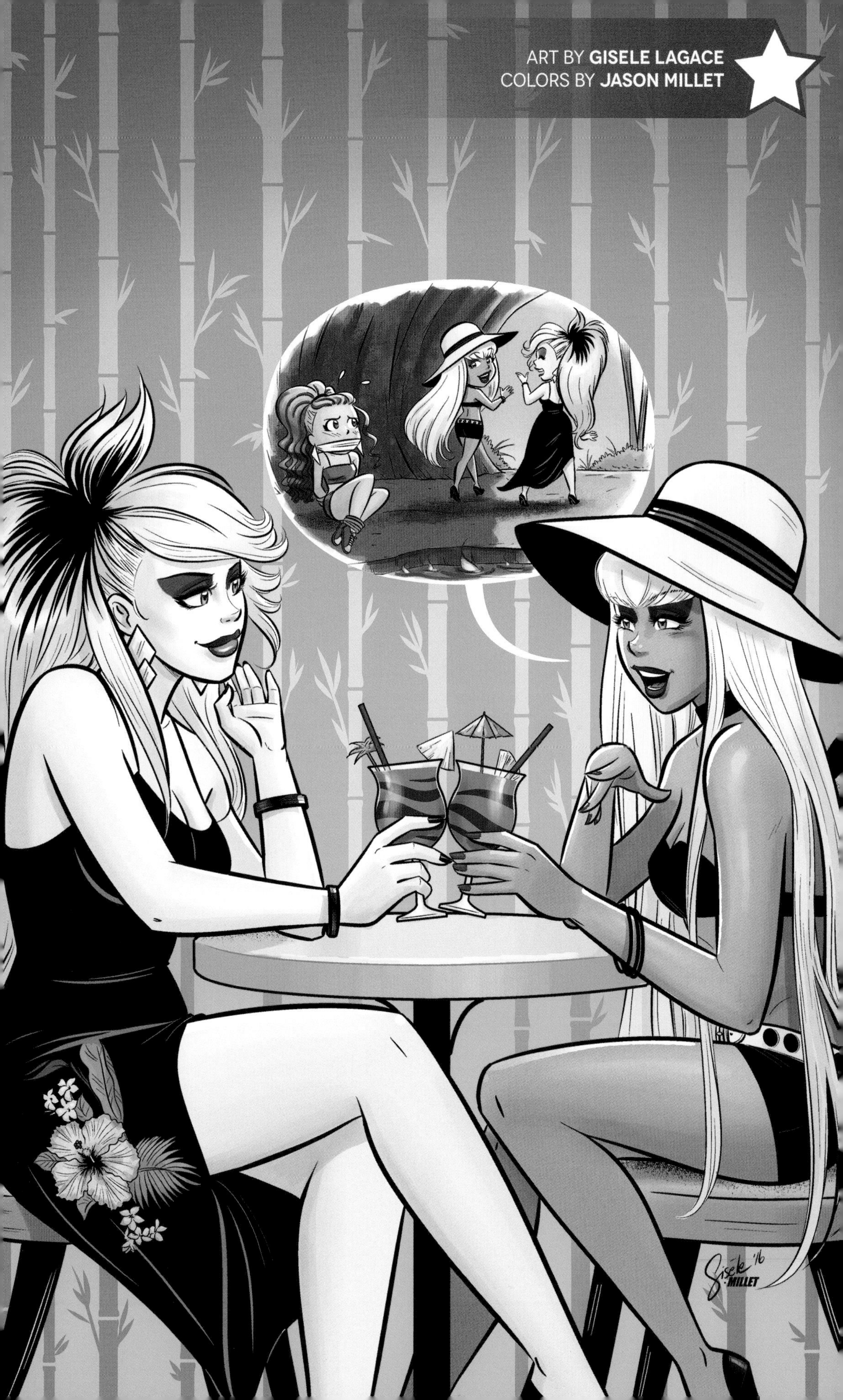
ART BY GISELE LAGACE
COLORS BY JASON MILLET
Gisele '16
MILLET

ART BY **SOPHIE CAMPBELL**

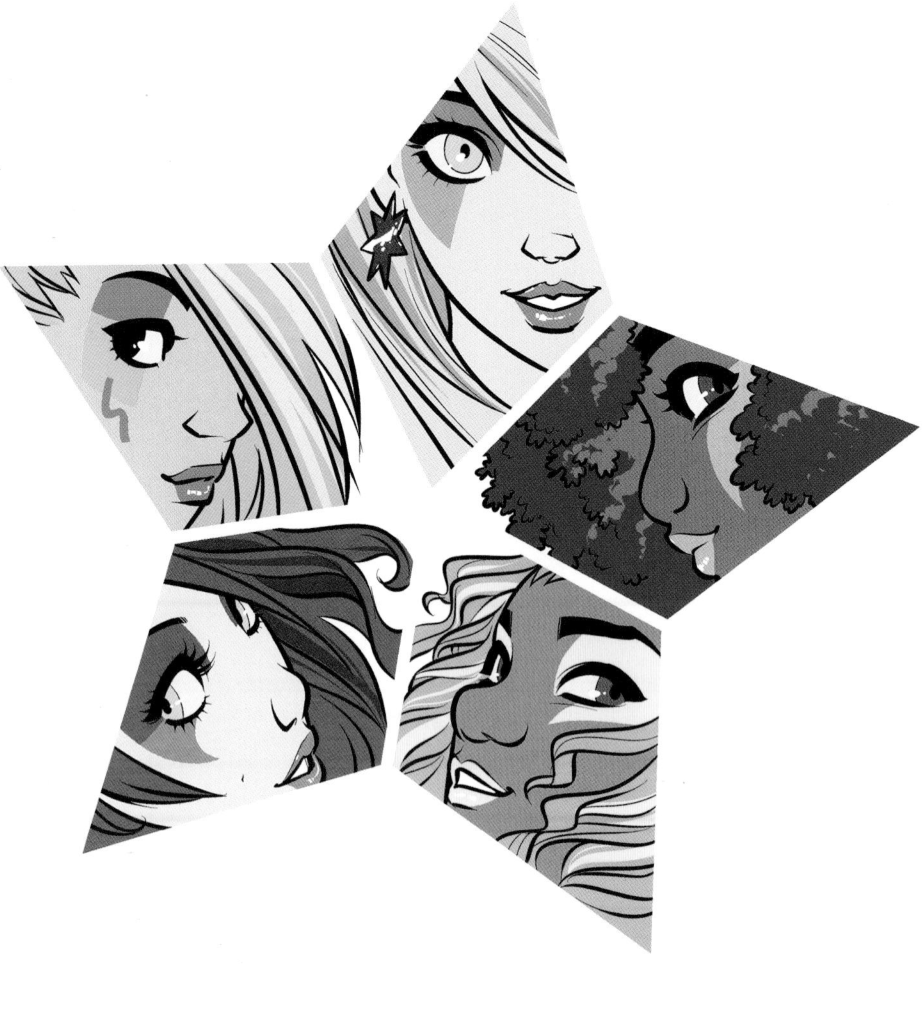

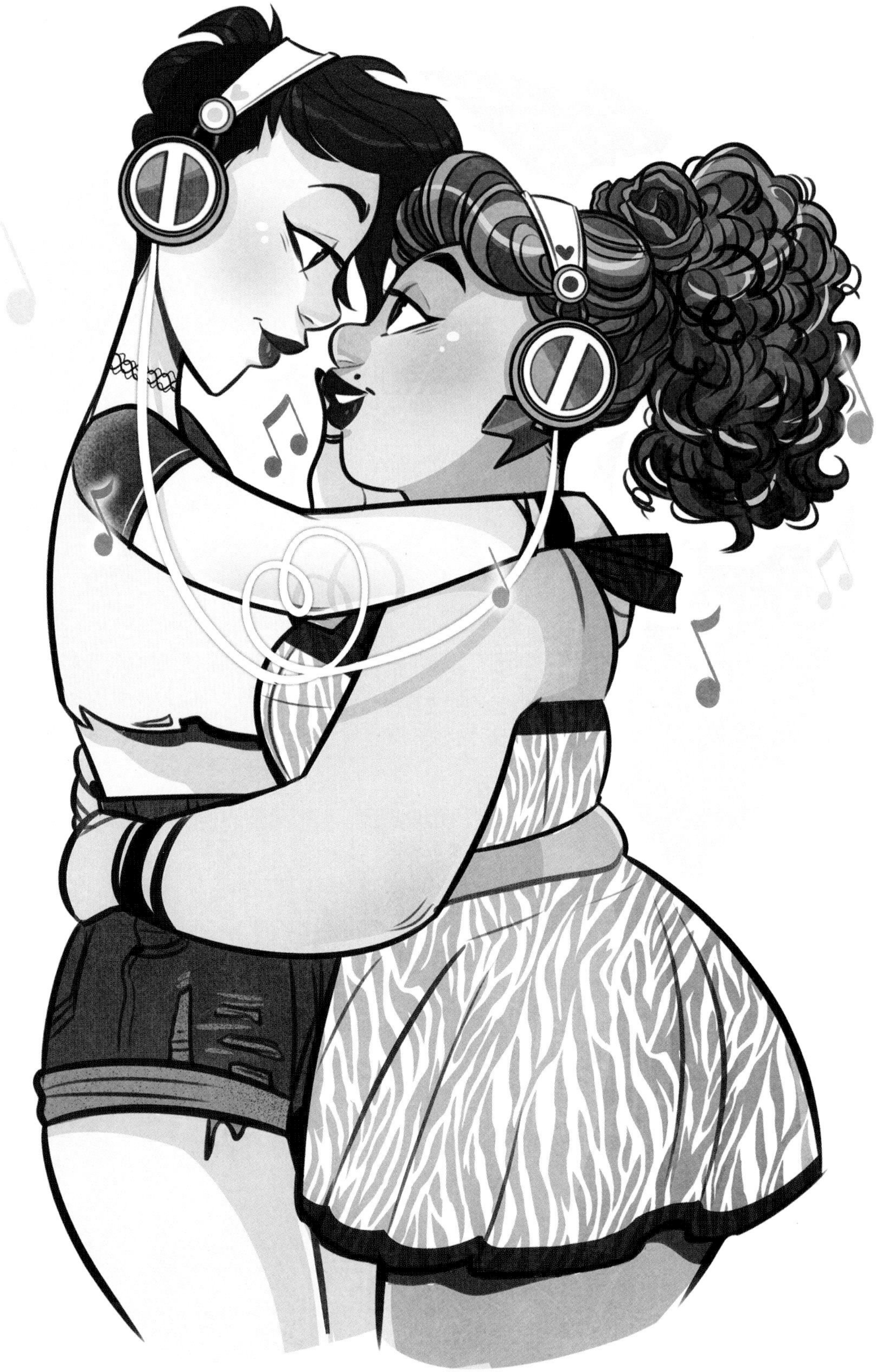

ART BY **BECCA FARROW**

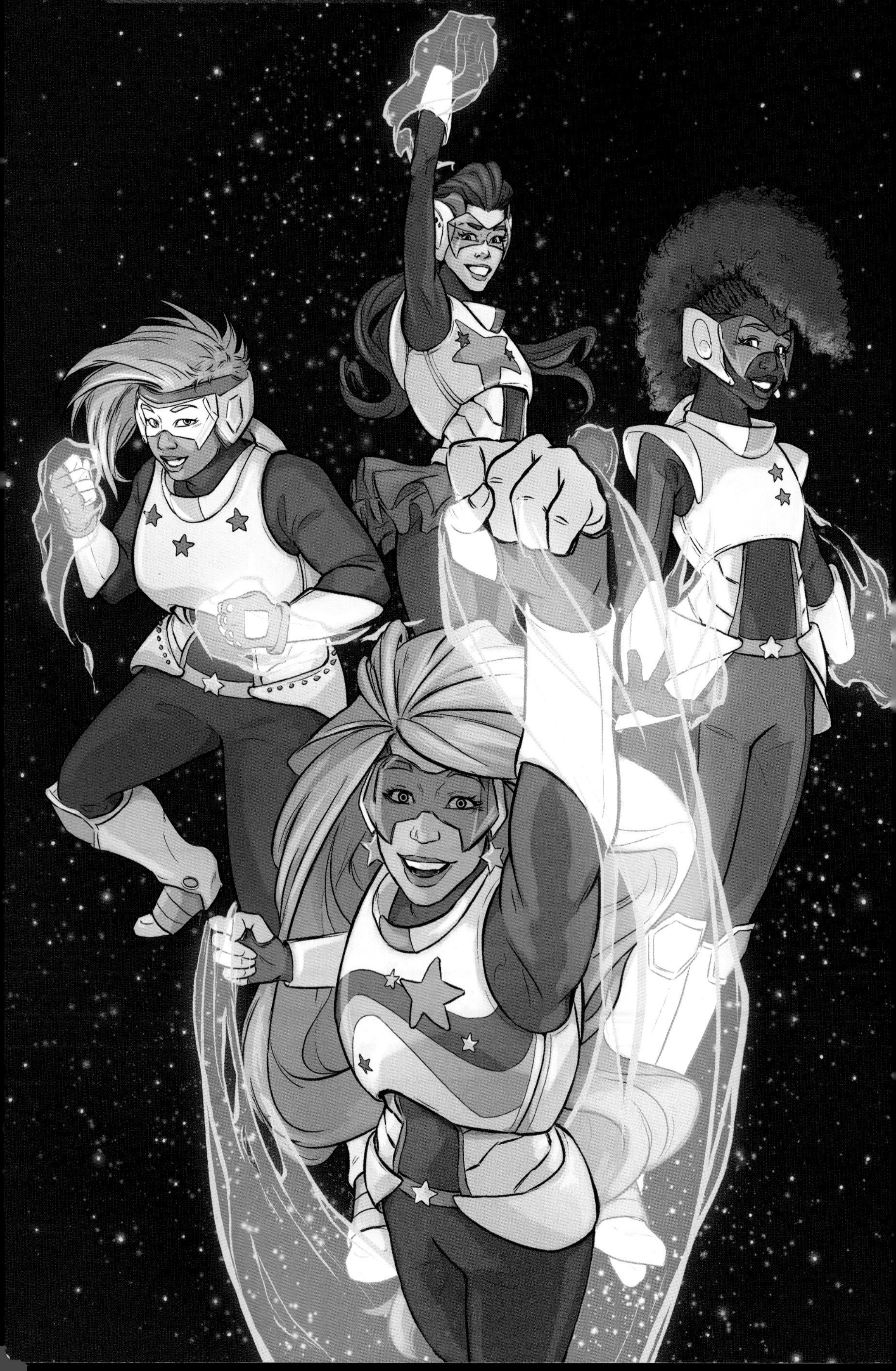